SINGLE ADULT MINISTRY

Jerry Jones, Editor

**SINGLES
MINISTRY
RESOURCES**

NAVPRESS ●*
A MINISTRY OF THE NAVIGATORS
P.O.Box 6000, Colorado Springs, CO 80934

Cover illustration: Cary Henrie
Those who assisted with the editing and production
of this book are: Michele Halseide, JoAnn Hill, Tom
Raabe, Paul Santhouse, Jean Stephens, Jon Stine,
Debby Weaver, and Steve Webb.

Scripture in this publication is from the *Holy Bible:
New International Version* (NIV), Copyright © 1973,
1978, 1984, International Bible Society, used by permission of Zondervan Bible Publishers; the *New American
Standard Bible* (NASB), © The Lockman Foundation
1960, 1962, 1963, 1968, 1971, 1972, 1973, 1975, 1977;
the *Revised Standard Version Bible* (RSV), copyright ©
1946, 1952, 1971, by the Division of Christian
Education of the National Council of the Churches of
Christ in the USA, used by permission, all rights
reserved; *The New Testament in Modern English*
(PH), J. B. Phillips Translator, © J. B. Phillips 1958,
1960, 1972, used by permission of Macmillan
Publishing Company; the *New King James Version*
(NKJV), copyright © 1979, 1980, 1982, Thomas Nelson
Inc., Publishers; and the *King James Version* (KJV).

Printed in the United States of America

The Navigators is an international Christian organization. Jesus Christ gave His followers the Great
Commission to go and make disciples (Matthew
28:19). The aim of The Navigators is to help fulfill that
commission by multiplying laborers for Christ in every
nation.

NavPress is the publishing ministry of The
Navigators. NavPress publications are tools to help
Christians grow. Although publications alone cannot
make disciples or change lives, they can help believers
learn biblical discipleship, and apply what they learn to
their lives and ministries.

Contents

Part Two: Leadership
for Your Single Adult Ministry

Part Three: Suggestions
for Programming Your Singles Ministry

Part Four: Single Adults: The Role They Play in Today's Church

Part Five: Making Small Groups Work in Your Ministry

Part Six: Outreach and Evangelism in Your Ministry with Single Adults

Part Eight: Divorce and Remarriage

Part Nine: The Single-Parent Family

Preface

On the following pages, you will find the best collection of guidelines, ministry philosophy, and practical information from more than fifty of the top leaders involved in ministry with single adults.

You will gain practical ideas, suggestions, and new perspectives that will benefit your own ministry. Specifically, you will learn how to:

- Build a healthy single adult ministry in your local church.
- Develop and train your singles ministry leadership team.
- Integrate your single adults into the life of the church.
- Reach the unchurched single adult.
- Counsel single adults.
- Consider various perspectives on divorce and remarriage (as well as implications for your ministry with single adults).
- Develop support systems for single-parent families.
- Address (and learn more about) some of the contemporary issues facing today's single adults.
- Increase your singles ministry budget.

And those are just highlights. If you're serious about building and nurturing a healthy ministry with single adults, this book is must reading for you.

This Material Did Not Start Out to Become a Book

In October 1983, a publication was born specifically to help the church be more effective in ministry with single adults. This monthly publication began as *SALT* (Single Adult Leadership Training) Newsletter. In September 1986, the name was changed to *Single Adult Ministries (SAM) Journal*.

Over the years, *SAM Journal* has become one of the most regularly sought-after sources of ideas, resources, and guidance for ministry with single adults. Thousands of pastors and lay leaders across North America have benefited from this publication since its inception (along with leaders from England, Finland, Israel, Australia, New Zealand, and Singapore, to name a few).

As *SAM Journal* continued to grow and become better known, an increasing number of people were requesting back issues. For several years we attempted to meet this need, reprinting issues as they ran out. It finally became apparent that we would need to reprint all of the back issues to continue meeting the requests that arrived on a weekly basis. Rather than reprint each individual issue, it made much more sense—to us and to the people requesting the information—to simply put all of the back issues in one handy volume, organized in convenient, topical categories.

You are now holding in your hands the end result of over eight years of the best articles from *SAM Journal*.

The writers in this book represent various—and sometimes opposing—viewpoints. In that respect, this is not an ordinary book. And that is its strength. You will not find the counsel of only one person telling you how to "do the ministry" just his or her way. Instead, you'll find a diversity of opinions and ministry models, representing a healthy range of theological, denominational perspectives within the evangelical community.

How to Use This Book

For some people, reading the book from cover to cover will be the best method. This is especially true for those who are just beginning a single adult ministry and need an extensive "A to Z" course. For others, this book might best be used as an "encyclopedia," by referring to the sections that specifically cover the information needed. That is why we have included an index to help you quickly find the subjects you are seeking.

A Special Thanks to Those on the Front Lines

Most of the writers in this book are experienced pastors and leaders who have helped blaze the trail in this growing ministry with single adults. They are pioneers, people who are some of the first to recognize and respond to needs in a changing world. My hat is off to each of them for taking time out of their busy schedules to contribute some of their thoughts, wisdom, and experiences to the readers of *SAM Journal*—and now with you.

These leaders are the ones, more than anyone else, who have made this helpful resource available to you. I think I can speak for each of them and say that our prayer is that this book will help you become a more effective instrument as you seek to take God's wholeness and healing to the single adults in your church and community.

If you would like to subscribe to *Single Adult Ministries Journal* and keep up on all that's happening in the field of singles ministry, you can find further information on the last page of this book.

Jerry Jones, Editor

PART ONE:

Building a Singles Ministry in the Local Church

ABOUT PART ONE

The baby-boom generation
has been and will remain one of the
most significant influencing forces during its
lifetime. As the largest generation ever,
it has had a profound effect on lifestyle, politics,
commerce, culture, and the issues
facing the church.

Youth ministry is one good example.
Following World War II, as the boom babies became
teenagers, the church recognized a growing need
for youth ministry. Then in the early seventies, as these
teens were becoming adults—remaining single longer,
experiencing divorce more frequently—the church began
to see the need for a specialized ministry
with single adults.

In fact, people in the baby-boom generation—
those born between 1946 and 1964—are 500 percent
more likely to be single than were those in their parents'
generation. Any church that does not have an effective
ministry with single adults is overlooking a large,
growing segment of the community.

Over the next few pages, several leaders look at
some of the foundational whys and hows of building
a healthy ministry with the single adults in
your church and community.

Why Today's Church Needs a Ministry with Single Adults

Singles Ministry Cannot Be Ignored

by Harold Ivan Smith
Founder of Tear Catchers
Ministry, Kansas City, Missouri

Any church that ignores single adults is signing its death warrant. That sounds like a rather strong and opinionated statement. Yet, what else can we say to those churches who treat single adult ministry as only a fad to replace their former fascination with bus ministry?

Nearly 64 million single adults cannot and should not be ignored. Businessmen, educators, Realtors, bankers, and brokers have not ignored this market. Why should the church?

The issue revolves around the psalmist's question, "How shall we sing the LORD's song in a strange land?" (Psalm 137:4, KJV). Yet, unfortunately, there persists in the church the subtle notion that to minister *with* single adults is to abandon our historic commitment to marriage. Here are five reasons why I believe the church must not ignore single adults.

1. *A church that ignores single adults fails to underwrite tomorrow's leadership.* A business must carefully groom its junior partners. Thousands of professionals—skilled, talented, capable—are pew-warmers not because they are unwilling to serve but because the church keeps them at bay with the attitude that one of these days they will either (a) "grow up" or (b) "settle down and get married." This attitude keeps the church from tapping into an army of talented, creative people able and willing to serve. Single adults are an investment in a healthy church for tomorrow.

2. *A church that ignores single adults fails to appreciate the pattern demonstrated by the early church in Acts 6.* After a painful confrontation with widows, the church *responded*, rather than reacted, to the *chera* (those without a mate),[1] and what they feared would not happen, happened. A revival broke out in Jerusalem with rather outstanding results—priests became converted and the church multiplied. God honors obedience.

It's hard to believe what Luke wrote in Acts: "There were no needy persons among them" (4:34); and "they gave to anyone as he had need" (2:45). However, the early church did follow the Apostle Paul's advice: "As we have opportunity, let us do good to all people, especially to those who belong to the family of believers" (Galatians 6:10).

Was it James who wrote, "The religion that God our Father accepts as pure and faultless is based on this: how high your steeple is, and how loud your praise choruses are"? No, not exactly; rather, James advised his readers "to look after orphans and widows [the *chera*] in their distress and to keep oneself from being polluted by the world" (James 1:27).

The attitude of the world we must

avoid is, "Let the government or Big Brother or fill-in-the-blank take care of it." The weight of Old Testament thought is summarized in severe curses on *anyone* who ignores the *chera* (Exodus 22:22).

When God accused the Jews of robbing Him, they demanded "How do we rob you?" Malachi responded, "In tithes and offerings" (3:8), which funded the care of the widows and orphans. God said, "Test me in this . . . and see if I will not throw open the floodgates of heaven and pour out so much blessing that you will not have room enough for it" (3:10). Maybe this explains why there are so many anemic churches—they aren't committed to God's priorities, which include today's single parent families.

3. *A church that ignores single adults fails to follow Jesus' example.* His dying words to the Apostle John were, "Here is your mother" (John 19:27). The words of a man delirious with pain? No—a man committed to God's priorities. If Jesus took time from His agenda of dying to remember the needs of a widow and to care for her, how much more should His church follow that example of caring for those without a mate?

4. *A church that ignores single adults is a slave to the past rather than a previewer of the future.* Much of the current hullabaloo over the "family crisis" is similar to the complaints of the Israelites after they had come out of Egypt—a pining for days of old. There is a sense in which the church is in exile from the nice nuclear family we so fondly imagine. However, God is always with His people in their exile. Jeremiah's words haunt us: "Seek the peace and prosperity of the city to which I have carried you into exile" (Jeremiah 29:7).

The church must painfully abandon some of its most cherished myths and cultural notions concerning the family in order to embrace the realities of twenty-first century living if we are to sing "to serve the *present* age, my calling to fulfill."

I do not believe that "a great revival" will send us back into nuclear family configurations. (We cling to the "traditional" fifties and sixties version of the family as if it were

> **"I believe singleness to be the permanent direction of the American population not because of some post-Vietnam or post-Watergate consequences but because the drift of American culture for more than 200 years has clearly been in this direction."**

the norm, when in reality, it was *the exception* to the norm.) I believe singleness to be the permanent direction of the American population not because of some post-Vietnam or post-Watergate consequences but because the drift of American culture for more than 200 years has clearly been in this direction.

We need to tackle the opportunity without hesitation or apology. We need to see the opportunity rather than the problem. We need to sense the urging of God to channel this great mass of people into Kingdom-building.

5. Finally, *a church that ministers with single adults will help singles*

mature, make spiritual commitments, and establish Kingdom priorities that will lead them into better marriages. Thus, the church's commitment to marriage will be strengthened. This is a paradox under the blessing of God.

Any church that fails to minister with single adults has missed an invitation to be God's leaven on earth and therefore has signed its death warrant as a thriving, growing community of believers in the years to come.

Singles Ministries Meet Needs

by Dennis Franck
Singles pastor at Bethel Assembly of God Church, San Jose, California

L et's look at the need for singles ministry from three perspectives.

The Numerical Need

- Approximately 66.3 million single and single-again adults live in the United States.
- Baby boomers—those Americans born between 1946 and 1964—are approximately 500 percent more likely to be single or divorced than were their parents.
- At least 60 percent of today's children will live with only one parent for some period of time before they reach age eighteen.
- About 50 percent of first marriages end in divorce.
- From 60 to 70 percent of second marriages end in divorce.
- From 70 to 82 percent of third marriages end in divorce. [2]

The statistics are staggering; single adults, and the issues they face, are here to stay. They can no longer be ignored by the church. We must be aware of the opportunities and benefits of ministry to this ever-growing segment of our society.

The Emotional Need

Some people ask, "Why do we need a single adult ministry? Why can't the single adults be content in the church's adult classes? Why do they need a special ministry?"

Many single adults feel like a fifth wheel in our churches' "family-oriented" atmosphere. Church leaders and lay people have a tendency to think, talk, and act out family thoughts and scenarios.

Just the other day an announcement was made in our church concerning an upcoming men's retreat. The announcer said, "Men, get your wives to let you go away for a couple of days." What do statements like this from the pulpit tell the single man? Why assume that all or even most men in our churches are married, when possibly as many as 30 or 40 percent are not? This attitude, among others, tends to keep single adults from feeling included in the mainstream of the church.

Also, classes that are composed of—

or led by—mostly married adults tend to focus on subjects that may not relate well to the single person. Singles often have different lifestyles and struggles than marrieds, especially in such areas as intimacy, companionship, and sexual fulfillment. This is also true concerning the needs of the single parent.

The Social Need

One of the biggest needs of the single adult is to establish a network of people who will provide support, friendship, and learning. Unlike marrieds, singles have no mate to help make decisions concerning finances, raising children, where to attend church, and many other areas. A single adult ministry is one way to provide an atmosphere for forming healthy relationships from which to draw strength, support, and help in both the major and minor decisions of life.

Specific Needs of Single Adults

A ministry needs to be built and directed toward meeting specific needs of people. Based on my involvement in singles ministry, the following primary needs and struggles need to be addressed with each of the specific groups.

1. *Never-marrieds:* dating, commitment, life direction, handling changes, goals, loneliness, managing money, relationships, sexuality, and vocation.

2. *Separated:* confusion, direction, forgiveness, loneliness, rejection, self-esteem, and sexuality.

3. *Formerly-marrieds:* self-esteem, bitterness, commitment, forgiveness, failure, guilt, identity, loneliness, managing money, parenting, rejection, relationships, and sexuality.

4. *Widowed:* grief, guilt, identity, loneliness, parenting, relationships, self-esteem, and sexuality.

Although separated people are not legally single, they have a hard time fitting in with the marrieds. In my opinion, separated people need to have the option of attending a single adult ministry for support and direction.

Starting a Ministry with Single Adults in Your Church

Building an Emotionally Healthy Ministry

by John Splinter
Associate pastor and director of singles ministries at Central Presbyterian Church, Saint Louis, Missouri

In desiring to create a ministry with single adults, many churches are now responding to the fact that one-half of the adult population in most major cities of our country is single. (Some estimate that single adults may comprise 50 percent of the total adult population soon after the year 2000.)

Yet building a ministry with single adults is, in many ways, significantly different from standard models used by many churches for ministries with other groups—couples, youth, or almost any other segment of the church population.

I have seen many churches begin a singles ministry, only to see it attract such a conglomeration of lonely chronic losers that, if the group did not collapse under its own emotionally unhealthy weight, the church decided to terminate it.

Why is this such a common experience? Why do many of the sharpest singles in any community shun church singles programs? Why do so many chronic failures gravitate toward church singles ministries?

Not a Counseling Shop

The first step in analyzing this problem is to look at a factually operational definition of singles ministry. By "factually operational" I mean that, as one analyzes how his or her time is used, he or she should ask: What activity takes the bulk of it? Counseling? Offering friendship to lonely people? Handling crises in the lives of singles? Trying to figure out just how to reach singles?

If the singles ministry is seen as a counseling shop, the singles pastor will soon be overwhelmed with people who feel a need for counseling. In this scenario it is not unusual to see a singles pastor burn out quickly as he or she tries to manage a counseling load of twenty or thirty individuals who are more than willing to cast full responsibility for their lives and problems upon the minister.

In most cases it is wise for singles ministries to have an active roster of professional therapists to whom the vast majority of counseling cases may be referred. Most pastors, singles pastors or otherwise, are not equipped to handle the variety and depth of problems inherent within the counseling process in singles ministries.

Neither are most singles pastors able to commit the amount of time necessary to accomplish ongoing, long-term therapy, maintaining even an active "case load" of fifteen or twenty people. Sadly, in many cases where counseling is considered the functional definition of singles ministry, what is actually created is an atmosphere of emotional dependence upon the singles minister.

There is little if any growth but a lot of time spent counseling.

If the functional definition given to singles ministries is that of providing an emergency room for people dealing with acute trauma, then that will become the predominant activity of the ministry. For example, many singles ministries become homes for people going through divorce, a place where they may vent some of their feelings, or find others going through similar circumstances, struggles, and emotional upheaval.

One problem with this definition is that healthy single adults usually leave the ministry once it is determined that its predominant function is to help those in acute stress. Another problem with this definition is that it can actually promote an atmosphere wherein people are allowed to fixate on their problem. I know of singles ministries that started out as "divorce-recovery groups," and four years later the same people were still in the same group, still talking about their divorces. That's not ministry.

Not a Separate Church

Some singles ministries talk in terms of being a "separate church" for singles. This is not a healthy approach either, since singles need the married community and vice versa. Singles are isolated enough without a church providing further isolation by creating a special church just for them.

Other singles ministries define themselves in terms of providing a place of welcome and acceptance for the chronic, lonely losers whom nobody else will take in, or who command such refined skills at alienating others that nobody will willingly accept them.

Before progressing any further, it must be stated that all of the above are certainly aspects of any singles ministry. Certainly, there is a need for counseling, and a need for helping people progress through acute crisis in their lives. Certainly, there needs to be a place for the "lonely loser," and anyone who has worked with singles knows that there is a place for a singles-only fellowship. But these items dare not become the functional definition of a singles ministry.

Forming an Effective Growing Singles Ministry

So how does one go about forming an effective and growing singles ministry? Many churches have begun with, for example, a Saturday evening get-together for singles. At the first meeting they may have thirty in attendance. At the next meeting there are twenty-three, then fourteen, and finally a "really committed core" of eight that comes to every singles function. Frequently, that core is composed of two or three relatively sharp people, and about five weird types who scare off all the other singles who don't have enough personal security to allow themselves to become identified with a group in which there are so many weirdos.

> "Why do many of the sharpest singles in any community shun church singles programs? Why do so many chronic failures gravitate toward church singles ministries?"

Then the singles minister or leader is left with solving the following dilemma: "The weird ones seem to drive off the normal ones, and the really sharp ones don't even come around. They're too busy, and they don't seem to have a need for a singles ministry. So we're left with a residue of emotionally lame and sick people who don't have anywhere else to turn. This is ministry?"

Here are some tips for starting and maintaining a thriving singles ministry.

Target Your Ministry

Do you want a small-group Bible study for singles or a divorce-recovery group? Will your meeting be aimed toward never-married singles in their twenties, or will it be for those from thirty to fifty with kids? Will the meeting be primarily for social purposes, or do you want to emphasize spiritual growth? What do you wish to accomplish? What is your target?

Don't make the mistake of just starting a singles ministry and hoping it will take off. It probably won't. The singles community is as varied and complex as the married community. Targeting ministry is perhaps even more important within singles ministries than within other church ministries.

For example, one ministry I know of operates the following targeted ministries:

- A fourteen-week divorce-recovery program.
- A program for the children of divorce.
- A program for single parents.
- A program for blended families.
- A program for tying together single parents and married couples for the purpose of providing support for the

---

WHEN A MINISTRY WITH SINGLES IS A THREAT TO THE CHURCH LEADERSHIP
an interview with Larry Crabb
Founder of The Institute of Biblical Counseling, Denver, Colorado

As you travel and speak, do you sense that church leaders feel comfortable or uncomfortable with single adult issues and needs?

If I'm sensing anything, it's that the leadership feels caught in a real bind. On one hand, they feel they ought to do something to help address and meet single adult needs. But on the other hand, they feel threatened. They don't know what to do with single adults. Some, it seems, even wish the issue didn't exist.

Many churches today are putting a heavy emphasis on the Christian home and strengthening the family unit. In truth, there is a real need to do so. But another primary reason for this emphasis is because most pastors—who are usually married, family men—are teaching in their areas of competence and staying away from areas of incompetence. Consequently, single adults often feel uncomfortable—like they don't quite fit. It's a little like the patient who has a disease that the doctor can't diagnose or cure. The patient starts feeling very insecure with that doctor.

I think that singles are a real threat to the church leadership. What leaders need to do is admit that they are insecure and don't know what to do in this area, to be honest about that. They also need to meet with a group of single adults and say, "Help me."

single parent and healthy marriage modeling for the children of the single parent.

- A host of varied social and athletic programs to draw new people into the ministry via purely social activities.
- Several varied approaches to small-group Bible studies.
- A diverse program with many activities for people in their twenties.
- A program for people over fifty.
- Two retreats every year.
- Two Sunday school classes for singles only.
- A counseling referral network.
- Home potluck dinners for singles only.
- A women's support network for mothers whose husbands have recently left them.
- A fifteen-week program for people considering first-time marriage.

That's what is meant by "targeting" ministry. *Each one of the above programs will attract a different group of singles.* There is a principle involved in this concept: The more focused a ministry is, and the more it requires of those involved, the more likely it will succeed in its objectives. The weakest programs in most singles ministries are those that have no specific target, and also make no demands of any kind on the participants ("Ya'll just come on out and let us love ya").

Need Dictates Ministry

If the program's not working, there may not be the need you thought there was. Successful programs usually reflect needs. If something is not working, kill it and refocus your energy on another objective. If hardly anyone

---

If you were a senior pastor or church leader in that situation, what would you do to become more effective in ministering to the needs of the single adult?

First, I would find four or five single people—not necessarily the sharpest or the best but an honest random sampling—and see if they would meet with me in a small-group setting for about ten weeks. During that time I would attempt to develop a trust level so that I could draw out the honest questions and issues that are most on their souls. My goal would be to gain understanding, to get beyond the obvious.

Most people—including single adults—are fighting all kinds of private wars, and oftentimes they have no one to turn to. Many single adults struggle with bitterness, loneliness, sexual issues. Some may even be dealing with a subtle but deep rage, because they feel the church or their family is saying they don't fit in unless they're married.

Through this small-group time I would try to come up with a list of ten or twenty areas that are their burning issues and needs. Following the ten-week period, I would invite a larger group of singles—maybe for a Saturday workshop—and talk to them about what I had learned during the small-group sessions. Then I would tell them where I'm coming from on each item, admitting my own ignorance, doubts, and confusion, and listening to their responses, advice, and comments.

From there I would attempt to establish a more sensitive ministry with the singles in my church community on the basic premise that as Christians there is a biblical perspective that enables us to get through every honest question in life.

signs up or shows up, ask yourself what your objectives are and whether those objectives are being met. Perhaps they are and in time the program will take off. However, perhaps there is no real need for what is being offered.

*Leadership
Promotes Ministry*

Build on the best leadership you can find. One of the worst mistakes many singles ministries make is that of asking for volunteers. Those who make this mistake frequently end up with one or two volunteers who have very limited leadership potential and whom nobody would wish to follow or emulate. Nor are many of these volunteers able to determine the difference between good ministry and bad programming.

However, singles ministries *should* be run primarily by volunteers, whether single or married, and those volunteers should be the sharpest people available. If married, the couples should have a real appreciation for the struggle inherent in single life, and should not have too many quick answers.

The sharpest singles frequently have the least need for a singles ministry because they have already taken full charge of their lives and have surrounded themselves with friendships, activities, and personal growth objectives. Those very people should be encouraged to take on various leadership roles.

> **"The most needy people usually make the worst leaders. The least needy frequently have the most to offer. The challenge of recruiting leadership is to convince the sharp people that they should become involved at a leadership level, not because of their need for a singles ministry to fill a void in their lives, but because of their commitment to Christ and their desire to help build the Kingdom."**

The most needy people usually make the worst leaders. The least needy frequently have the most to offer. The challenge of recruiting leadership is to convince the sharp people that they should become involved at a leadership level, not because of their need for a singles ministry to fill a void in their lives, but because of their commitment to Christ and their desire to help build the Kingdom.

Then, tie the leaders to ministries that reflect interests or experiences of their own. Ask the healthy divorcees to begin a divorce-recovery program. (Give them two or three such programs or models to choose from and limit the duration of the program so that people won't fixate but will recognize that the best leaders in that kind of program are those who have been there and are now a few years away from their own struggles.) Ask the sharp single parents who have gotten their lives together to consider beginning a single parents' program for singles more needy than they.

Ask the jock to begin a jogging program or a softball program. Ask the socially suave lady to begin a program for training others to be good hosts or hostesses at singles functions. Ask the person who enjoys theater to begin a program of attending the best theatrical productions.

Give specific objectives. Build in checkpoints where leaders will be asked to report on their accomplishments. Help them form operational committees, but give them full ownership of the ministry. The two greatest errors commonly made in managing volunteer leaders are (a) unclear goal setting and (b) lack of accountability.

Begin Slowly, Build Slowly

Singles ministries with fifteen different forms of programs or ministries are not built in a month, or a year. It takes time to build good ministry. The best way to build is to take one objective at a time, build a leadership team, provide the equipping necessary to accomplish the objective, and then give 100 percent of the ownership to the leaders.

Once one ministry is up and running, begin building another. There are enough needs within the singles community for a wide variety of ministries within any church. Churches represent a host of resources—both physical and spiritual. Keep building and keep recruiting. Keep identifying resources available within the body, and keep tying those resources to specific needs within your singles community.

Aim for Long-Range Objectives

The goal could be to involve all singles in some form of small-group fellowship. One of the most predominant characteristics of singles who are hurting is social and spiritual isolation. The small group, whether drawn together for Bible study or simply for Christian community, represents a magnificent tool for meeting many of the needs of isolated individuals. It also represents the best way for a church to become a real "body" for singles.

Ministry to single adults is a complex issue. In no way can five points cover the need or define success. However, the five concepts outlined above have proven very effective in several singles ministries, including my own.

Overcoming the Obstacles

by Terry Hershey
Director of Christian Focus, Inc., Seattle, Washington

A species becomes extinct when its environment does not give it the opportunity to grow and thrive. The question we will examine is a simple one: *Are the churches in America creating an environment for single adult ministry to grow and thrive?*

Unfortunately, I believe the answer far too often is no.

As I travel, the reports continue to confirm my fears. Persons in single adult ministry leadership positions— clergy and lay persons—are finding themselves ignored, frustrated, understaffed, underbudgeted, and face to face with a ministry that appears to attract "losers"; yet they are still expected to perform programming miracles. So, what else is new?

Yet underneath my concern is a growing sense of hope. It is a hope which says that *God has not called us to His ministry to experience only ineffectiveness, barriers, and poor stewardship.* It is a call that is accomplished by His Spirit.

With that Spirit to guide us, let's attempt to bring clarity to the issue of how to build a healthy single adult ministry and develop the necessary leadership by focusing on two questions.

> "You can tell a church's theology not by the creed it posts in the narthex but by the theology it practices in its programs. Many singles ministry problems are not program problems; they are theology problems."

1. What specific issues prevent the church from creating a healthy environment for single adult ministry and leadership development? In other words, what issues threaten to make single adult ministers a doomed species?

2. What specific steps can the singles minister or leader take for leadership to develop, and for programming to blossom?

For the remainder of this article, I will suggest answers to the above questions, based on my observations.

Obstacles that Thwart a Healthy Environment

1. We attempt to erect single adult programming on foundations that are not yet ready, or we are not even open to discussing the issues relevant to single adult integration into the church body.

Ministry must—and can only—begin with an adequate foundation.

Having a single adult program because it's the thing to do is not an adequate reason. Too often, the question why is never asked!

Let me give an example (which is repeated over and over in real situations). Church A decides it needs a single adult ministry. It hires a minister for single adults. "You're free to create as you please," the new minister is told. Within six months, he is fatigued and frustrated and wants to quit. He wonders why. What has gone wrong?

A program for single adults, by implication, connotes that the church believes in integration and equality, but the pastor's Sunday sermons reflect just the opposite. He holds up marriage as God's only "ordained" option and continues to wonder aloud in staff meetings why the new singles minister can't get his single adults to come to church.

You can tell a church's theology not by the creed it posts in the narthex but by the theology it practices in its programs. Many singles ministry problems are not program problems; they are theology problems. The example I gave reflects this reality. Is it any wonder that a leader in a single adult program will become frustrated when the system itself mitigates against integration and singleness as a valid lifestyle?

2. We live on the uncertain ground that comes from doing day-to-day battle with the issues of divorce and remarriage.

Single adult programming, by its very nature (we're referring mainly to a "thirty and older" single adult ministry here), magnifies the time one needs to confront the issues surrounding divorce. This ongoing confrontation can subtly take its toll; we need to be aware of its consequences.

There are two primary consequences. If the single adult leader is conservative in theology (remarriage is seldom or never allowed), he will find it very difficult to support his formerly married single adults, unable to offer them any hope for marriage, while at the same time questioning the reason behind their single status. Thus, leaders find themselves antagonizing with their divorced participants.

If, on the other hand, the single adult leaders attempt to wrestle with the implications of grace in the issue of

---

QUESTIONS TO ASK BEFORE YOU START
by Doug Fagerstrom
Minister with singles at Calvary Church,
Grand Rapids, Michigan

Here are ten questions the church leadership needs to consider before beginning a ministry with single adults.

1. Do we really know the needs of our singles, regardless of their age or status?
2. Are we forsaking the pain of some singles in order to protect the prestige of our church or some of our established programs?
3. Will our singles ministry—our ministry "with" singles—be confined to a singles group, or will we need to begin growing into new areas of departmentalization and integration?
4. Is our primary mission to seek and save the lost (Luke 19:10) and make disciples (Matthew 28:19-20), or is it to house and maintain the believers already in the door? How will this answer affect our attitude toward, and treatment of, "unacceptable" lifestyles among our single adults?
5. Are we guilty of imposing the "youth model" of ministry on our single adults?
6. Are we considering a new form of ministry directed to the particular singles in our church, or are we trying to follow the model of another church's ministry built upon the needs of their singles?
7. Are we still hung up theologically with the divorce/remarriage issue and can't (or don't want to try to) resolve this conflict?
8. Are we operating from the premise that this "singles phenomenon" will pass in a few years?
9. Do we really conduct our ministry as if all believers are ministers (1 Corinthians 3:5-9)? What are the implications of this with our single adults, even those previously married?
10. Is the focus of our ministry primarily on our programs or our people (1 Corinthians 16:15, Ephesians 4:11-12)? Where is most of our time and energy expended?

Honest discussion of these questions (with both your singles and key church leaders) will help you lay the groundwork for a healthy ministry with your single adults.

remarriage, they often find opposition from the senior pastor or church board. Singles leaders become labeled as "liberal" or as "encouraging the people to divorce and remarry." Is it any wonder that there is stress in single adult ministry?

3. We expect single adult leaders to "be all things to all men"—that is, leaders are to be responsible for effective programming with all the single adults in the congregation.

The effect of this expectation is simple: The programming is so broadly based that it never addresses specific needs and issues, which vary greatly in a community of people from ages twenty to eighty.

Today's adult singles are dealing with everything from single parenting, divorce, and death of a mate to the concerns of professional career singles who choose not to be married. Do we know who we're aiming at, and why we're aiming at them?

We've said enough about the obstacles. Now let's look at the steps to overcoming them. The following recommendations are directed at the leaders in single adult ministries. If there is to be reform, we must affirm the fact that it will begin with us.

Overcoming the Obstacles

1. *When taking a single adult ministry position in a church or beginning a new program, never assume anything about the church's philosophy of ministry.*

Be confident that you know where the church stands. Ask questions. What does the church mean when it uses the word *family*? What is its theology of personhood, commitment, divorce, and evangelism? Spend time with the senior minister. What does he mean when he refers to single adult ministry? Be informed.

2. *Commit yourself to the ongoing task of educating the church body.* People by nature revert to comfort zones and stereotypes. Continuing education is a must for any church. Ask if you can make a presentation regarding single adult issues at the church staff meeting. Twice a year, teach one or two of the married Sunday school classes to help raise their level of awareness concerning the various needs within your singles ministry as well as the kinds of things that require your time and attention.

Are your single adults able to participate in planning worship? Are single adults on your church board? Ask. It never hurts to ask. Lobby for the single adults in your church.

3. *Get together with other staff members on a regular basis for no other purpose than to be a support group.* Support among staff members is far more important than staff meetings. And antagonism—due to sensitive theological issues and differences—can be diffused in the presence of an ongoing supportive staff environment. How does the support begin? You start it.

4. *Spend time in other areas of the church program where integration with single adults is necessary.* Visit the college group. It helps diffuse their stereotypes about single adult groups. Involve your singles in church small-

group programs. Develop a good relationship with the children's ministry and explore ways to be colaborers in reaching single-parent families.

A CASE STUDY:
Energizing the Apathetic Church

**with a suggested solution
by Doug Morphis
*Counselor at First United Methodist Church in Wichita, Kansas***

The Problem

"I'm the volunteer lay leader of our single adult ministry. (I became involved after noticing the growing number of singles in our church and community who were being overlooked by our 'family-oriented' church.)

"The senior pastor is a good man, but he seems to want to keep single adults at arm's length. It's almost like he's uncomfortable with the idea of a ministry with singles, and he seems blind to the fact that the need exists. His messages are always very 'family-oriented' and he seldom—if ever—acknowledges the single adults in our congregation. Consequently, the church as a whole does not seem to be very enthusiastic or supportive of a ministry with and for single adults.

"What can I do to help the senior pastor and church leadership catch the vision? Is it even possible? How can I help my church recognize the need and provide the moral (and even financial) support necessary?"

A Possible Solution

It's very easy to be discouraged if you are alone with your vision. First, I would suggest that you gather a support group of from three to six other persons who share your vision (or with whom you can share yours). It sounds as if you already have a possible group among the single adults in your church, but you need to be more intentional about selecting a core group. That group will do the following things:

Pray, Study, and Dream Together

Intentionally form a close-knit support group (if possible, invite a member of the staff to be a part of this group). Share your own dreams and invite the others to share their honest feelings, thoughts, and dreams.

Study Your Community

Get the statistics on the number of single adults and single-parent households in your community, the number of active and inactive singles in your congregation, and the number of divorces and loss of mates by death per

> "The senior pastor is a good man, but he seems to want to keep single adults at arm's length. It's almost like he's uncomfortable with the idea of a ministry with singles, and he seems blind to the fact that the need exists."

year. Talk about what this means for your church. Explore the barriers that may be keeping your church from reaching these single adults.

Visit Other Church Ministries

Along with other members of your core team, visit several churches' singles ministries in your community. Learn from other churches that have active and positive singles programs. Share together what you learn from these visits. Meet with the senior pastors of these churches and ask them why the singles ministry is important to them.

Involve Your Senior Pastor

Approach the senior pastor of your own church, or better yet, have him come to you. Invite him to visit your core-group meeting and have him listen to all that you have learned (statistics, programs, insights, and advice from other senior pastors). Offer positive suggestions as to how he and the church can better reach out to the growing singles population. Ask him if you can share the information at the next church administrative body planning meeting.

At the appropriate ministry planning committee, discuss such specifics as
• financial support,
• child care,
• secretarial help, and
• church meeting facilities, if needed.

Your senior pastor and church leadership will be more likely to catch the vision if you have done your homework, laid the groundwork, presented the information in a positive way, and helped others to catch your vision. Well-presented statistics and facts will speak for themselves; the other people involved with you can help provide the necessary support.

Remember, you are not alone. Gather those people around you who share your vision, prepare your facts and game plan, and be sensitive to God's leadership.

Launching the Singles Ministry

by Dennis Franck
Singles pastor at Bethel Assembly of God Church, San Jose, California

This is not intended to be a comprehensive guide to beginning a ministry. But here is an overview of several key steps I recommend.

1. *Take a Sunday morning census.* Survey your entire congregation on one or more Sunday mornings. Find out who your single adults are. Also ask your people to let you know about friends or family members who are single and unchurched. Include them on your mailing list.

2. *Analyze the census data.* What is their average age? What pockets of need seem to be most noticeable? (For example, do you have a significant number of single parents, widowed persons, or young career singles?)

3. *Plan the first meeting.* Based on the information you obtain from the

survey, gather a group of interested single adults to plan a social activity and discussion time to learn more about their interests and needs.

4. *Select a leader.* Singles as well as marrieds can serve effectively as leaders. A married couple may provide a healthy stability and model marriage that single adults can respect. On the other hand, a single man or woman may have a burden for this ministry and provide strong leadership.

Leadership is probably the most crucial area of single adult ministry. Without effective leadership the ministry will fail. Furthermore, the pastor or director does not have the time nor talent to do everything. Giving ownership to the ministry by delegating responsibility to others is crucial.

Probably more than any other ministry within the church, the singles leader—due in part to the high turnover of people in singles ministry—must continually recruit, train, and motivate the leadership team.

5. *Hold regular weekly meetings.* It is important that momentum be established. One of the greatest desires of the single adult is fellowship and relationship-building. Therefore, a weekly meeting is much better than a monthly get-together. If the weekly meeting is held in a local church building, you will primarily draw people from your church. If it is held outside the church building—in a restaurant, for example —the unchurched may feel more free to attend.

6. *Develop a mailing list.* Regularly send a letter or monthly calendar to your single adults so that they are aware of upcoming activities.

7. *Develop other ministries.* Ministries can be started as leadership becomes available. These could include social activities, Bible studies, retreats, seminars, divorce-recovery workshops, children's classes or activities, and single-parent classes. Find every possible way to get all of your singles involved in some kind of ministry. The more they are involved, the more ownership they will feel in the ministry. With ownership comes a higher degree of commitment and involvement.

Establishing Goals, Priorities, and Objectives

by Charles Bradshaw
Management and organizational consultant, Diamond Bar, California

D o you sometimes feel like you're lost in the forest or driving in a fog? Leaders have those feelings when they have not adequately defined their purposes. The following steps, taken from an interview with Charles Bradshaw, president of The Bradshaw Group, will guide you in setting goals, priorities, and objectives for your ministry with single adults.

Planning Is Important
• Planning helps you move from being

managed by the urgent to managing the important.

- Planning helps develop a sense of belonging and team play. It gets everyone playing off the same sheet of music.
- Planning improves communication. A planned ministry leaves less room for mistaken assumptions.
- Planning helps you become a more effective leader.

Here are six steps that will enable you to plan a more effective ministry with the single adults in your church and community.

Step 1: Identify Needs

Your ultimate goal as a single adult minister is to meet the needs of the single adults in your church and community. Consequently, you begin by identifying the needs around you.

Seek Christ's heart. Visualize Christ sitting on top of your church building, looking out over your community. What would most break His heart as He looks at the single adults there? What needs would concern Him most?

Get in touch with singles. Mingle among the single adults in your church and community. Visit key singles hangouts in your area. Invite singles out for coffee and a visit. Listen as they identify their needs, hurts, pains, desires, and dreams.

Brainstorm. Bring a small group of key people together to talk about singles' needs. Write down the ideas, group them into categories, and prioritize them. Use this time to list all the possible needs and opportunities for ministry you can think of. Don't try to solve the needs during the brainstorm session. Remember, you may never be able to meet all these needs.

Study demographics. Study your community at your local library. What are the statistics about singles in your community? How many of them are there? What are the demographic trends unique to your particular community? What needs do those statistics reveal?

Focus on the needs that make you most passionate. What needs are you most likely to cry over or pound the table about? These may be the best areas for you to focus on. Put names beside each need you write down. Until you attach to the needs the names and faces of real people whom you intensely care about, you will lack the motivation required to do anything about meeting those needs.

Jewish psychologist Viktor E. Frankl said, "People can put up with a lot of the what if they know the why."[3] When you have a rough day and wonder, "Why am I doing this? Is it worth it?" go back to the needs you've identified as a reminder of why you're in this ministry.

Step 2: Write
A Purpose Statement

After you have identified the needs, formulate a purpose statement. A purpose statement completes the sentence, "We exist to _____."

Keep it simple. Your purpose statement should be like a "cocktail party answer." When I was bogged down in the details of my doctoral dissertation, my advisor suggested that I prepare a one-sentence answer for a person at a party who would ask me, "What is your dissertation about?" If you want to maintain your focus and get others interested in your vision, you should be able to answer the question "Why does your ministry exist?" in one easy-to-understand sentence.

A purpose statement provides unity, direction, and focus. When it's concise, your leadership team will understand it and work together more effectively to accomplish it.

People tend toward extremes when writing a purpose statement. Either they are too grandiose, or they say too little. "We exist to glorify God" is not an adequate purpose statement. The challenge is to say something unique about your ministry while keeping it simple.

How to write your purpose statement. Use the "hot pen" technique. For fifteen minutes, rapidly write down everything you can think of that describes the purpose of your ministry. From what you wrote, choose the three words that best describe your purpose. Then select one word. Finally, write one nontechnical sentence describing why you exist. Keep the sentence free from theological jargon. Make it something that the average person can understand.

Step 3: Define Objectives

Now you need to decide in which categories of your ministry you will set specific goals. These categories will be called objectives. Think of objectives as umbrellas under which your goals will fall.

Guidelines for setting objectives. Write down several areas where you must continually be working in order to accomplish your purpose as defined in your purpose statement. Some examples are: education, crisis intervention, fellowship, outreach, care, research, and development.

Don't make your objectives too narrow. For example, "Wednesday night Bible study" or "Sunday school" are not good objectives. Instead, make "education" and "Bible study" your objectives. You may not always have a study on Wednesday nights, but you will always maintain some form of education or Bible study.

Set between three and seven objectives. Ideally, put a person in charge of each objective area. In my opinion, you will want no more than seven objective areas because your ministry will begin to suffer if you have more than seven people reporting directly to you.

> **"Visualize Christ sitting on top of your church building, looking out over your community. What would most break His heart as He looks at the single adults there? What needs would concern Him most?"**

The benefits of objectives. Objectives provide balance so that your ministry does not become lopsided. You may be a great caretaker but weak in education or study. Maybe you're great in crisis intervention but poor in providing fellowship or nurture after the crises. Some churches are zealous evangelists, winning many people to the Lord, but they don't adequately feed and disciple new believers. A well-planned, closely followed set of objectives will help keep you balanced and on track.

Step 4: Brainstorm

Now is the time to explore every idea you have in each objective area. Bring your key people together for a brainstorming session.

Keys to Effective Brainstorming

Numbers matter. Research shows that only from 6 to 8 percent of the ideas listed are good and workable. So, if you come up with only six or seven ideas, the odds are that none of them will be workable. But if you can brainstorm 100 ideas, you may come out with six or seven powerful winners.

Do not judge. To get a good quantity and to help keep ideas flowing, don't critique ideas at this point. Outlaw these expressions: "That's a dumb idea," "We tried it last year," "That costs too much," and "The pastor won't let us do that." Don't be afraid of the wild or unusual ideas. They may turn out to be your best ones.

Step 5: Goals

Goal-setting puts feet on your objectives. What are the specific, measurable steps required to accomplish your objectives? Objectives are not measurable, but goals must be. Attach a time, date, or number to each goal so you know when you have reached it.

> **"Your goals are tools—not whips. Don't be afraid to change them or make adjustments as needs and circumstances change."**

Keys to Setting Goals

1. *Goals fall into three time frames:* short-range, mid-range, and long-range. Set goals for each.

2. *Don't set too many goals.* Limit your goals to three per objective per time frame.

3. *Be realistic.* Keep your goals attainable. It's better to err on the side of making the goals too easy to achieve. You will be motivated to set new goals when you are able to reach existing ones.

4. *Write your goals in pencil.* Your goals are tools—not whips. Don't be afraid to change them or make adjustments as needs and circumstances change. (Remember to always keep your goals compatible with your purpose statement and objectives.)

Examples of Objectives and Goals

Remember: Your goals *must* be measurable.

- *Objective:* Crisis intervention.
- *Goal:* Begin one six-week divorce-recovery workshop no later than September 1 with at least twenty-five people attending, ten of whom are from outside this church.
- *Objective:* Education.
- *Goal:* Start a Sunday morning forty-and-older singles class by April 1.
- *Objective:* Outreach.
- *Goal:* Recruit at least fifteen singles to go to Mexico over Memorial Day weekend for a mission project.
- *Objective:* Research and development.
- *Goal:* Talk to twenty unchurched single adults in the community by March 15 to learn more about their

felt needs and their attitudes toward the church.

Once you've established goals, compare them with your purpose statement and objectives. It's easy to set goals and say, "Look at all I'm accomplishing," while going in the opposite direction from your objectives. The more you go in the wrong direction, the farther behind you will get.

Step 6: Record Milestones

One of the greatest causes of burnout in ministry is the lack of closure. There are always more people, more crises, more divorces, more pain. Measurable goals give you a sense of completion and accomplishment. Every time you reach a goal, you reach a milestone. You may not have met every need in the world, but you *have* met a specific need that God placed on your heart and within your reach.

Write down your milestones so that you can keep track of each goal that has been accomplished. On those days when you wonder, "Am I doing any good? Am I accomplishing anything of value?" pull out your milestones sheet and say, "Yes, with God's help, I've accomplished this, and this, and this."

SUMMARY

The amount of time required to

WHO NEEDS PLANNING?
YOU DO IF YOU ANSWER YES TO MORE THAN FIVE OF THE FOLLOWING
by Charles Bradshaw
Management and organizational consultant, Diamond Bar, California

☐ 1. I experience frustration, tension, and/or pressure because my leadership team makes assumptions different from mine as to their roles and responsibilities.

☐ 2. I feel overwhelmed, burned out, and/or apathetic.

☐ 3. Energy and resources are being wasted because there is no clear, agreed-upon direction for my ministry.

☐ 4. Decision-making is often inadequate or even postponed because there is no framework for it.

☐ 5. I experience a great deal of miscommunication because of differing assumptions of what should be happening.

☐ 6. I am frustrated or angry because people don't really know what a great job I am doing.

☐ 7. I put most of my creative energies into putting out fires.

☐ 8. I know some good things are happening, but at times I feel like I am spinning my wheels.

☐ 9. At times I wonder if I am on the right track and if I am making the best use of my time.

☐ 10. I have days when I wonder, "Why am I doing this?"

complete this goal-setting process will depend on you, your staff, the number of people involved in the process, your experience, and the size of your ministry.

You don't have to put in a lot of time at first. Your purpose statement, goals, and objectives don't have to be perfect before you begin. You don't have to start with a Mercedes. You can begin with a stripped-down Chevy. The process can be constantly refined and improved as you go and grow. But you *must* begin. Plan to begin planning today.

Principles for a Lasting Ministry

by Jim Smoke
Founder and director of The Center for Divorce Recovery, Phoenix, Arizona

Building a singles ministry has a lot in common with building a wall. In the book of Nehemiah,[4] we read about one man's struggle to rebuild a wall—the wall of Jerusalem. Nehemiah's first step: He accepted the challenge. Then he got down to business. Along the way, he overcame physical and human obstacles. His prayer, uttered in the midst of rebuilding the Jerusalem wall, was simply, "O God, strengthen my hands!" To those who sought to detract him from his goal, he responded, "I am doing a great work, I cannot come down!"

How often in the midst of a busy week do we need to re-echo those words of Nehemiah? As I look at the life of Nehemiah the builder, several principles to his success become clear.

Establish Clear Objectives and Priorities

First, he got his objectives and priorities clearly in mind before he started. He knew what he was called to do, and he shared it freely with those willing to help him.

Have a Specific Goal

Next, his goal was firmly set. He knew what he was shooting at. He knew a wall was not a wall until it was completed. Nehemiah was not a half-wall man!

Recruit Others to Help You Build

Third, Nehemiah enlisted his workers. He never intended to do the job by himself. You cannot build walls or ministries without a task force. There will always be those who want to watch and those who want to build. Enlist and involve the builders!

Develop a Unique Ministry

Next, Nehemiah was careful not to get blown off course by other people's agendas. It is dangerous to try to adopt someone else's ministry because it seems to work for that person. Develop a ministry based on the needs and concerns of your own people—not someone else's. What is your own ministry style? What are the abilities of your leadership? What are the particular circumstances and needs in your church and community? Pay attention to those. Remember, each ministry is different; it cannot be xeroxed.

Be Persistent
in the Midst of Distractions

Finally, Nehemiah had learned to watch out for distractions and interruptions. He seemed to face a new one every day, and so will you. Some come from within the ministry and some from without. People, failures, and success are the most common distractions to both ministry growth and wall-building.

Along with the above principles, let me add some questions for those building a ministry with single adults. Spend some time reflecting on your answers. What areas in your ministry need to be changed or fine-tuned? What can you do to make sure your ministry is being built on a solid foundation? (It may even be a good idea to discuss these questions with your leadership team.)

1. Am I building this ministry primarily for myself and my own reputation or glory?
2. What will I leave behind for others to build upon when I move on?
3. Who am I really training and discipling in this ministry?
4. Do others understand what I am trying to build? Have I clearly communicated my vision? Have I encouraged and allowed my people to share their own dreams and goals for this ministry? Do they feel a part of the process?
5. Do the people I am building this ministry with know that I love them and care for them?
6. When I leave this ministry, will people say, "Look at the mess he left!" or will they say, "What a foundation he left behind for us to build upon."

Welcoming New Singles

by Bill Flanagan
Minister with singles at Saint Andrew's Presbyterian Church, Newport Beach, California

One of the most important aspects of beginning and building a healthy ministry is to develop an environment that can keep your visitors involved. The more visitors who take an active role in your ministry, the better you will grow.

Three ingredients can help newcomers feel at home in your single adult ministry.

The Personal Touch

We are called to be shepherds, not ranchers. A shepherd knows the flock by name. A rancher only knows how many head are in the herd.

The personal touch is crucial no matter how large or small a group may be. The welcome mat must always be out, with committed single adults warmly welcoming, integrating, and following up visitors. Name tags are essential.

Finger Food

Coffee and finger food are necessary ingredients for nervous people who may have thought about coming for a long time and finally gotten up the courage to do it. Acts 2:42 indicates that "the breaking of bread" was a key dimension in the growth of the early church along with teaching, fellowship, and prayer.

> "We are called to be shepherds, not ranchers. A shepherd knows the flock by name. A rancher only knows how many head are in the herd."

This is particularly true in a ministry with singles. We never have an activity without food. Food facilitates fellowship and the building of authentic relationships. Simply holding a cup of coffee in your hand eases nervousness and helps create a spirit of warmth.

Being Needed

I remember a young single named Dave who came to our group several years ago and wasn't sure whether he would return. A member of our social committee roped him into bringing mashed potatoes to the potluck the following Friday. Dave reluctantly accepted, and being a responsible person, decided the group was depending on him for mashed potatoes. It gave him a reason to show up. It also gave him an opening line as he went into a house full of strangers.

Suddenly, the group became "his group" because he was making a contribution to it. (Incidentally, Dave later met June. They fell in love and got married. Months later, Dave shared with me how it all started with a bowl of mashed potatoes.)[5]

What Should Be the Goals of a Local Single Adult Ministry?

Priorities for Singles Ministry

by Bill Flanagan
*Minister with singles at Saint
Andrew's Presbyterian Church,
Newport Beach, California*

Somebody once said, "Shoot at nothing and that's exactly what you will hit." Unfortunately, many of us shoot at a singles ministry before we have a target in sight. When the mandate is handed down by heads of staff to get going with a singles program, many of us are quickly off and running to build a viable ministry. But we often get sidetracked and into trouble when we act before taking a closer look at our reason for existence and the broader needs within the church and community.

Personally, I have decided that ministry involves four key areas:
• teaching,
• counseling,
• program administration, and
• the development and equipping of lay leaders.

Whenever I'm asked to pursue an area other than these, I carefully consider it in light of what I have already determined to be my priorities (which means I often have to say no to activities that pull me off course). I have come to terms with the fact that my gifts and energy need to be carefully focused and channeled.

Our congregation has done much the same thing. We have established a clear and simple statement of who we are and why we exist. Any ministry within the church needs to do the same thing. Our congregation has established the following as its clearly stated purpose:

1. The reaching of people with the gospel and indwelling power of Jesus Christ.
2. To nurture and enable people to grow in what it means to be a Christian.
3. To reach out in service and touch the needs of our community, nation, and world by translating our doctrine into action.

With this as the foundation, our single adult ministry seeks to flesh out our Christ-centered purpose and provide a program that will reflect a microcosm of the Christian life—meeting the felt needs of people while being obedient to the biblical calling to reach both inward and outward.

Specifically, this takes form in four ways:

1. *We want to raise the consciousness of the whole Church of Jesus Christ to understand that singleness is natural and healthy.* One is a whole number, and single people are more than simply a target group needing a special outreach ministry. Rather than simply viewing singles as people who need our help, we want the whole church to understand that all of us need to learn from one another.

Single people have much to teach and offer to the total Body of Christ. One of our goals is to help the whole church understand, as well as believe, that unmarried, separated, divorced, or widowed persons are not always less fortunate than married persons. We are committed to modeling that personal fulfillment and wholeness is not realized just when one is married.

2. *We also want to bring the entire congregation to a deeper biblical understanding of marriage, divorce, and remarriage.* We seek to raise, within the context of love, the issues of unconditional fidelity, and where and when to go for help in a marriage or personal life when things begin to fall apart.

We want to model in our words and actions what God really says about grace, forgiveness, and wholeness, and to live effectively in the tension between legalism and freedom. We want to demonstrate the openness that comes when we accept people where they are and not where we want them to be or wish they were.

3. *We are totally committed to the integration of single people into the whole life of the church.* Because of the sheer size of our singles ministry and the number of singles who are becoming an active part of the congregation, we've been forced to rethink the way we have done things for many years.

Events such as family nights are still a part of our church's program, but our people understand that "family" has a larger meaning than mom, dad, and the kids. Many congregations find themselves less than whole because they minister only to a narrowly defined constituency or specialty group. When the church reflects the community around it, it then becomes not only more representative but balanced and whole as well.

4. *Single adult leaders need to clearly understand that the predominant goal of the people in their programs is to find and develop new relationships, usually with the hope that they will eventually lead to marriage.*

Pastors and leaders will find the previously mentioned points helpful for goals and ministry strategy, but they also need to realize that many singles who do not have spiritual or church-related motives are also coming to these groups. We need to capture the special opportunity that is ours to provide a seedbed for developing relationships, while at the same time speaking to the spiritual vacuum and human needs of the singles we influence.

> **"Events such as family nights are still a part of our church's program, but our people understand that 'family' has a larger meaning than mom, dad, and the kids. Many congregations find themselves less than whole because they minister only to a narrowly defined constituency or specialty group."**

Any single adult ministry is a "meet market," which, I believe, is a worthy purpose for ministry as we bring Christian men and women together in authentic relationships. We hope our groups will not become "meat markets" but will illustrate a community similar to that of the early church, where the secular world looked at it and said, "See how they love each other."

Three Goals for Ministry

by Johnny Crist
Senior pastor of Vineyard Christian Fellowship, Atlanta, Georgia

As the number of single adults continues to increase, so does the pressure within the church to have something for them. But a word of caution is advised.

The first step toward developing a healthy ministry with single adults is to examine the goals of the ministry. What gives justification to this effort? In my opinion, there are three valid goals for the existence of a single adult ministry in a local church.

Evangelism

A single adult ministry must serve as a point of entry into the Body of Christ. Nationwide, 40 percent of all married couples attend at least one religious service each week, but among those who are divorced, only 28 percent attend.[6] *The single adult ministry is to be an extension—an arm—of the church reaching out into the community drawing people to Jesus Christ.*

Church growth experts Donald McGavran and Win Arn coauthored the book *Ten Steps for Church Growth*, in which they cite several helpful principles of church growth for the local church. McGavran and Arn write,

The church has two ministries: Caring for those already in the church and reaching out to the lost. It's helpful to think of these as ministry *to* the Body and ministry *through* the Body. . . . It is necessary that we begin to see unreached people and then pray, plan and program. . . . Unless we find ways to bring them in, there won't be significant growth.

To accomplish this task . . . we must discern the various homogeneous parts of the Body.[7]

The singles group within the local church may well be one latent homogeneous unit that can and should serve as a powerful evangelistic arm of the church. Singles can reach other singles; thus the singles ministry functions as a key ingredient in the growth of the church.

A dynamic singles ministry can provide an excellent evangelistic tool in the hand of the local church. It becomes possible to reach the newly divorced person who would have little interest in attending the annual Mother's Day banquet, but would welcome the opportunity to attend a divorce-recovery workshop and small-group discussion.

What, then, is the nature of a single adult ministry? It is a bridge between the world and the church. The single adult ministry is to be an extension of the church reaching out into the community to bring singles to Christ.

Incorporation

The single adult ministry must integrate singles into the life of the local church. The end goal of a single adult ministry should never be self-contained. I am critical of the local singles ministries with members who are very active participants in events for singles but make no commitment to the local church that gives it life.

Numerical increase has always been one of the more thrilling aspects of a single adult ministry. Leaders, especially, have the tendency to rejoice as increasing numbers of singles are drawn to their well-planned functions. Numerical increase is good. It is justified. It is approved by God, for surely His Church will not grow unless more are won.

But, *the singles ministry of the local church must not perceive numerical increase as the end product.* A singles ministry does not exist for itself. Too frequently, the singles ministry is in competition with the church that gave it birth. It would be interesting to determine the percentage of singles who attend the singles events *and* the worship services of the sponsoring church.

What is ultimately accomplished if those involved in the singles ministry find themselves unrelated to the other members of the local body? Can the singles ministry fulfill the various needs of all who come its way? I think not.

Ministries to single adults should be only the path or doorway by which singles enter into responsible membership in the Body of Christ. Those in ministry with single adults should have as their goal the incorporation of singles into the larger Body of Christ. Herein is the challenge the single adult ministry leadership must face.

Nurture

The single adult ministry must develop singles as Christians. In the advertising jungle of attractive offers to join the latest clubs or discussion groups, what right does the church have to enter the private world of the singles lifestyle? What does the church have to offer them?

The single adult ministry must be the vehicle through which singles are encouraged to grow as Christians. (Here we enter into a discussion that requires scrupulous discernment so as not to reject the use of the most creative methods of our day.)

To build an effective singles ministry within the context of a local church, the builders or craftsmen must first decide the nature of the structure they wish to construct. It is difficult, if not impossible, to radically alter the building when it is half-constructed.

The equipping/developing ministry of the church must be a cornerstone upon which the singles ministry will stand. Every "method" or "tactic" one employs to attract singles must be related to the local congregation's foundational goal.

Herein lies the great difference between a singles "program" and a

> "Herein lies the great difference between a singles 'program' and a 'ministry.' 'Program' allows anything to happen as long as more singles are attracted to swell the ranks. Gimmicks that smell and taste of local clubs may attract singles, but how can Jesus Christ change the lives of those attending if the message is never presented?"

"ministry." "Program" allows anything to happen as long as more singles are attracted to swell the ranks. Gimmicks that smell and taste of local clubs may attract singles, but *how can Jesus Christ change the lives of those attending if the message is never presented?*

The gospel, to me, must be the primary goal of a local single adult ministry.

Setting Your Ministry's Goals

by John Westfall
Pastor of adult ministries at University Presbyterian Church, Seattle, Washington

I am a person with an incredibly short memory and an immense ability to lose sight of what is most important. I have found that without clearly defined goals, I am prone to spend my time either "blowing on embers" trying to start a fire under someone or some group, or "putting out fires" in reaction to the pressures and problems that continually clamor for attention.

Rewards of Goal Setting

Before going further, let me share four reasons why I've found goal setting to be so vital.

1. *Determining goals provides freedom from nearsightedness.* Thus, we can focus on the long-range perspective and release ourselves from the "tyranny of the urgent."

2. *Goals provide a focus for agreement that unites those with differing perspectives and priorities for ministry.* We can acknowledge our unity of purpose, though we may sometimes disagree on how best to accomplish it.

3. *Goals become a measuring stick to determine our effectiveness in ministry.* When our goals are clear, it is possible to see whether or not our ministry is doing what we in faith have set out to accomplish.

4. *Establishing goals can be a tremendous group-building experience.* When single adults are allowed and encouraged to set their own goals for ministry, ownership and accountability are established from the beginning. As leaders we are no longer trying to sell something to our people, rather we and our people are partners in ministry working together in serving Christ.

Goal-Setting Questions

When setting goals, I've personally found it best to begin by considering the Lord's direction for my own life and that of my group. I use these questions (or others like them) to begin exploring where God is leading me.

- What does God want to accomplish in me?
- What does He want to have happen in us as a group of single adults?
- What difference would God like to make in our church, city, and world through our single adult ministry?

These questions help us move beyond our own personal agendas and begin to focus on God's priorities for His work.

Stating Your Goals

Here at University Presbyterian Church we have one primary goal statement followed by three subgoals.

Our goal is not to build a strong single adult ministry; rather, we are striving to *build strong single adults* who are ministers.

Our emphasis on the upbuilding, encouraging and equipping of people in ministry is a reflection of our church's understanding that *our final product is people not programs.*

Our three subgoals are as follows:

1. *We are called to be an open door.* The classes, workshops, activities, and small groups in the singles ministry are intentionally designed to draw in those outside the immediate group. We are becoming an open door through which people enter into the fellowship of Christian community and a personal relationship with Jesus.

We realize that people come to groups for differing reasons. For example, some are lonely and seek friendship, others want to grow in their understanding of God's Word, and others still are seeking someone to love and hope to find a life partner.

By being an open door, we embrace people at their point of need and proclaim that there is indeed a place for them to enter and belong.

2. *It is our goal to be a sliding door.* Singles ministry can become a passageway to growth. Just as sliding doors allow us to move from one room to another, we provide opportunity and encouragement for people to move along in their Christian growth as their needs and circumstances change.

Perhaps the notoriously high turnover of singles in our ministries is not because singles are flaky or uncommitted but rather because our range of programs is too limited to handle all their needs.

Maybe we need to slide open more doors, encouraging singles to explore and take steps as they grow. There can be no significant growth when we need to feel safe.

3. *Our goal is to be a revolving door.* Recognizing that ministry with singles is only a small part of the church's life, we encourage singles to move out of singles ministry into new areas of service and investment.

We have become a commissioning center from which singles are moving into significant involvement and investment in the church, the city of Seattle, and the world. Believing that every Christian is a minister, we are releasing people to discover or create new ministries.

> **"Our goal is not to build a strong single adult ministry; rather, we are striving to *build strong single adults* who are ministers."**

Keeping Your Ministry on a Healthy Course

Fourteen Reasons Why Your Ministry Can Fail

by Jim Smoke
Founder and director of The Center for Divorce Recovery, Phoenix, Arizona

At least once a month, someone tells me that he or she used to have a singles ministry in his or her church, but it died! When I hear that, I wonder who killed it.

As you work to build your ministry with single adults, let me share what I believe are the pitfalls, the things that can kill it. Use this as a midcourse checkup to see how your ministry is doing.

1. *Fad-born.* If your singles ministry was started as a "jump-on-the-bandwagon fad ministry," the chances are great that it will fizzle out when some other new ministry pops up in your church. A ministry must be founded on need and vision—it exists to find a need and fill it, to find a hurt and heal it. The commitment level is more than fad-deep.

2. *Inappropriate lay leadership.* Lack of trained and knowledgeable leadership in the ranks of the laity will send a singles ministry down the drain. A single adult ministry must be owned by a laity that is trained in equipping and understanding this unique ministry. A good way to do this is through leadership retreats.

Also, some groups use a lopsided number of women in leadership roles. As a result, the men often quit coming. Leadership needs to be divided between both men and women.

3. *Leadership by committee.* A failure to put someone at the helm of the ministry will cause confusion in the ranks and ultimately scatter the troops in disarray. Whether it is a layman or a staff professional, it must be understood that the buck stops on someone's desk. Committees don't lead. They have committee meetings. Leaders lead!

4. *Weak clergy support.* The failure of the senior pastor and pastoral staff to understand and support the ministry will cause it to fail or at best sputter and chug along. The "you can do it but don't bother me" line that clergy are prone to spout will put a singles ministry right next door to the church broom closet. Verbal support and encouragement must come from the senior pastor and church staff.

5. *Unfounded congregational fears.* The failure of the congregation to understand the ministry and its goals will raise such a wall of doubt and questioning that the ministry will self destruct. People fear what they don't understand. A ministry must be interpreted and explained to the congregation in order to gain its vital support and encouragement.

6. *Poor integration.* Failure to incorporate the singles ministry into the larger life of the church will cause it to

fail. It cannot be an appendage ministry tucked away in a back room, even if you have only ten singles. There must be a way for your singles to be integrated into the total life of the church. This also means providing opportunities for them to serve in positions of church-wide leadership.

7. *No budget.* Lack of proper financial support and incorporation into the church budget will cause a ministry to die a slow death. Ministries cost money if they are done properly. The surest way to kill any ministry is to keep it out of the church budget. When this happens, the message is, "It's not important enough."

8. *Inadequate counseling.* The lack of a counseling or referral system for troubled singles will cause the ministry to fail. Many singles come to a program with hurts. They need to know that there is a way they can get help. If no one seems to care, they will move on.

9. *Unbalanced program.* Lack of a balanced program will kill a singles ministry. You must have a broad integration of biblical teaching, social structure and events, small-group and educational opportunities, and camps, conferences, seminars, and retreats. Monthly potlucks and Sunday school classes do not make a singles ministry. People get bored with the same old thing.

10. *No new blood.* Too many veterans from years in the singles wars can send your ministry down the drain. They are the kind of people who know it all, have done it all, and now want to complain about it all. This is why I believe there is a time for some singles to get out of the group and take a sabbatical. New people are adventurers. Veterans tend to be settlers. Set some limits on how long your leaders can remain in leadership positions. Keep the new blood flowing.

11. *Poor outreach.* A failure to capture what I call the "arms out to one another concept" will sink a singles ministry fast. People becoming whole need to keep reaching out to those coming in the door in need of wholeness. If they forget to be wounded healers themselves, they will become ingrown, and new people will feel excluded, causing them to go elsewhere.

> **"Too many veterans from years in the singles wars can send your ministry down the drain. They are the kind of people who know it all, have done it all, and now want to complain about it all. This is why I believe there is a time for some singles to get out of the group and take a sabbatical. New people are adventurers. Veterans tend to be settlers."**

12. *Ducking hard issues.* The fear that singles coming into a ministry will bring a bag of problems with them can send sane people running for their lives. Yes, you will have to deal honestly and openly with divorce and remarriage, sexuality and singleness, and a host of other struggles. A singles ministry does open a grab bag of issues. But if they are not openly and honestly dealt with, the ministry will collapse.

13. *Inadequate direction/purpose.* The lack of long-range planning and vision will cause the demise of a

singles ministry. The question is, "Where are you going beyond the next potluck?" A real ministry is planned for the present and the future. Your program should be planned at least three months in advance and even further for special events. Most good speakers cannot even address your group unless given from four to six months advance warning.

14. *Programs.* A ministry will also fail if it doesn't create programs that answer the pressing needs in the lives of single adults.

Is Your Ministry on the Road to Success?

by Bret Avlakeotes
Singles pastor at Fellowship Bible Church of Park Cities, Dallas, Texas

The story is told of a farmer who used to shoot his bow and arrow at the side of his barn every day. A friend visited and was impressed that each arrow was in the center of a bull's-eye. When he asked about the farmer's incredible ability to hit a target, the farmer told him, "I just shoot the arrow and wherever it hits, I draw a bull's-eye around it." The saying is true, "If you aim at everything, you are sure to hit something."

In today's ever-changing single adult culture, failing to plan is the same as planning to fail. The following seven questions are designed to help you and your leadership team chart your course. They are not intended as a road map telling you everything you're supposed to do, but rather as a compass, telling you if you are heading in the right direction.

Spend time discussing them together and then consider sharing them with your entire group.

Question 1: Why Do We Exist?

The answer to this question should reflect how your particular group is unique. What sets you apart? What are your group's basic purpose and core values? How would someone define the group? What specific needs is the group trying to meet?

For example, our ministry to singles is guided by four purposes:

- *Relationships*. We want to provide an atmosphere where healthy Christian relationships are encouraged, nurtured, and developed.
- *Spiritual nourishment*. We emphasize biblical teaching and application.
- *Evangelism*. We want to be a group where seeking nonChristians can come to learn about Jesus.
- *Involvement*. We would like to see every person in our class involved either inside or outside the church using his or her spiritual gifts and talents for the Kingdom of God.

These four purposes help tell us when to say yes to various opportunities that come along, as well as when to say no. They also guide us in how to spend our money, time, and energy.

For example, we recently relocated one of our single adult classes to a nearby hotel. The availability of tables to meet around for interaction was one of the main reasons we chose the place. Our stated purpose of developing relationships guided us in this decision. So, knowing why you exist is key to knowing who you are and where you should be going.

The answer to question number one should also reflect your target audience. Describe the singles you are trying to reach in terms of age, place in life, and values. Examples might include: single parents, singles in their twenties, early career singles, singles from ages thirty to forty, or divorced.

Our church used to have only one singles group that was for any single adult of any age in the church. When a second group was started for singles in their thirties, there was growth in both groups. The original group now targets the needs of singles in their twenties, and the second group targets singles thirty and over. The needs of these two groups are different and need to be defined and addressed accordingly.

Once you have answered the "why question," you are ready to structure the rest of your ministry. Don't attempt anything else until you have sufficiently answered the first question.

Question 2:
Where Are We Going?

Robert Schuller defines leadership as "thinking ahead, planning for the future, exhausting all possibilities, envisioning problems, dreaming up solutions to them, and then communicat-ing the possibilities and the problem-solving ideas to the decision makers."

Before you can lead your group, you have to know where you are going. My wife and I have gone on mini-retreats to pray and ask God what he wants to do in our group over the coming weeks and months. After spending time in prayer, we write down every impression the Lord gives us. We try to be open to the Holy Spirit and to listen to His voice.

"Vision" has been defined as "a mental image of a desirable and future state." Vision is what Hebrews 11:1 calls faith: "Now faith is being sure of what we hope for and certain of what we do not see."

Knowing where you are going will accomplish three things. It will

• attract people,
• establish priorities, and
• define success.

The bigger the vision, the more attractive it is to others. People like to be a part of something that is stretching and exciting. When we walk through these seven questions with our singles group, helping them see the larger picture, people come up to me with excitement—making fresh commitments to be involved in our ministry. The smaller your vision, the smaller number of people you will attract to your ministry.

Vision defines success. By stating your vision, you encourage and invite others to help it become reality. No one wants to see a worthy goal go unreached. With a clearly defined direction and purpose, you will also be able to chart your progress and know when you have succeeded. This can become a wonderful source of encouragement for both your leadership and your group.

Question 3:
Why Are We Going There?

Why are we doing all the things we're doing? Are our goals worthy and biblical? What difference will our ministry make? How would people's lives be different if our ministry did *not* exist?

I recently challenged our group with the fact that only 6 percent of the singles in our city go to church. That means that 94 percent do not. Thousands of single adults in our town face a Christ-less eternity. But our

---

HERE'S HOW OUR SINGLES MINISTRY ANSWERED "THE SEVEN QUESTIONS"
by Bret Avlakeotes

The following is an abbreviated look at how our singles ministry leadership team addressed each of the seven questions:

Question 1: Why Do We Exist?
1. To reach single adults, from age thirty to their early forties, who live in Dallas with the good news of Jesus Christ, and to teach them how to live a meaningful and useful life for the glory of God.
2. To provide a place where Christian singles can meet one another in a network of healthy relationships.
3. To provide spiritual nourishment by teaching the life-changing truths of the Word of God.
4. To provide avenues for meaningful involvement both inside and outside the four walls of the church.

Question 2: Where Are We Going?
1. Eighty percent of our class will be involved in some kind of small group for accountability, fellowship, and spiritual nurture.
2. Our class will fill the hotel ballroom (our meeting place) to capacity.
3. Our class will spin off a new group for single adults in their late forties and early fifties.
4. Eighty percent of our class will be involved in some meaningful ministry either inside or outside the four walls of our church.
5. Eighty percent of this group will be equipped to lead another person to Christ by sharing the good news.

Question 3: Why Are We Going There?
1. There is a tremendous amount of loneliness in the city of Dallas.
2. There are so many people who do not know right from wrong and are suffering the consequences of bad decisions.
3. We care that so many are going to a Christ-less eternity with no one telling them where to find life.
4. It is not enough just to be a Christian; people need to learn how to please the Lord in their daily lives.

group can help make a difference!

Dale Galloway, in his book *20/20 Vision,* tells the story about a gang of laborers digging a hole five feet square by ten feet deep. After grueling hours of hard labor, they finally got the hole dug. The boss had never bothered to tell them the purpose for digging the hole. In fact, after they got the hole dug, he looked at them and said, "Fill it back up." Immediately, the men said, "We quit, we want our pay now! Digging holes and filling them up again only makes fools of us." When the boss took the time to explain to them the purpose for digging the hole, which was to locate a leaking gas line that was endangering the health of the

Question 4: What Does It Feel Like To Be Going There?
It feels
1. fun
2. exciting
3. powerful
4. worthwhile
5. satisfying
6. contagious
7. difficult
8. overwhelming
9. humbling

Question 5: What Can You Do?
1. You can be a table leader.
2. You can become part of our hospitality committee and reach out to help others feel at home here.
3. You can be one of our small-group leaders reaching out with love and help to from eight to twelve people.
4. You can offer your home or apartment for meetings of small groups and social activities.
5. You can help pass out flyers and materials at the Hilton hotel (where we meet) on Sunday morning.
6. You can pray and begin a ministry of prayer for the others in our group.
7. You can give financially.

Question 6: How Are We Going To Do It?
1. We will organize a group of table leaders and have a training meeting.
2. We will develop a small-group strategy that is attractive and can accommodate a continual flow of new people.
3. All of our leaders will seek to model in their personal lives the vision that we have.

Question 7: What Will The Rewards Be?
1. People who do not know Christ will find Him as their Lord and Savior.
2. More and more people will be part of a supportive network of healthy friendships.
3. More and more people will mature and become like Jesus.
4. Jesus will say to each of us, "Well done, thou good and faithful servant."

people who lived nearby, the laborers remained on the job; they learned there was a purpose.

Since it only takes the members of a group about one month (or less) to forget why it exists, remind them regularly.

Question 4: What Does It Feel Like To Be Going There?

For this question, come up with as many descriptive adjectives as possible. Words such as *exciting, challenging, meaningful, difficult, disappointing,* and *worthwhile* help a person to emotionally feel the impact of the journey. Use them often.

Question 5: What Can You Do?

How can the people in your group get involved? What specific jobs need to be done so the vision can be accomplished? Work together as a leadership team to define as many of these job descriptions as possible. This enables your people to own the vision in little "do-able" bites. People want to help make a difference; they want their life to count for something. Sometimes all they need from you is permission.

I remind myself that my singles are saying, "Use me or lose me."

Question 6: How Are We Going To Do It?

This is a strategy question. It answers the question of how. What plans will lead to the accomplishment of our vision, to ensure that success is realized? Be as specific as possible. Take time with your leaders to brainstorm creative ways to accomplish what God is calling you to do. Be sensitive to your particular cultural context. We live in the fast-paced nineties. What worked in the seventies may not work today. Be fresh. Put your feet up often to think, pray, and dream.

Question 7: What Will The Rewards Be?

Whether we like it or not, people are tuned into WII-FM—"What's in it for me?" People want to know that their hard work will bring rewards. Remind them often about both the tangible and intangible benefits, both for today (see box) and for eternity, for their own lives as well as for others. Singles want to know that their lives count, that what they do really matters. Everyone

---

BENEFITS OF HELPING OTHERS

People who exercise vigorously often describe feeling high during a workout—and a sense of calmness and freedom from stress afterward.

New evidence reveals that these same emotional and physical changes can be produced with activity requiring much less exertion—helping others.

The feel-good sensation [from altruism] is most intense when actually touching or listening to someone. . . . Interestingly, altruism's pleasure does not appear to arise from donating money, no matter how important the cause, nor from volunteering without close personal contact.[8]

wants to hear from Jesus, "Well done, good and faithful servant."

Asking these seven questions will not solve all the problems or challenges associated with your singles ministry. But they are guaranteed to provide helpful discussion and interaction—first among your leadership team, and then with your entire group.

Singles Ministry and Church Discipline

by Scott Last
Minister with singles at
Emmanuel Faith Community
Church, Escondido, California

How can church discipline and singles ministry be intelligently discussed in the same article? After all, how could anyone expect to build a viable ministry by seriously insisting on biblical standards of conduct to a segment of society notorious for its relaxed style of living?

On the other hand, if a ministry has already been developed that has effectively drawn in large numbers of unchurched singles, wouldn't the enforcement of biblical morality tend to drive away those same people?

Several years ago I went to a seminar at which the leader (a singles minister of some stature) as much as said that you have to choose between discipline and singles ministry. You can't have both and really expect to grow. With all due respect to my colleagues who share this view, I would like to say, "Baloney!"

In fact, my belief is that without discipline a Christian singles group cannot survive as a legitimate ministry. Without discipline a group can quickly degenerate into a "meat market." At best it may become a social club that, perhaps, speaks "Christianese" and attempts some gospel presentations but bears few of the marks of authentic Christianity.

In our attempts to attract the unchurched, sometimes I wonder whether we are influencing them as much as they are influencing us. Is the church reaching the world, or is the world reaching the church? Now before you brand me as a legalist, or at least a "fightin' fundy," and turn to another page, let me tell you that I hate having to confront or discipline anyone. Those who know me know that I am not big on rules. Being the heavy is not my idea of a good time.

Based on these reasons alone, I would love to be able to completely avoid this topic—along with the accompanying responsibilities—if I could. But there are deeper issues at stake here than my own personal comfort.

I too have a heart for evangelism and would love to reach as many singles as possible for Jesus. But at what cost? Should you and I sacrifice the integrity of God's commands upon our lifestyles in order to make our groups comfortable to nonChristians? Certainly, reaching out is of the highest priority, but isn't "teaching them to obey" also part of the Great Commission?

My view is that the pendulum between outreach and discipline usually swings too far in one direction or the other in our ministries. What I'd like to propose are some principles to help us reach a balance between the two that is gracious yet uncompromisingly biblical in its approach.

The Purpose of Discipline

As I see it, the purpose of maintaining church discipline within a singles group or any other Christian group is twofold.

1. As Galatians 6:1 and Matthew 18:15 discuss, the restoration of a brother or sister in Christ from the trap of sinful behavior or attitudes is paramount. Even in the case of church expulsion, as is discussed in 1 Corinthians 5, discipline is not to be used vindictively or with hostility. Verse 5 of that chapter shows that even the harshest discipline is designed to ultimately benefit the recipient.
2. The purpose of discipline is to protect the rest of the local body from being divided or defiled by internal corruption. We all know what one bad apple can do to the rest of the barrel. Ephesians 4 and 5 tells us that the church's unity and purity are top priorities in God's mind, and we need to "make every effort" to maintain them (Ephesians 4:3).

The Limitations of Discipline

One of the dilemmas facing those of us who believe in church discipline is the fact that if we tried to confront every sin or problem in our groups, our jobs would soon become limited to full-time moral law enforcement. This would give a new and unwanted meaning to our positions as church officers.

An alternative is to run the sin or problem through the following grid (based on my understanding of the purpose of discipline). Ask yourself these questions:

• Is an individual's sin a repetitive problem that could seriously damage him or her and/or others?
• Is the unity or purity of the group threatened by the problem behavior or attitudes?

When we process the matter through this type of grid, it is much easier to determine, for example, how smart it would be to get involved with a conflict between Bill and Mary over their dating relationship.

The Practice of Discipline

As I discuss the practice of discipline, I will assume that you are familiar with the steps of confrontation and church action described in Matthew 18. With that as a foundation, let me give some tips on implementing these steps for the maximum positive effect with a minimum number of confrontations. (Remember, I hate confrontation too.)

1. *Have as few rules as possible, but make sure everyone knows them and the consequences for breaking them.* My people know they will be confronted by me for very few reasons. But they know I will confront them

concerning the following:

- sexual immorality or sexual harassment,
- dating when one or both partners are still legally married to someone else (usually due to unfinalized divorces),
- drug or alcohol abuse, or
- for teaching or doing something that creates division in the group.

We actually talk about these rules from time to time in our large group meetings. When they are explained clearly and shown to be for the good of all, I get very little objection from even our newest members and visitors. I have also found that when the rules are clear, the group tends to become self-policing in a positive way. There is a real sense of security and identity within a group that stands for something and knows its rules.

2. *Encourage accountability and support within your group.* People get into big trouble when they are living as "lone rangers." But when they get involved with each other in small groups and as friends, supporting and building each other up as brothers and sisters in Christ, I have found that many potential and real problems have been solved without my personal involvement. What a strength-builder it is for the body that develops its own immunity to spiritual sickness.

3. *When a problem comes to your attention, it is wise to proceed gently and leave room for growth.* But don't let gentleness be an excuse for procrastination.

Some time ago I discovered that a very influential man in our group had become disenchanted with what our church and I taught in certain areas of doctrine. Instead of keeping his disagreement to himself or finding another fellowship more in line with his opinions, he felt compelled to try to use his influence to turn others toward his way of thinking. Needless to say, his activities soon began to cause confusion and problems within the group.

After speaking gently with him about what he was doing, I thought it best to give him some time to work it out. This proved to be a good strategy because he really seemed to have a sincere heart and had the sympathy of many in our group. To have come down hard on him right away might have caused a split among us.

As it turned out, we eventually did have to expel him. It was a very difficult experience. But because my people knew that I had given him every opportunity to work out his disagreements and stay in our fellowship, when it came time to take final action, he had already worn out his welcome in the eyes of the group. In fact, I had almost total support since many had seen me dealing with him gently without procrastination.

> "Several years ago I went to a seminar at which the leader (a singles minister of some stature) as much as said that you have to choose between discipline and singles ministry. You can't have both and really expect to grow. With all due respect to my colleagues who share this view, I would like to say, 'Baloney!' "

4. *When you do confront, communicate as clearly and lovingly as possible.* Don't hint around and expect the person to know what you want. Communicate exactly what you expect of him or her, when you expect it, and what the consequences will be. Write it out and rehearse it in advance if necessary.

Try to remain calm and loving in your presentation. I haven't always succeeded in this. During some confrontations I have gotten more overheated than I would have liked. But at least the person I confronted knew what I was thinking and feeling.

> **"Church discipline does not make a group less loving (which tends to be our fear). Rather, it makes a group more loving because people know we care enough to do something about problems and people who are messing up."**

5. *If expulsion becomes necessary, do it as publicly as possible.* This doesn't mean that you drag all the dirty laundry before the church on Sunday morning and risk being sued for slander or libel. But making your disciplinary actions public will accomplish the following three things for you and your singles ministry.

- It will let your people know what action has been taken and give them guidance on how to deal with the person acted upon should they be friends or just cross paths.
- It will enhance your spiritual authority, showing your people that you are serious about God and His priorities.
- It will let your people know that along with the privileges of being a member of the local Body of Christ also comes responsibility. If they want to stick around to enjoy the fellowship, they will need to behave in a responsible fashion or face the consequences.

6. *Always make it possible for disciplined people to return.* Leave the ball in their court. Let them know that if they decide to repent or change their behavior in an appropriate manner they will be restored to fellowship. Restoration is always the ultimate goal of discipline.

If the disciplinary action was made public, make sure that restoration, if it does come, will be public as well. I thank God that we have experienced many private restorations, although I am still waiting for our first public one. (I have heard of public restoration happening in other fellowships with dramatic impact.)

7. *Don't forget to bathe this whole process in thought and prayer, seeking wisdom and insight from God and counsel from sources you really trust.* Without divine wisdom and protection, you can get badly burned in the fires of church discipline. I know that God has bailed me out more than once by preventing me from acting in anger without sufficient preparation. I praise God for the times I have gotten a busy signal or no answer when I would have undone the discipline process with my anger. With nothing left to do but pray, it's funny how my perspective of a situation seems to improve.

The Results of Discipline

When I look back over the results of maintaining discipline within our singles ministry, I can see why God's Word outlines the process so clearly. Church discipline—when properly and consistently applied—really works. Whether or not the offending brother or sister is restored (which happens more often than not), I have seen it pay dividends over and over within the rest of the group. The more consistently discipline is practiced, the less often it seems to be needed.

Church discipline does not make a group less loving (which tends to be our fear). Rather, it makes a group more loving because people know we care enough to do something about problems and people who are messing up.

I am not saying that our numbers have jumped as a direct result of our willingness to show tough love. Discipline does not take the place of outreach. But there is no doubt in my mind that, because we have demanded a higher quality of commitment, we have helped some people live a higher quality of Christianity. And high-quality Christianity can be a considerably attractive lifestyle for Christians and nonChristians alike.

I am not saying that we have this thing whipped. We still have wolves who show up and try to hit on our women. We still have long-time members who get into trouble.

As I write this article, I am aware of a situation that will demand my attention within the next twenty-four hours. I really wish the problem would go away by itself. But if I procrastinate, it will probably get worse. Unfortunately, I really like the person I have to confront, and she should know better than to be doing what she's doing. Yet I know that I must proceed quickly but gently with a lot of prayer. Hopefully, she will respond to our little talk in private. If not, I know that I need not fear the process because it is in God's Word, and I have seen Him glorified in it.

So let me encourage you. I don't think you need to choose between outreach and discipline. I think you really can have both. It is a delicate balance that depends to a large degree on your own ministry setting. But don't let the fear of "turning someone off" cause you to compromise the quality of your ministry in the truest biblical sense.

Vital Signs of the Healthy Ministry

by Jim Dyke
Minister with singles at College Avenue Baptist Church, San Diego, California

In 1976, C. Peter Wagner authored a book that became a basic handbook for ministers interested in helping their churches grow. In *Your Church Can Grow: Seven Vital Signs of a Healthy Church*, Wagner stated two premises:

- A church is like a human body and must be healthy in order to grow.

- One can detect the health of a church in the same way one detects health in a human body—by looking for the right "vital" signs.

(I have found these vital signs to be valuable in measuring the vitality of a department *within* a congregation as well.)

The following are my adaptations of Wagner's seven "vital" signs for a healthy single adult ministry (SAM).

> "Cliques can be devastating to a new person. If your SAM is one large clique, it is tough for new people to 'belong' and therefore difficult for your ministry to grow in numbers."

Vital Sign 1:
Decisive Direction

Are you a leader with faith and vision who is willing and able to mobilize others and motivate them to action?

This is probably the most critical of all the vital signs. There must be one person who is willing to accept the responsibility to lead the SAM. Committees are great, but they rarely provide visionary, decisive direction. They work best as they provide counsel and support for an *identified leader.*

This leader may be the senior pastor, a staff member who is the minister for single adults, or a gifted lay leader. The leader should be

- willing to accept responsibility for the ministry;
- an individual of faith and vision;
- able to mobilize the gifts, talents, and resources of others; and
- able to motivate people to active and effective involvement in the singles ministry.

Vital Sign 2:
Serving Singles

Do you have singles who are discovering, developing, and employing their spiritual gifts for ministry?

Ephesians 4:16 makes it clear that every Christian has something of value to contribute to the ministry of the group and to the spiritual growth of its members. Your SAM will grow and prosper only if individuals use their spiritual gifts in active ministry.

A wise leader will help individuals discover their spiritual gifts and teach them to employ those gifts in appropriate ministry opportunities.

Spiritual gifts and ministry make good psychological sense. Spiritual gifts are God's way of demonstrating that all the members of His body are important and have something to contribute. Ministry can be great therapy for hurting single adults who need to recover a sense of self-worth and personal value.

Vital Sign 3:
A Growing Group

Is your SAM big enough to provide the range of ministry and relationships necessary to meet the needs and expectations of its members and newcomers? Many such ministries are just too small to grow and prosper.

Part of the problem is psychological. People in our culture are more attracted to a large group because it communicates a feeling of success, particularly in a social setting. This has obvious application to SAMs, where single adults are very interested in interacting socially with other singles.

A second part of the problem is sociological. Large groups provide a different dynamic of interpersonal interaction. We'll take a closer look at this in vital sign 4.

A third part of the problem is programmatic. Large single adult ministries find it easy to attract new people because they have more to offer (e.g., a divorce-recovery group, a single parents fellowship, a young professionals group).

If your SAM cannot survive on its own—especially if you are in a smaller church or community—you may choose to combine with other churches in an intercongregational singles ministry.

Vital Sign 4:
Clear Of Cliques
Does your organizational structure make effective use of groups and group dynamics?

The key is to have a group large enough to be a "group of groups," where a newcomer can find different clusters of relationships to belong to.

A SPIRITUAL CHECKUP FOR YOUR MINISTRY
by Jim Dyke

How are the vital signs of your single adult ministry? Success in single adult ministry depends on the health and vitality of the group. Perform a spiritual checkup today on your ministry. Ask yourself the following tough questions about leadership, membership involvement, ministry potential, group life, local church integration, evangelism, and ministry priorities.

1. Am I mobilizing the singles in my group to become strong leaders, or am I "taking over the reins" myself?

2. Is the single population in my area really big enough to support a vital SAM? Do I need to concentrate my efforts in developing a special segment group to minister to, rather than trying to "be everything to all people"?

3. Is teaching my group about spiritual gifts part of my upcoming lesson plans? Do I have ways to relate the different spiritual gifts to specific ministry opportunities that are available in our church?

4. What kinds of groups are part of my SAM? Are they diverse enough to make a variety of newcomers feel they could fit in? If my ministry is one large clique, how can I encourage it to split into several groups?

5. What percentage of the members of my ministry is actively involved in the sponsoring church? How can I encourage those who are not to become more involved?

6. What evangelism programs are currently being encouraged in my SAM? What kind of assimilation programs do we have for new converts?

7. Are my SAM's priorities in order? Am I focusing first and foremost on helping individuals to grow in their personal relationship with Christ? Do the topics of my lessons reflect these priorities?

This diffuses the negative impact of cliques in your ministry.

Cliques can be devastating to a new person. If your SAM is one large clique, it is tough for new people to "belong" and therefore difficult for your ministry to grow in numbers.

Groups can take many forms: a small-group Bible study, a social committee, a musical ensemble, a ministry team, a single adult softball team, or an evangelism team. The more groups, the more possibilities for assimilating new people.

Groups provide jobs for people to do. Church growth consultant Lyle Schaller reminds us that people come to a church for many reasons, but they stay for two reasons: They know someone or they have a job to do. Groups in your SAM can help in these two critical areas by introducing people to new friendships and giving them opportunities to serve.

> **"As a leader, you must develop and communicate a positive attitude toward your sponsoring congregation. If you cannot support your church in good conscience, or if you really don't feel your ministry is a true reflection of that church, then maybe you are in the wrong place of leadership!"**

Vital Sign 5:
Local Links

Does your SAM have strong identification and integration with the sponsoring local church?

As a leader, you must develop and communicate a positive attitude toward your sponsoring congregation. If you cannot support your church in good conscience, or if you really don't feel your ministry is a true reflection of that church, then maybe you are in the wrong place of leadership!

Help your people feel a part of the church. Encourage them to become members of the church. Support them in finding roles of ministry in the church.

If you are working with a nondenominational singles ministry, it is still important to have a good working relationship with the churches and pastors in your area. Remember, a nondenominational SAM (like all other parachurch ministries) is not a substitute for a local congregation. Your people still need to participate in a local church where they can worship, minister, and experience meaningful fellowship.

Vital Sign 6:
Effective Evangelism

Are you experiencing evangelism that culminates with the integration of new Christians into active participation and relationships in your fellowship?

The first consideration is evangelism itself. Is it happening in your group? Is there a vision for helping people on the most fundamental level? Are the gifted evangelists being mobilized, trained, deployed, and encouraged?

The second consideration is assimilation. Are new Christians being incorporated into the group socially and spiritually? Are they being ministered to with patience and understanding? Is their infectious experience of conversion allowed expression among the "old-timers"?

Commitment to evangelism requires special investment in new converts. This could include a "basics" class led by a mature Christian with a gift for shepherding, a one-on-one teaming of new converts with stable members of your fellowship, or a special home Bible study group for new Christians.

Provide entry-level ministry experiences for new converts as well. They can contribute to ministry in such areas as visiting a convalescent home, helping in a children's Sunday school class, or cooking for a social get-together.

Vital Sign 7:
Renewal That Reaches Out

Do you have spiritual growth and renewal that culminates in ministry and service?

In his book *Lord, Make My Life a Miracle*, Ray Ortlund presents three priorities for the Christian life. The first priority is commitment to Christ; the second is commitment to the Body of Christ; and the third, commitment to the work of Christ in the world.

Ortlund says these priorities must be established in order. Your single adult ministry should first facilitate the individual spiritual growth of its members, and then lead them into ministry experiences that will mobilize them for service. It is no good trying to construct an aggressive missions program unless there is a strong element of love and commitment within your group. Similarly, it is useless to try to build strong small groups unless your people are being nurtured in their individual relationships with Christ.

These priorities call for effective ministry on each level. The first priority requires a strong emphasis on Bible teaching, worship, and prayer, while the second demands a vital element of face-to-face Christianity, usually through strong small groups. Priority number three calls for a major focus on spiritual gifts and ministry opportunities and a well-supported missions program.

PART TWO:

Leadership for Your Single Adult Ministry

ABOUT PART TWO

Few areas are more crucial
in your singles ministry than trained,
empowered, nurtured leaders.

In fact, leadership development and training
is an ongoing, week-by-week process.

In this section, several leaders provide
suggestions and guidelines on how to
select and train leaders.

But this information goes beyond that and looks
at how to empower your people for ministry—
how to give the ministry away.

The last part of this section offers
some advice on how to keep yourself
and your leadership team on track
spiritually and emotionally.

Working with Your Leadership Team

Equipping Your Singles

an interview with Frank Tillapaugh
Senior pastor at Bear Valley Baptist Church, Denver, Colorado

What can a leader do when his single adults come up with great ministry ideas or projects but don't know how to make them happen? It seems they don't have the motivation or organizational skills to get going. How can he help them follow through on their ideas and develop new ministries without doing it all for them?

In my opinion, if they don't have the ability to keep it going, then it's not God's time for them to do it. I really believe in this principle called "relaxed concern." When Jesus went to the cross, not every blind person could see, not every crippled person was healed, and not every sinner was saved. Yet in John 17, we read where Jesus said He had finished the work given Him to do. We need to relax and do what He wants us to do.

How do we determine what God wants our people to do?

We look at the burdens God puts on people's hearts and the ability He gives them to carry it through. If you look at your ministry as an organism rather than an organization, death is as natural as life. We shouldn't be afraid to let things die; it's natural with any organism. Some ideas or ministries should not survive.

If God (the Head) isn't enabling me or someone else to do something, that can be a good indication that it's not what He wants us to do. It needs to be allowed to die. And when any of us tries doing something He hasn't enabled us to do, it simply becomes a frantic, fleshly effort.

How does the principle of "relaxed concern" fit in with the concept that leaders are to equip their people for ministry? Aren't we as leaders responsible for seeing that they get the job done?

If you can help get a ministry or project running on its own, that's okay. But if, by going in, you create lines of dependence back to you, that's a different story. What I'm saying is, avoid the stuff that creates lines of dependence back to you. If you are enabling people to operate without you, that is true equipping.

> **"If you are enabling people to operate without you, that is true equipping."**

I also believe leaders should spend most of their time equipping a person's character rather than teaching him or her the mechanics of how to get something done. The most liberating thing I can say to people when they are frustrated and can't figure out how to do something is, "I don't know." That way, in agony on their knees, frustrated, God gives them some mechanics; something that works best for them; something they own.

Thus, when equipping, focus on developing a person's character.

Two Phases of Leadership Training

by Doug Morphis
Counselor at First United Methodist Church in Wichita, Kansas

I cannot stress enough the importance of having a good, strong core of lay leaders for the health of your singles ministry. I've been involved as a singles pastor for several years and have seen my singles group at both its best and its not-so-good times. The best has been when a committed, Christian leadership team is at the helm (not just one leader, but a core or group of leaders).

The not-so-good times have occurred when the lay leadership was weak, or when I tried to do too much for the singles on my own. During these times the entire singles program seemed to suffer. (Today, after learning several things the hard way, I see my primary role as one to encourage, support, train, and guide my lay leadership team.)

I believe there are two phases in building strong lay leadership in a singles group. The first phase involves recruiting and training leaders for a new group; the second involves leadership training for the ongoing group. (There is a difference in lay leadership development between these two different types of groups.)

Phase One: Leadership For the New Group

There are seven steps that I recommend when building a strong core leadership team for a *beginning* singles group.

1. Before recruiting lay leadership, meet with persons who are interested in forming a group. (This might include staff, the senior pastor, interested singles, or a combination of the above.) Help them identify the primary purpose for the group as well as the target audience in terms of age, sex, and other specific variables.

2. Make a list of singles in that target group who exhibit leadership skills or potential. If, for instance, we were trying to begin a group for single parents from age thirty-five to forty-five, I would list about twelve people—an equal number of males and females—who are potential leaders for that group.

I have found that the best leaders do not necessarily need a group but have the capacity to attract and to minister to others in that group.

3. Next, meet with these persons individually to get to know them better and to share with them the various new ministry opportunities. Emphasize the importance and potential of each ministry position and the positive attributes they have to contribute, should they become involved.

4. Explain that they need to make a nine-month commitment. (This includes three months for training and six months to serve in the leadership position.) Furthermore, the commitment requires one evening a week during their term of office.

ARE YOU A SPIRITUAL LEADER?
by Lawrence O. Richards
Author of more than fifty books, including **The Believer's Guidebook**

Leadership is often defined as the art or skill of getting things done through other people. The leader is viewed as one who plans and organizes, assigns, delegates, and supervises to accomplish tasks. This concept of leadership is appropriate in government, in business, in the military, and in clubs or work groups. But it's not appropriate in the church or the family. It's important for us as Christians to have a biblical understanding of the leadership God expects us to provide in these relationships.

Which Of the Following Are You Most Like?

Secular Leaders
• focus primarily on building organizations and structures,
• focus primarily on organizing people to get jobs done, and
• tend to be concerned with controlling behavior.

Spiritual Leaders
• focus primarily on building and nurturing people,
• focus more on helping people grow, "to prepare God's people" for works of service, "so that the body of Christ may be built up . . . and become mature" (Ephesians 4:12-13), and
• are concerned more with motivating others towards discipleship and responsiveness to Christ's leading.[9]

5. Once you receive six commitments, begin the three months of leadership training. This includes Bible study, reading materials to help them become more familiar with the needs and issues of their target group, visiting and observing other area singles ministries, and developing the master plan, organization, program, and publicity to be used during their six-month term.

6. At the end of the three-month training period, have the leaders begin inviting members to join their group. The core leaders are encouraged to assign job descriptions to other members so that group ownership is developed and everyone has the opportunity to participate, invite, and care for group members.

7. Trust the core group to form its own structure, train its own leaders, and set its own program. You should continue to attend weekly planning meetings and evaluations for the purposes of overall coordination and support.

This is the primary way we have launched the various groups in our singles ministry.

Phase Two: Leadership For the Ongoing Group

The ongoing group will already have an established purpose, target group, and core group of leaders. But how do we maintain that core group of leaders as the group becomes larger and as leaders rotate? The method that has worked best for us is as follows:

1. Make it a policy that leaders not

be involved longer than their nine-month commitment (or whatever length of term you choose to set). Some exceptions may be made. However, accepting this nine-month limit will help keep you better prepared for the ongoing process of developing a new leadership team.

2. Since current leaders have a good understanding of the purpose and leadership needs of their group, encourage and challenge them to recruit their own replacements (with your participation).

3. I consistently remind my core group that every first-time visitor is a potential leader. That is where the leadership development process begins. To help facilitate this, take the following steps:

- Have one of the members of the core leadership group contact all first-time visitors.
- As soon as is appropriate, invite them

HELPING THEM TAKE THEIR ROLE SERIOULSLY: A COVENANT FOR LEADERS
by Deane W. Ferm
Author of Alternative Lifestyles Confront the Church

In my ministry, there are seven people on the single adult ministry leadership team. To serve on the team, each leader is required to covenant with each other as follows:

1. I will commit myself to living in community with the others of the ministry group. (Living in community includes such things as mutual support, accountability, being vulnerable, life-sharing, gift-evoking, planning for ministry, and group prayer. Meetings of the ministry group will include all of these and others, though not necessarily in the same meeting.)

2. I will attend the weekly meetings of the singles ministry group.

3. I will use my personal gifts regularly in one or more ministries of the ministry group.

4. I will use my material assets generously with 10 percent of my income (a tithe) being the minimum I will give in any year. (Persons not currently at a 10 percent giving level may have one year of grace to move up to that level so as not to shock their budgets too severely.)

5. I will be open to God daily for my growth, choosing one or more of the following avenues:
   - quiet meditation,
   - prayer,
   - journaling,
   - Scripture reading,
   - worship.

6. I will be intentional about my personal growth and training for ministry by participating in workshops, institutes, and events at the church and elsewhere.

7. I will participate in the parish life of the church.[10]

to join the singles group or Sunday school class and ask them to fill out a survey form that helps you get to know them better, learn about their interests and skills and where they might eventually like to serve in the singles group. (Visitors who join our church also fill out a talent survey to be used in the church's overall ministry.)

4. Twice a year offer a leadership training event open to anyone interested in working in the singles ministry. This training need not be for specific jobs, but rather, it should serve as a basic Christian training course for effective ministry with single adults. With this training event on the calendar, you can begin ongoing recruitment of people who seem to have the leadership potential needed for your singles group. (Once a year, our entire church holds a nine-week leadership development training course, to which many of our singles are recruited as well.)

5. Provide your core group leaders with the names of all single adults who have attended any of these training events. Many of your new leaders can be recruited from this pool of names.

6. To help make leadership transitions smooth, each core group has a month overlap. For example, new officers are installed in December, while old officers leave their office in January. This provides a one-month on-the-job training period where new and old officers are working together.

7. Hold an installation service for the new officers and a celebration of the past six months for the old officers. This gives you and your singles a chance to say thanks to the leaders, to affirm them, and to raise awareness for the important roles they have played within the ministry.

Six Keys to Recruiting and Selecting Your Leaders

by **Terry Hershey and Lisa McAfee**
Terry is director of Christian Focus, Inc., Seattle, Washington Lisa is coauthor of How to Start a Beginning Again Ministry

We recommend six keys to recruiting and selecting your ministry leadership team.

1. *Choose your leadership.* We can't overemphasize the fact that good leaders must be chosen. We have to avoid the age-old method of "If you want to be a leader, raise your hand." At best, such "recruitment" produces a mixed bag of leaders. Leadership is best recruited when we approach as individuals the people who model the requirements we have established.

This model, in fact, is straight from the New Testament: Jesus chose His disciples; He didn't ask for volunteers. Of course, we don't want to keep people from volunteering, but we do want to avoid leadership out of desperation.

2. *Let your leaders recruit leaders.* We have found that our best leaders

are those recruited by current leaders. They understand the qualifications for the position and are therefore able to see people who could effectively serve as leaders. Furthermore, in choosing leaders, current leaders have an opportunity to reproduce themselves, as it were, by encouraging and aiding in the development of leadership potential in another person.

3. *Define the qualifications.* Leadership suffers when qualifications are not consistent or clearly defined. Consistency allows for unity and shared direction within the leadership team. Clearly defined qualifications help you know exactly what you are looking for as you search for leaders.

4. *Outline the lines of authority for your leaders.* Each leader should know who is responsible for what, who has been given authority to perform which functions, and who has the responsibility for handling problems or conflicts.

5. *Clearly set forth expectations.* You capitalize on leaders' potential by defining the expectations you have for them. Leaders should know their areas of responsibility.

6. *Select leaders who can be positive role models.* Above all, leaders are role models. And it is encouraging to know that role models do not necessarily "have it all together." They, too, are in the process of growing and becoming whole. To the extent that they are faithful in that process, their lives become models to those around them.[11]

Twelve Steps for Developing Leaders

by John Etcheto
Singles pastor at Reno Christian Fellowship, Reno, Nevada

The heart of my singles ministry is the leadership T-E-A-M:
T=teach
E=each
A=a
M=ministry

Our team of twelve single adults plans and coordinates most of the singles ministry functions. Over the years, I've found the following twelve principles and guidelines helpful in developing a successful leadership team.

Before the Team Is Selected

1. *Don't rush it.* Recognize that recruiting and training quality leadership takes time. I invest four months each year specifically for this purpose. The more time put into selecting and training the leadership team, the less likely they will be to drop out.

2. *Be prayerful.* Two months prior to my annual leadership training retreat, I encourage my singles to begin praying specifically about the new team and whether God might be leading them to be a part of it.

3. *Be selective.* Following this two-month period of prayerful consideration, I invite several of my singles (the

potential leadership team) to a leadership retreat.

4. *Provide role models.* Prior to the retreat, I give each participant several tapes to listen to—tapes by teachers like Chuck Swindoll and Howard Hendricks—on such topics as motivation and leadership.

5. *Discover strengths and gifts.* Also prior to the retreat, I ask each participant to complete a Taylor-Johnson Temperament Analysis (TJTA).[12] (The tests should be scored, returned, and charted prior to the retreat.)

6. *Build community.* Prior to the retreat, I ask each participant to prepare a five- to ten-minute "history." During the course of the weekend retreat, each person shares his or her history with the group. This is done for two reasons: to allow the group to begin the bonding process, and to teach the concept that the Lord uses our past to equip us for His future.

7. *Discuss the role and responsibility of a leader.* During the retreat, I have the group examine and discuss leadership, servanthood, motivation, and expectations of both the team and the pastor. During one session we also go over the results of the TJTAs to learn more about the strengths and characteristics of each person.

8. *Present the leadership challenge.* Near the end of the retreat, I challenge the participants to spend the next two weeks prayerfully considering a one-year commitment to be on the leadership team. Then, I make the final team selection.

After the Team Is Selected

9. *Organize the TEAM.* After commitments have been made, we take a second weekend retreat (or weekend session at the church) to organize the areas of ministry. I divide the team into subgroups (we have five in our organi-

---

INSTILLING ACCOUNTABILITY IN YOUR LEADERSHIP TEAMS
by Andy Morgan
Director of Single Point Ministries at
Ward Presbyterian Church, Livonia, Michigan

We design each leadership team as a small group. People are working together and, as they do, they are developing community and trust. Let's say one of the leaders is responsible for a white-water rafting trip. On the trip the leader does something that others feel is wrong or inappropriate. Long before they talk to me about this, they will have talked to the leader in question.

This is because I have a standard policy: if people come to me with a complaint about somebody, the first thing I will do is ask if they've talked to the person about it. Only after they've talked to the person, can they come talk to me (if they still need to). This immediately reinforces accountability among our leaders. They have to learn to confront people when it's needed. I'm not here to patch up all of their problems or fix everything.

This policy also removes me from the gossip chain. There are a lot of things going on that I never hear about. And that is okay. My singles realize I don't need to know who is dating whom, that I am more interested in developing a relationship of trust and integrity with them.

zation) to handle the major ministry areas.

10. *Develop goals and objectives.* At this second retreat, I have each subgroup write a brief overall goal and statement of objectives for the single adult ministry, as well as one for its specific area.

11. *Training and discipling.* Following this second retreat, I spend an additional six weeks in group and one-on-one training and discipling. Areas of training for the team include such things as communication skills, goal setting, small-group dynamics, and planning productive meetings. Some of this training is often provided by team members who have expertise in needed areas.

12. *Commission the TEAM.* Following the six-week training session, I formally present the new leadership team to the church and singles ministry.

I've found that investing four months in recruiting and training my team has resulted in tremendous improvement and growth in our ministry. When the team is trained and equipped to effectively plan and coordinate the many activities and functions of our ministry, I am then freed to concentrate on teaching, counseling, and long-range planning.

Selecting and Training Singles Leaders

an interview with James Richwine
Minister with singles at Coral Ridge Presbyterian Church, Fort Lauderdale, Florida

VISIBLE MALE LEADERSHIP IS ESSENTIAL

What do you consider to be the keys to developing effective leadership in a singles ministry?

I think a healthy singles ministry requires a considerable amount of visible male leadership. If men come to visit a group and see women in leadership, they will tend to think the group is primarily for women and often will not return.

But if men are in leadership, they are more likely to assume that it is a place for them too. In the vast majority of cases, if your visible leadership is primarily female, you will ultimately have a women's group. Women, on the other hand, are more likely to return regardless of the leader's gender.

Are you saying that women are not capable or effective leaders?

Not at all. In fact, half of the members on our leadership team are women. And they do a tremendous job. (Most of our leadership teams have male-female coleaders.) I'm talking about the visible leadership, the people who are primarily up front making announcements, teaching, and setting the tone for the meeting.

How would you deal with a situation where the men in a group do not accept a leadership position?

This is where we need to follow Saint Paul's example. Go out and pick two or three men. They may not even be Christians or a part of your group yet. Share the gospel with them, lead them to Christ, then take the next year or two to disciple them, invest in them, help them struggle through their problems and issues, pray with them. Help bring them to a place where they are spiritually mature. Then train them in the nuts and bolts of leadership.

I think, unfortunately, that we too often expect people to come to us ready-made. We want instant ministries. But that is not reality. What we need to do more often is to work at laying the groundwork, building the foundation, nurturing and discipling our leaders from conversion.

Personal fellowship has worked best for me. On a weekly basis, I meet with a group of men for lunch. We talk about whatever they are experiencing. After every meeting, we have a brief time of prayer, either at my office or in the car. This includes praying for one another. It's amazing how men grow in spiritual maturity when they meet together regularly to encourage each other in their faith and to pray for one another. The only real way for me to disciple people is to spend regular time with them, letting whatever leadership skills I have spill into their lives.

Let's say there is a woman in a church who sees the need for a singles ministry, but she does not know of any men who can (or will) provide the necessary leadership. What advice would you give her?

There are two steps I would suggest. First, she needs to determine if the pastor and church leadership are supportive of starting this singles ministry. If they are supportive, she should present the need to them and ask that they either hire someone to serve as the singles pastor or appoint one of the elders to be responsible for this area.

Second, if that door seems to be shut, then I would counsel her to pray and wait for God to raise up the leadership. Let it be known that the position is open and that you are waiting for God to raise up the leadership. If need be, allow the position to remain vacant. In my opinion, both biblically and practically, this must happen if the ministry is ever to grow in a healthy way. If God does not raise up the male leadership needed, then there should be a reevaluation of the need for the ministry in this particular church.

> "In the vast majority of cases, if your visible leadership is primarily female, you will ultimately have a women's group. Women, on the other hand, are more likely to return regardless of the leader's gender."

Have you found it difficult to develop good male leadership?

Not at all. I believe that male leadership breeds male leadership. The battle is in the beginning when you establish your leadership policies and requirements. Insist on visible male leadership and get started on the right foot.

> **"Surprisingly, we have not found it any more difficult to get a two-year commitment than to get a six-month commitment. And it has given our leadership positions more respect and status."**

Much of my ministry is focused around men. This is not just a principle for singles ministry, but for the church at large. If a senior pastor focuses most of his energy on training and building up men in their faith, then the women will also be involved and the church will be stronger overall.

QUALITIES AND CHARACTERISTICS

What qualities or characteristics do you look for in new leaders?

There are two key things I look for: someone who has demonstrated a love for the Lord and someone who has shown responsibility.

How do you discern that your prospective leaders have a love for God?

My leadership team and I discern this by observing how they demonstrate faithfulness to the ministry and to others. How do they relate to people? How interested or concerned are they about making new people feel welcome? Do their relationships with people signify a serious deficiency in their relationship with God? How do they respond when a leader suggests that they do something differently?

As they move up in our leadership ranks, before their name is even allowed on the ballot, they are interviewed by me or one of our other key leaders. At that time, we not only discuss what their responsibilities would be if elected, but also their spiritual life.

This process, the observations over a period of time as well as the interview, provides us with a fairly clear picture of where they are in their relationship with God. If someone is turned down for a position, it is always done on a "for now" basis. We continually put it in terms of "here are some steps you can take to become prepared for responsibilities down the road."

How do you determine a person's level of responsibility?

We look for someone who has had small responsibilities on some committee or in another capacity. For example, we have some people whose only responsibility is to stand at the door and greet people on Sunday morning. How faithful and responsible have they been in this task? Do they arrive on time? Are they consistent? How much of their heart do they put into the job?

I believe a leader must primarily be a servant. Most of our leadership begins by doing mundane, menial kinds of things: purchasing the doughnuts and making sure they're out on the table in time, having the coffee made.

LEADERSHIP SELECTION AND REQUIREMENTS

How do you select your leaders?

In our particular church we do it by

elections. Nominations are received from the floor in writing several weeks prior to the actual election. As I mentioned earlier, everyone who is nominated is interviewed.

First, we have some constitutional requirements. For example, a person cannot be elected president or vice president unless he has served on one of our main committees for at least six months during the previous two years. That guarantees that he has come up through the ranks and has had an interest in and commitment to this ministry. We also require that all leaders regularly attend our weekly worship service plus some type of ongoing educational process (i.e., Sunday school, discipleship classes). The first nominations eliminated are those who do not meet our constitutional requirements.

Second, we approach the remaining nominees and ask them if they would be willing to serve. If they say yes, they undergo an interview with either myself or one of our key leaders. During this interview, we discuss the specific job responsibilities and time commitments required. (This includes attending our two annual leadership re-

WHAT MAKES A LEADER?
by Warren Bennis
Professor of management, University of Southern California School of Business Administration

Based on a study of ninety top executives in both the public and private sectors, leaders possess similar qualities.

- They focus on doing the right things versus doing things right. While most managers concern themselves with doing things right, leaders focus on doing the right things.
- They have a compelling vision and a dream for their work.
- They are the most results-oriented people I ever encountered. They are highly conscious of what they want.
- They share an ability to communicate. An effective leader has to be able to communicate ideas in a way that people can understand. The leader doesn't have to be articulate, but he must have a knack for using the right metaphor.
- They help their followers feel important. Those who work with them feel significant and empowered.
- They are committed and persistent. Leaders are able to hang in there and stay the course.
- They know their own worth; they have positive self-regard. They realize what their strengths are and know how to nourish and nurture them. They are also able to discern the match between what they are good at and what an institution's needs are.
- They don't think about failure; it's what I call the Wallenda factor. Like Karl Wallenda, the tightrope walker, leaders put all their energy into walking the tightrope; they regard almost every false step as a learning opportunity and not the end of the world.[13]

THREE QUALITIES OF SPIRITUAL LEADERS
by Lawrence O. Richards
Author of more than fifty books, including **The Believer's Guidebook**

Spiritual Leaders Have Close, Intimate Relationships
   Spiritual leaders are called to live among (not over) others, and to build close, caring relationships. Coming to know others well and being known well are both basic to effective spiritual leadership (cf., Matthew 20:25-26, 2 Corinthians 1:3-9, 1 Thessalonians 2:7-12).

Spiritual Leaders Set Clear, Consistent Examples
   Spiritual leaders are called to live the Word of God, thus providing examples of the way of life toward which they guide others. As 1 Peter 5:3 puts it, the church is to have no little tin gods, for elders serve "not [by] lording it over those entrusted to you, but [by] being examples to the flock." The importance of example is constantly stressed in the New Testament. We are even taught to recognize as leaders only those whose lives have taken God's truth to heart (cf., 1 Timothy 3, Titus 1).

Spiritual Leaders Provide Gentle Guidance (Teaching)
   Spiritual leaders are called to share the Word of God, explaining it to show others how to live godly lives.[14]

treats.) We also discuss the kind of spiritual warfare that leaders may face, how they feel about this, and whether they are spiritually prepared for battle. And finally, we talk about their devotional life and try to identify personal problems that might affect their leadership ability.

Once the constitutional requirements have been made and they have passed the interview process, their names are placed on the ballot. Then we trust God in the election process.

How important is skill or training in the selection of your leaders?

One thing we don't look at is lack of skill. Over the years I have observed many of our singles who appeared to have little or no skill in providing leadership up in front of 200 or more people. But there is something that happens when they are elected to a position. It gives them a boost of confidence, an affirmation. It spurs them on to develop and rise to the challenge. I've enjoyed watching our people blossom and develop into very capable leaders once they were elected.

Our nation has recently witnessed something similar with George Bush. After the election, he seemed to develop a new confidence, and has surprised many who did not previously perceive him as a capable leader.

MAINTAIN HIGH EXPECTATIONS

How long are the terms of office for your key leadership?

This is an area where we are bucking a trend in singles ministry. It used to be that we had six-month terms, as do probably the majority of other singles ministries across the country. But we are now electing people for two years.

Why did you decide to move from six-month to two-year terms?

We found we were expending a lot of energy holding elections twice a year. Since people could be elected for a second six-month term, most of our leaders were serving for one year anyway. But we were still going through the time-consuming process every six months.

As a pastor, I found that process to be extremely frustrating. It seemed that we were always starting over, that our ministry was being short-circuited. So I met with my leadership team and got their advice. Out of that meeting we came up with our current leadership structure.

Surprisingly, we have not found it any more difficult to get a two-year commitment than to get a six-month commitment. And it has given our leadership positions more respect and status. Our people have responded to the higher level of expectation in a most positive way. The more you expect from your leadership, the more you will get. We expect quality and we get it. The Lord continues to provide us with capable, qualified leaders.

We have also structured our leadership teams into two groups. One has the responsibility for things that happen every week: Sunday school and our weekly Bible studies; the other has responsibility for all of our ancillary activities: retreats, socials, and intramural sports.

Do the leaders have a training period during their two-year term?

Yes. The first year of each term is spent serving as an assistant or trainee to the leader beginning his second term. This means that half of our total leadership council are always experienced and trained and half are providing new blood and ideas. (All of them have an equal vote and say on the council.) We've found that this provides our ministry with both freshness and continuity.

ADDITIONAL SUGGESTIONS

What else have you found helpful in developing your single adult leadership team?

Here are three other things that I'd recommend to other leaders. First, take your leadership team (and any other interested singles) on at least one short-term mission trip each year. I have watched our single adults come back from these trips with a new outlook on life. I'm not quite sure what it is, but something happens when a team of people spend that kind of intense time preparing to go, then actually work on a project together in a Third-World country. In some ways,

> "I judge the success of our ministry by how effective we are in moving people out into ministry. If a single adult is still in the receiving mode two years down the road, then we have blown it. We want to get them involved in one of the many ministry opportunities in our church. The singles group should not become a destination point."

this is the way Christ trained His disciples—through intense time together.

Second, don't encourage your singles to stay involved in the singles group for more than two or three years (unless they are involved in a leadership capacity). I judge the success of our ministry by how effective we are in moving people out into ministry. If a single adult is still in the receiving mode two years down the road, then we have blown it. We want to get them involved in one of the many ministry opportunities in our church. The singles group should not become a destination point.

Finally, learn to turn your leaders loose to do the job. Don't lead with a heavy hand. I try not to overburden my leaders with a lot of requirements once they have been elected. Rather, I do everything I can to set them free to do the things God has called them to do in their specific areas of responsibility. My primary responsibility then becomes to pastor them, to help them grow personally in their faith, and to counsel them when they have needs.

A CASE STUDY: "How Should I Handle a Leader with Child-Support Trouble?"

with a suggested solution from
Jim Dycus
Senior associate minister of education at Calvary Assembly of God, Winter Park, Florida

The Problem

Recently, I learned that one of the single men in my group is considerably behind in his child-support payments. In my mind, the issue is of even greater concern because he, as part of my leadership team, is something of a role model.

This leader is a good man and, for the most part, reliable. But, by allowing him to be in leadership, am I supporting in some way his irresponsibility as well as hurting the cause of single parents who often struggle to survive financially?

I'm in a tough spot. I don't want to lose one of my hard-to-find male leaders. Nor do I want to build barriers or unnecessarily meddle in his affairs. Yet, as his pastor, I feel a responsibility to help him take more seriously his moral and legal responsibility to his children.

How can I best deal with this situation?

A Possible Solution

I expect my leadership to set an example of responsible, mature Christian living based on biblical principles.

My first course of action would be to set up individual counseling sessions with this man to determine the facts. It would be impossible to assess the situation accurately without this discussion.

My counseling sessions have the following goals:

1. *I would discover at what point of recovery this individual is from his divorce or separation.* (I would already know this about anyone on my leadership team. In my mind, recovery would be a necessary qualification for a leader before he is ready to minister to others.)

I feel it is necessary for my leadership to be beyond post-divorce or separation hostility, bitterness, resentment, and anger. These emotions could cause a person to arbitrarily choose to ignore child-support payments. This attitude would disqualify a single adult from my leadership team.

2. *I would discover the reason for the overdue support payments.* In ministry to the single-again, these problems often arise and require understanding, grace, and patience from the single adult leader.

3. *I would see if the leader was willing to sit down with me and work out a reasonable payment schedule.* Many variables can affect child-support payments, and the following would have to be considered:

- other financial obligations,
- loss of job or temporary layoff,
- emergency financial problems,
- misunderstandings of court actions,
- temporary illness,
- changes in job status, and
- temporary freezes in wages due to transfer.

4. *If the individual desires, I would contact the ex-spouse and mediate, thus helping the two of them work out a satisfactory solution together.*

5. *I would share scriptural principles.* For example, the Apostle Paul writes, "But if any provide not for his own . . . he hath denied the faith, and is worse than an infidel" (1 Timothy 5:8, KJV).

I believe the key to solving this situation is finding out if the leader has acted irresponsibly, or if he has some needs of his own that have precluded his ability to pay.

The spirit of the person is the greatest factor for whether or not he remains in leadership. He must exhibit a willingness to fulfill his legal and moral responsibilities, as well as his spiritual leadership responsibilities.

Only then can God truly honor his leadership.

> **"I feel it is necessary for my leadership to be beyond post-divorce or separation hostility, bitterness, resentment, and anger. These emotions could cause a person to arbitrarily choose to ignore child-support payments. This attitude would disqualify a single adult from my leadership team."**

Four Building Blocks for an Effective Leadership Team

by Dan Chun
Minister with singles at Menlo Park Presbyterian Church, Menlo Park, California

I consider the following to be my four building blocks for effective singles leadership.

1. *One-to three-year leadership terms.* When I first came to this church in 1985, the term of leadership for those in the singles ministry was six months. The belief held by many groups across the country was that you can get singles to make only a six-month commitment in a leadership capacity.

I found that this philosophy catered to one of the primary weaknesses of singles by reinforcing their transiency, expecting only short-term commitments. It also meant that if they served six months, by the fourth month I was already looking for their replacements. As a result, there was very little continuity.

Few or none of the leaders had survived an entire calendar year and didn't know what it was like to go through Christmas, Easter, and summer, nor the accompanying seasonal ups and downs in attendance. Lack of experience in this area created policy making that was very short-sighted.

I'm convinced that catering to the six-month syndrome is unhealthy for our singles ministries. Consequently, I changed our system to one-year terms of leadership, with the option of serving up to three years. At the end of each year, there is a review in which the leaders themselves say no or yes to continue for another year. (I have asked some people not to continue for another year due to failed responsibility or some other factor, but that rarely happens.)

Although there have been skeptics about a longer-term commitment, I have found that the hardest part is getting the leaders to quit. That is because our leadership team is not just a working group, it's a family unit. We pray for one another and laugh together—along with conducting our business.

Interestingly, about 90 percent of all the weddings in our ministry are between singles serving on the leadership team. Having emotionally and spiritually mature people work together side by side can create an attractive situation. The flip side is the frustration in losing so many key leaders by marriage. (We're the only ministry in the church that has such a high turnover in leadership due to these unions.)

2. *Build a strong relationship between yourself and your leaders.* One of the most important things I do with my leadership team is meeting monthly in someone's home. This makes our time together much more relational. As a team, we meet on a regular basis and

encourage prayer requests and praise items.

To further build our team relationship, we have an annual leadership retreat. During the two-and-a-half days that we meet, I let them see my vision, I share with them my pastoral heart for the ministry, and together we decide how to implement our ministry. We select a retreat facility that does not provide our meals. We build a sense of community when we cook, clean up, and play together. This also strengthens the trust levels so that if we hit a tough time later in the year we can say, "I know this guy is not trying to mess me up. He just disagrees with my idea."

3. *No parking lot politics.* The greatest sin a member of a leadership team can commit is to create divisiveness. Unity among team members is one of the things I stress most. I would rather delay a vote than allow it to divide us. I encourage my leaders to stay away from "Parking lot politics." By that I mean I urge them to share their hearts and be honest in our meetings. Lay all the cards on the table in front of everyone (with diplomacy and gentleness). They know they won't be jumped on for disagreeing.

Everything must be said in the meeting; it is forbidden to talk about it in the parking lot and tell someone how they really feel about what "Sally or Roger said." It is unfair to share something outside that has not been shared inside the meeting. This simple rule has helped us cut back on a lot of unnecessary background tension and gossip.

When discussing unity with my leaders, I often use the metaphor of crew. Crew or rowing is the only true team sport. In basketball, if one person is not pulling his or her weight, a Magic Johnson or a Larry Bird can make up for it. But in crew, everybody has to pull on the oars in the same rhythm in the same direction. One person can't compensate for someone else who's rowing at a different cadence and angle. Everyone has to carry his or her load and pull in the same direction. This is the kind of unity we work for. Once a decision is made, although we may privately disagree, we all publicly support it. Even I have had to back decisions I didn't like.

4. *Be the leader and set the vision.* This is what I call my gold nugget of leadership. In seminary, I was taught that pastors are to be facilitators—we facilitate the laity and let them plan all the policies, issues, and agenda. However, I have found that in real life this seldom works if you want a quality ministry. People want direction from the pastor; they need a vision. They need to know where to row.

Max De Pree, in his book *Leadership Is an Art*, says the leader's two main responsibilities are to (1) set the vision and (2) say thanks. The leader must set the vision. Imagine if Moses led the Israelites based on a Gallup poll or a consensus vote. What if Jesus did

> **"The leader must set the vision. Imagine if Moses led the Israelites based on a Gallup poll or a consensus vote. What if Jesus did the same? The Jews would still be living in Egypt, and the church would be a civic club."**

the same? The Jews would still be living in Egypt, and the church would be a civic club.

We obviously have group participation as a team, researching the needs of our singles and brainstorming a wide variety of ways to meet those needs. But at some point someone must make the decision after weighing the options. And that someone is the shepherd of the flock, the pastor. I know not all singles pastors would agree with this.

The strongest metaphor for the pastor is that of coach (which my singles call me). I work hard to help them maximize their skills and abilities and give them opportunities. But someone has to call in the play and give the overall game plan. It is not done on a majority vote in the huddle. The coach listens to the players, watches them, and helps identify their skills and gifts. My observation is that far too many leaders are not really exercising their leadership role. They are not communicating a vision to their people, and they are waiting for someone else to decide.

The basic leadership strategy I use is to:
• receive a lot of input from my team,
• present an architectural plan based on all the information, and
• help the team to carry it through and to do it all with their gifts and creativity.

If one were to ask who is planning our twenty outreach programs a month, our four social options, the seminars, the retreats, and the small groups, I can honestly say, "I didn't lift a finger. The team did it all. Say thanks

to them." My job ended when the game plan they helped design was formed. My job is to thank them like crazy and affirm and encourage them through dinners, gifts, and public acknowledgment.

SINGLE MEN IN LEADERSHIP: How Important Is It, and How Do You Develop It?

A MAN'S PERSPECTIVE
by Andy Morgan
Director of Single Point Ministries at Ward Presbyterian Church, Livonia, Michigan

I'm convinced strong male leadership is vital to a healthy, growing single adult ministry. Female leadership can work, but from my observations predominantly female leadership primarily attracts only females.

When men come to our group, they are enthused to find male leadership. Male leaders attract both men and women.

Develop Male Leadership

First, I visit them where they work. (Jesus sought out most of His disciples where they worked.) A man's workplace is such a big part of his self-image. Visiting them at their workplace helps me earn their respect and friendship.

Second, we intentionally plan some activities for men: motorcycle or fishing trips, sporting events, board game tournaments.

Third, I challenge them to participate in a "men's discipleship ministry" that meets on Friday nights. We meet together for dinner and fellowship. Then we spend two to four hours serving members in our fellowship: painting a room, helping someone move, fixing minor house repairs. (If necessary, we complete the job on Saturday.) Later in the evening, we have a short Bible study and prayer time. From this, strong fellowships develop, plus a feeling that they belong and are needed.

Fourth, I teach and encourage men to accept the biblical model of spiritual leadership. (I even encourage them to be open to full-time Christian work —which several have chosen to do.)

Fifth, to get quality leadership, you have to expect it. People usually rise to meet expectations. So I make it clear that I expect my men to take bold, responsible leadership roles. It works.

Finally, I personally must keep myself readily available, one on one or in group settings. Sometimes I ask several to attend a baseball game or play board games and eat pizza with me so I can spend time with them. I must set the example of praying with them, loving, counseling, and encouraging them.

A WOMAN'S PERSPECTIVE
by Mary Randolph
Director of singles ministry at Asbury United Methodist Church, Tulsa, Oklahoma

I believe single adult ministries are most effective with male leadership "up front." Men can lend an image of strength. New men, perhaps coming reluctantly, will feel better to see other men in visible positions. Those who can identify and encourage male participation at all levels can be more effective.

Make It Work

To qualify what I've said, women also make excellent leaders. I'm in the people business. People are both male and female and my commitment is to help build up both. Since women make excellent leaders too, we generally have male—female leadership teams. This approach has proven very effective for us.

Find Male Leaders

I constantly visit with our singles, asking, "Which men should be plugged in? What are their gifts?"

Then, intentionally, I get to know them. How committed are they in their faith and to our group? What are their personal goals and dreams? What challenges them?

Finally, if I feel they are qualified to serve in our ministry, I invite them to serve in a particular position. (If they accept, they are expected to attend a Saturday or evening leadership training session.)

When You Can't Find Enough Quality Male Leaders

This can happen even in large churches. When it happens, I just make sure our most visible teams always have male leadership. This is especially true for our Sunday morning leadership team. I'm sure that nearly every church can find at least one or two good men to serve as leaders.

How to Have a Productive Staff Meeting

by Jim Smoke
Founder and director of The Center for Divorce Recovery, Phoenix, Arizona

Meetings are an important part of your ministry. The preparation for them is sometimes as important as the meeting itself. It is important to ask yourself a few questions before calling a meeting, however. Here are a few to help serve as a checklist:

1. *Do we need this meeting?* I've been to many meetings that were unnecessary—a phone call or a letter can sometimes work just as well.

2. *What issues need to be addressed at this meeting?* Be sure you have focused on the central issues. It helps to write down what you need to accomplish. This will also keep you from packing too much into one meeting.

3. *Has the proper homework been completed to assist in making needed decisions?* Be sure that someone has collected all available facts that could affect your meeting outcome. The better prepared you are, the more wisely your time will be used.

4. *Who needs to be there?* This seems obvious, but time and time again I've wished I would have invited Mr. A or Miss B. Think this through beforehand.

5. *Is there time to give enough notice?* Poor attendance is not always indicative of poor interest. Heavy schedules must always be considered. Be fair to your people. Give them adequate advance notice.

6. *Have you effectively communicated the time, date, and place?* Many meetings are rendered ineffective for just this reason. People have short memories. It helps to send a written notice and to call them the night before the meeting. Be sure to communicate starting and ending times so they will know how to plan.

7. *What room would best suit this meeting?* The physical environment is very important. A meeting planned for ten should not be held in a room built for 200.

8. *Is a blackboard needed?* Know what equipment you need in advance. Make sure the equipment is in place and in working order. A blackboard without chalk is not very useful.

9. *Should refreshments be served?* In most cases refreshments help warm up a group for the business ahead. We recommend it.

10. *Should I stick to the agenda*

once the meeting begins? I've found it helpful to negotiate the agenda with the group at the beginning of the meeting. Share the agenda with those attending and allow them to determine priorities and help make additions or deletions. Remember to keep the clock and your priorities in mind. If possible, save time by sending agendas to participants ahead of time.

11. *Should someone plan to take notes?* Yes, definitely. I've lost more important information by failing to designate someone to take notes. It's best to ask someone in advance to do this, so they can come prepared.

The above are just a few considerations. Add your own and have a productive meeting.

Equipping Through a Leadership Retreat

by Jim Smoke

One of the reasons that single adult ministries fail is due to poor leadership and leadership training. Many groups operate on the premise that whomever is available and popular and has been around the group for over fifteen minutes should be elected or appointed to a leadership position. The reality is that groups that operate in this way either never have officers for long, or have officers that are weak and not fully aware of what is expected of them.

One of the best ways to promote effective group leadership is to conduct a leadership training weekend after the new officers are elected or selected. A weekend retreat—Friday evening through Sunday noon—can help equip your new leaders for a solid six-month term of office. (In my opinion, six months is the best length of time for a commitment to serve as a single adult officer.)

The following outline will give you an idea of what should take place once you get your officers to Camp Gittchee Gumee for the weekend. The presence of all officers and committee chair people should be required. Exceptions are death.

Friday Evening

Arrival by 8:00 p.m. for a buffet dinner followed by a presentation from the singles minister (layman or professional) regarding goals, objectives, and purposes of your singles group. Why is your group in existence and what are its goals and intentions? How does it operate in your church structure? What are your dreams for the year? All these things need to be clearly defined so that everyone can focus on a common objective.

Saturday Morning

Saturday's format should include team building through small groups, a discussion concerning principles of good leadership, and an explanation of the various officer job descriptions and how the chain of command in your organization works. It would also be helpful to discuss how to deal with the problems that occur in every singles ministry.

Saturday Afternoon and Evening

You should include some recreational time along with group or class meetings to plan the calendar of activities for the coming weeks and months. Evenings can be devoted to warm times of group study, growth, and personal challenge.

Sunday

This day can be reserved for group worship, committee meetings, goal setting for the coming six months, and plans for the officer installation when you get home. A final time of prayer and communion is usually the tie that binds your people into a community and team.

Each group must decide what needs to be covered at a leadership weekend. The basic idea is to build a team, explain and plan the ministry, and grow spiritually with each other. It's also a time for your leaders to get close to each other.

Leadership is no accident. It is trained. Your leaders need to be a closely knit team to have an effective ministry and program. A clear definition of "Who does what?" will give you clear sailing for the months ahead. The challenge of leadership will always be there in your ministry. If people cannot do their jobs, offer to let them out and replace them with others who can.

Poor leadership will scuttle your ministry fast.

YOU CAN'T DO IT BY YOURSELF: Delegating Responsibility Is the Key to Getting Your Single Adults Actively Involved

by Rich Hurst
Singles ministry consultant, Pasadena, California

Single adults are not teenagers. Many single adult leaders continue to operate as if they were involved in a youth ministry. That will not work over the long haul with single adults. Treat them as adults and expect them to be full partners in the ministry. One key to accomplishing this is to delegate significant responsibilities to them.

Delegation is an interesting, multi-step process that begins to unfold when one person decides to trust another to own a project. By following these steps, you can "win" with delegation and motivate your singles to be much more committed and involved in helping build your ministry.

1. *You can't do it all.* Realize that you can't do everything by yourself. Even if you could, it would keep someone else from experiencing the pleasure of

learning and growing. When you attempt to do it all, you miss one of the most important tenets of Scripture: to train and equip others for ministry (Ephesians 4:11-12). It is not our goal to do everything but rather to teach others how to "win."

2. *Dumping does not equal delegation.* Consider what form your delegation will take and to whom you will delegate. It is gutless behavior to dump on anyone, even a support person. Even though you may feel rushed and in need of someone to help bail you out, to dump instead of to delegate leadership is inappropriate.

Choose the people you invest in, making sure you are ready to commit to their success. If you are not willing to stand behind those to whom you delegate and offer them the support they need, then simply do not delegate.

3. *What exactly do you want done?* Decide exactly what the job is that you are delegating, and share all that you know about it with the person to whom you are delegating it. Don't assume that a person knows all about the job and will just bounce in and handle everything the way you want it done.

4. *Delegating means letting go.* If a person is in charge of producing and promoting an event, meet with him or her early in the planning process and discuss your hopes and insights. Then give that person the trust and freedom to carry out the job. There is nothing more unmotivating than to hear someone give you a go-ahead, then follow it with litanies of "no" and "that won't work."

5. *Delegation demands support.* Delegating something to others demands that you support them. This is very different from giving someone an ongoing job. With a job, you give someone a set of rules and tell him or

---

SEVEN STEPS TO A "WIN" DELEGATION
by Rich Hurst

1. Decide what your own involvement will be. What kind of input do you want in the decisions and choices that are made?

2. Make things clear from the beginning through a written job description. Verbal ones are often misinterpreted.

3. If you set guidelines and rules, don't change them in the middle of the project. Wait until the next project.

4. Be flexible. There will always be some miscommunication and subsequently there will need to be some changes. Find a way to work with that.

5. Provide regular support in the form of questions and concern. Ask each person what it is he or she needs to feel supported.

6. Remember, it is people that are important, not programs. Your primary goal is to build people.

7. It is important to give credit to the person doing the job. When you steal credit from someone, it robs him or her of dignity and self-respect.

her what you want done. With delegation, you generally want a project accomplished a certain way in a certain amount of time. Therefore, delegating often requires a lot more support and encouragement than normal day-to-day activity.

6. *Debriefing the delegate.* Remember, a project is never done until the person responsible for the task feels some kind of completion. This means a debriefing time is necessary, a time when the person can give you advice and suggestions on how the delegation process can work better and how he or she feels the task went. It is also a time when you can give the delegate feedback on how you feel you worked together as well as offer suggestions about future working relationships.

> **"Delegation is an interesting, multi-step process that begins to unfold when one person decides to trust another to own a project."**

There is nothing more exciting than to watch a person to whom you have delegated a task succeed. People are the method God wants us to use. We can't say enough about our purpose: to help equip our singles to win.

Skills Your Leaders Need to Help Hurting People

by French A. Jones
Counselor in Dallas, Texas

Good leadership training includes recruiting good leaders and teaching them skills that they can utilize in the healing process.

One practical way to recruit leaders is to use an "involvement survey," which follows. Once leaders have been recruited, the single adult pastor needs to help them develop three specific skills:

1. *Listen to the hurting individual.* Listening is hard work, but it promotes significant healing. The leaders must actively pay attention to people sharing their hurts. Eye contact, empathy, understanding, and acceptance are all vitally important in helping people to get in touch with their feelings. Silence is not necessarily an invitation for the leader to "stop and share a verse," although there are times when that may be appropriate.

At this stage, the individual just needs to know that he is loved and accepted despite his pain. A leader's sensitivity to the ministry of the Holy Spirit is important during these times of listening.

2. *Be vulnerable by sharing practical*

steps that you took to receive healing. Even though the problems may not be the same, the leader can have a significant ministry of healing by opening up and explaining what she did to get through her difficult times. The hurting individual may think that "time heals all wounds." Not true! Over time, submerged painful feelings often manifest themselves in unhealthy ways. If a person is angry from past hurts, it may surface in several negative ways such as overeating or depression.

3. *Assist the individual by providing practical day-to-day help.* One of our groups helps people get assistance in finding jobs, providing manpower for people who are moving, and even fixing things for people in their homes. These are areas that can be overwhelming to someone who is depressed and hurting.

HANDOUT:
Involvement
Survey

by French A. Jones

Why Use This Survey?

Involvement generates commitment. The more involved your single adults are, the more they will sense personal ownership in—and enthusiasm for—the ministry. The challenge is to find a meaningful job for every person in your singles group. This survey (see next page) is designed to find out who in your group has the time and interest to serve in a particular job function, as well as to learn about their interests and skills.

Find Places of Service and Involvement for Your Singles

As a steering committee, brainstorm every possible way someone could become involved in your group. List all possible activities (such as sports and socials), logistical problems (setting up chairs and tables), Bible study groups, committees that need helpers—anything and everything where someone's skills and abilities might be used.

How Often Should This Survey Be Given?

Give it every three or four months. Keep the class needs and opportunities in front of your people. (It would also be helpful to give this survey to all newcomers, asking them to complete it at their convenience.)

When the Survey Is Completed

Make certain that one of the leaders contacts each person *the following week*. If the follow-up is not done promptly, people will think the group really does not need them. The benefits from something as simple as this are fantastic.

> "Involvement generates commitment. The more involved your single adults are, the more they will sense personal ownership in—and enthusiasm for—the ministry."

Involvement Survey

_____
Your Name

_____
Home Phone

_____
Work Phone

_____
Address

_____
City

_____
State   Zip

How often do you attend this singles class?
❑ Every week   ❑ Twice a month
❑ Once a month   ❑ Visitor

Are you interested in being in a "care group" that enables the members to have weekly contact by phone or in person?
❑ Yes   ❑ No

Please let us know which of the following opportunities to serve you would be willing and able to participate in.

1. Assist with physical arrangements for each class: ❑ (weekly)
2. Assist with decorating tables for potluck dinners: ❑ (twice a month)
3. Musical accompaniment for singing:
   ❑ Yes   ❑ No
   If yes, which instrument do you play?_____
   Have you had any experience in song-leading? ❑ Yes   ❑ No

4. Assist with helping any of our singles move out of or into another apartment or home. (This generally involves Saturdays, once a month maximum.) ❑ Yes   ❑ No
   Sometimes; call me first: ❑
5. Assist with producing our monthly newsletter: ❑ Yes   ❑ No
6. Serve as a greeter or welcome-table helper each week: ❑ Yes   ❑ No
7. Visitor follow-up (helping to call and/or send a card to visitors):
   ❑ Yes   ❑ No
8. Assist with prayer list requests and answers (keeping a journal):
   ❑ Yes   ❑ No
9. Hospital visitation committee (occasional visits): ❑ Yes   ❑ No
10. Assist with planning socials and activities: ❑ Yes   ❑ No
11. Serve on the missions committee:
    ❑ Yes   ❑ No
12. Serve on the care committee:
    ❑ Yes   ❑ No
13. Take responsibility to assist and/or teach a Bible lesson to children of single parents during some of our meetings on a rotating basis.
    ❑ Yes   ❑ No
    Teach a lesson: ❑
    Assist in some other way: ❑
14. Be involved in a weekly Bible study:
    ❑ Yes   ❑ No
    What evening and time is best for you?
    Evening: _____

    Time :_____

15. What two topics would you like to see our group study/discuss/address in the upcoming months?

_____

First topic:

_____

Second topic:

16. I would like to be a weekly prayer partner with someone of the same sex in this group (weekly phone contact or meeting for prayer): ❏ Yes   ❏ No

17. I would like to head up and coordinate or assist a committee that assists others in finding jobs (receive resumes, get the word out, make needs known): ❏ Yes   ❏ No
I would be glad to be in charge of coordinating this area: ❏
I would be glad to assist someone in this area: ❏

Other Ways To Provide a Ministry To This Group

1. I have access to a pickup truck that could be used occasionally to help people move: ❏ Yes   ❏ No

2. I have some skill related to my job that others might benefit from (i.e., "I am a CPA and would be glad to assist group members with their taxes"). ❏ Yes   ❏ No

_____

Skill(s)

3. I would be glad to be contacted before a retreat or seminar to assist in offering money for scholarships for those who cannot afford to go otherwise: ❏ Yes   ❏ No

4. I would be glad to share my testimony/faith story during some upcoming class: ❏ Yes   ❏ No

5. I would be glad to help with home needs such as car tune-up, mowing grass, painting projects, fix-up needs: ❏ Yes   ❏ No

6. I have some typing skills and would be glad to assist in typing resumes or other needs you may have (from two to three hours per month maximum): ❏ Yes   ❏ No

7. I would be glad to do something else to minister in some practical ways to folks involved in this group. ❏ Yes   ❏ No
List your area(s) of expertise:

_____

_____

_____

_____

_____

_____

_____

Thanks!

Your Role as the Leader

Do as Little as Possible in Your Ministry!

an interview with Andy Morgan
Director of Single Point Ministries
at Ward Presbyterian Church,
Livonia, Michigan

I*n this interview, singles pastor Andy Morgan talks about how the role of the singles pastor is not to do the ministry . . . but to give it away.*

With fifteen years of experience in singles ministry, you've had an opportunity to observe many various ministries across the country. What are some concerns you have about some of the attitudes and approaches among leaders in singles ministry?

One of the things that grieves me most is the fact that so many single adult leaders and ministers think it's up to them to do the ministering, thinking, "If I don't do it, who will?"

My position is that if the single adults don't do it themselves, then they don't want it done. All ministry is born from need. If people feel a need for something, they will come forth and express that need, and then come up with a way to meet that need.

That sort of environment breeds involvement and community. If a paid staffer is doing everything for me as a single adult, I'm going to feel like a forty-five-year-old fifteen-year-old with permission to hang around and do nothing. On the other hand, if the ministry depends on my involvement, I don't have permission to hang around. I have to contribute, be involved, take ownership.

It sounds nice, but aren't you being a bit idealistic? Suppose I'm in a small church of two or three hundred. I'm a volunteer lay leader and sense a God-given desire to build a ministry with the single parents in my church and community. The few single parents in the church are either not interested in providing any leadership, or they are already involved in teaching a Sunday school class or singing in the choir. None of the single parents is bringing specific needs to me, yet I remain convinced that there is a need in the community for this ministry. And I have a genuine desire to do something. Are you saying I should do nothing?

Let's look at the truth. First, currently there is not a single-parent ministry in your church. Second, if those single parents don't feel the need, you—regardless of your good intentions—are just trying to raise a corpse. I think it's much easier to hold down a fanatic than it is to raise a corpse; but, unfortunately, that's what we try to do much too often in ministry. We try to raise the dead, thinking the dead want to be raised. Many times we defeat ministries from the beginning because we think we have to do it; in reality, it may only be our agenda and not theirs.

Where does God come into the picture? This guy feels a genuine burden for this single-parent ministry. What is he to do?

First, we need to find out his definition of ministry. If I truly have a burden for the single parent, I can find one and say, "May I take your child to the zoo, or offer two nights a month of child care to give you time out?" Instead of doing that, we usually define ministry as program. That is not ministry. Ministry is a relationship.

If we start out with a relationship where we help that one person, that person will most likely tell a friend, and the friend will say, "Can you find someone to help me and maybe we could go out together for shopping or Bible study or whatever?" And, suddenly, the beginnings of a baby-sitting co-op is established. Out of that beginning, some of the single parents may start talking about their need for a class or support group. In many ways you are giving birth to this ministry because of your relationship with people for whom you have a burden, but you are not "doing" the ministry.

We have an example of this sort of thing in our ministry here at Ward. Historically, this church has always had a single adult ministry. But it has not always had a ministry specifically with single parents. Sometime back, some single parents came to me and said, "We want to do something." I said, "Okay, you have my full support, but what do you want to do?" They said they wanted to begin a monthly support group. I said, "Great. What will the purpose of this group be, and who do you want to lead it?" They put their heads together and got this group started. Then they said they needed baby-sitters during this support-group meeting and for other times throughout the month. I said, "Great, what will it take for you to make this work? How can this become a reality?" So they got together and started a baby-sitting co-op. Then they said they wanted a single-parent vacation. So they put that together.

This year they said they wanted to begin a seminar on effective single parenting, so they did it. Other than simply giving them my full support and encouragement, I've not had one ounce of input or responsibility in developing the children-of-divorce program, the single-parent ministry, or the single-parent vacations.

Today we have hundreds of single parents who are involved in this ministry. They do all their own planning, arrange for the buses, take care of all the details. This ministry has succeeded because they saw the need themselves, took the necessary initiative, and recognized that they could have a powerful ministry to one another.

> "My position is that if the single adults don't do it themselves, then they don't want it done. All ministry is born from need. If people feel a need for something, they will . . . come up with a way to meet that need."

In your previous ministry positions, did your single adults take this same kind of initiative in beginning ministries out of their own need and relationships?

No. But it was because I didn't give them permission to do so. It's taken me a while to learn this. I used to be a leader-director rather than a student-leader. When I came to Detroit, I came to a ministry that was well-established, recognized, and organized. Timm Jackson, the former singles pastor here, did a wonderful job of develop-ing this ministry. I came in not having any idea what was going on, and I had to come in as a student-leader.

I can remember one lady coming to me and saying, "This is the way we do divorce recovery here. It works and you'd better not touch it." She is a wonderful lady, and she had a healthy sense of ownership with that ministry.

A SELF-EVALUATION:
WHY ARE YOU IN LEADERSHIP?
by Terry Hershey and Lisa McAfee
Terry is director of Christian Focus, Inc., Seattle, Washington
Lisa is coauthor of How to Start a Beginning Again Ministry

How are your attitudes and motivations as a leader? Are you in a leadership position for the right or wrong reasons? The following guidelines will help you make that self-evaluation.

Wrong Motives for Leadership
1. I'm leading so that others will admire me or think well of me. (This motivation implies that we are seeking the glory of men, be it social recognition, prestige, popularity, or status.)

2. I'm leading so that I will experience acceptance or approval; I lead to fulfill my own emotional needs.

3. I'm leading so that I will obtain power and authority (again, a self-seeking or self-gratifying motivation).

Right Motives for Leadership
1. I am a leader because of my desire to serve: "For even the Son of Man did not come to be served, but to serve, and to give his life as a ransom for many" (Mark 10:45).

2. I am a leader because I desire to please and love God: "We speak as men approved by God to be entrusted with the gospel. We are not trying to please men but God, who tests our hearts" (1 Thessalonians 2:4).

3. I am leading because of the love of Christ, which controls me and pushes me forward: "This is how we know what love is: Jesus Christ laid down his life for us. And we ought to lay down our lives for our brothers" (1 John 3:16).

4. I am a leader because I seek to be like Christ: "Whoever claims to live in him must walk as Jesus did" (1 John 2:6).

5. I am a leader because my desire is to advance the Kingdom of God wherever and whenever possible: "Therefore go and make disciples of all nations . . . teaching them to obey everything I have commanded you" (Matthew 28:19–20).[15]

It was important for me to relinquish the title and become a servant. But several years ago—due to my own control issues and immaturity—I couldn't have done that.

What is the difference between a leader-director and a student-leader?

First, being a student-leader means I go into a ministry position with as few preconceived ideas and notions as possible. I don't go in thinking and acting as though I'm the expert, as the leader-director might. I may have had a very successful singles ministry in Chicago, but what works in Chicago may not work in Detroit, or New York, or any other place. So I must first go in as a student, to learn from the people, to listen—really listen—to what they are saying about their needs, concerns, hopes, and dreams. I also want to understand where they are socially, economically, spiritually, and relationally.

As a student-leader, what would you look for when you first go into a new singles ministry leadership position?

Here's an example. A few years ago I was on staff at a church in Aurora, Illinois. This church is in a lower-middle-class, very blue-collar area. There are a lot of pickups and motorcycles around. It was country and cowboy boots and night shifts. One of the ministries we had there for single men was called MOM—"Ministry on Motorcycles." That worked great there because it fit the community.

A few years later I moved to serve on a church staff in Arlington Heights, still in the Chicago area, but thirty miles north of Aurora. It is very much upper middle class with sport coats or suits and ties. Motorcycles were not in. BMWs were. I didn't go up there saying, "MOM was a wonderful ministry idea in Aurora, so I'll do it here." Instead, I went as a student-leader with the focus to learn and understand where these people were coming from, what some of their particular needs were, and how to most effectively build a ministry with them.

> **"We usually define ministry as program. That is not ministry. Ministry is a relationship."**

Very few of the singles actually worked in Arlington Heights. Instead, they got up early five days a week, caught a train in to Chicago, and worked to be promoted from the fifteenth floor to the thirtieth floor of some tall office building. From the time they wake up until they go to bed, they are in competition—achievement-oriented. So the ministry there was quite different from the one in Aurora only thirty miles away. When I came to Detroit, the same student-leader skills were required.

How does being a student-leader help your ministry grow in healthy ways?

A student-leader is first a relationship-builder, gift-discoverer, and nurturer. As a student-leader, I am spending much of my time meeting with people, saying, "I've really been enjoying this opportunity to get to know you. I've

SIX KEYS TO BEING A SUCCESSFUL LEADER
by Mary Kay Ash

Mary Kay Ash, founder and owner of Mary Kay Cosmetics, calls the following six suggestions her "Golden Rules" for successful leadership:

1. *People will support that which they help to create.* Develop and promote people from within your organization. Upward mobility builds loyalty. People give you their best when they know they'll be rewarded.

2. *Recognize the value in people.* People are your number one asset. When you treat them as you would like to be treated yourself, everyone benefits.

3. *Create a stress-free environment.* By eliminating stress factors, you can increase and inspire productivity and dedication to the task.

4. *Praise people.* Recognition is the most powerful of all motivators. And don't ever criticize in front of other people. Sandwich every bit of criticism between two heavy layers of praise.

5. *Share valid ideas with others.* As Woodrow Wilson said, "I use not only all the brains I have, but all that I can borrow."

6. *Imagine each individual is wearing an invisible sign that says: MAKE ME FEEL IMPORTANT!* This is an absolute priority for everyone. No matter how busy you are, you must take time to make the other person feel important.[16]

been watching you, and I've noticed you have a tremendous gift of hospitality. I think you could contribute greatly in the area of making people feel at home. Would you assist us?"

As my relationship with them continues to grow, they discover that they can use their gift and—this is key—that they have authority, responsibility, and ownership. I'm convinced that the reason many ministries have difficulty in finding good quality leadership is because they don't give the singles responsibility or authority. Instead, the message is, "Will you do my grunt work for me?"

What does it look like when you give people responsibility and authority?

Let me give you an example. On Friday nights we have a big ministry called "Showcase." It is the biggest

event—attendance-wise—that we have in our singles ministry. For each Showcase we bring in a top speaker or musician and provide dinner. We have a Showcase coordinator who has the freedom and the authority to choose the speaker or musician, to produce each program throughout the year within our budget guidelines, to make all travel arrangements, to take care of all the details. I don't tell this person who they should or shouldn't have. The coordinator and Showcase ministry team really "own" this ministry.

But many outside people don't know how to handle this. For example, some booking agent might call me and say, "I would like to have so-and-so come." I will tell him, "You'll need to call the person in charge of that." He will often say, "Oh, aren't you in charge; aren't you the director of this ministry; can't you make that decision?" I simply tell him that if I do that then I am usurping the authority of the person who has been given that responsibility. Sometimes as ministers or leaders we give the person the responsibility but take away the authority when our ego gets threatened or hurt.

It seems that this would be very difficult to do, especially if you have a particular vision for the ministry and someone is not making it happen the way you think it should be done.

Sometimes I have to bite the bullet because there are occasions when things are done in this ministry that I know I could do better. But if I did that, I would destroy my leaders' sense of ownership and responsibility. This is not my normal behavior. I've really had to work at learning this. I heard someone once say, "The responsibility of a leader is to catch a vision, share the vision, find a leader, and then say thank you." I have to remind myself of this now and then.

Are there times when this style of leadership will not work?

Yes. First, if you are not able to trust your single adults with leadership positions and with responsibility, it will not work. Letting go and trusting others is essential. Second, if your senior pastor and church are more concerned about programs than ministry and is highly director-leader oriented, it will not work.

Far too many pastors and leaders are pushed to produce. (And production is usually tied to programs be-cause programs are more measurable.) There is one singles leader I know who, when he was hired, was told he had three years to build one of the most significant ministries in the country. Under that kind of pressure you be-come an idiot-leader-director. It's absurd, unhealthy, and un-biblical. I couldn't and wouldn't work under this kind of leadership. If you want to focus first on true ministry versus program, then you need to make sure you are in a church where the leadership understands the dif-ference and encour-ages you in that direction.

How do you deal with problems that arise among your leadership team?

I find that we have very few problems. And I'm convinced this is because we really focus on rela-tionships rather than behavior. I think we only need to "police" people when we do not have a relationship with them. When you take the time to build relationships with people, they respect you and you respect them. People get to the point where they wouldn't do anything to intentionally hurt you. When they do, they either change their

> "Sometimes I have to bite the bullet because there are occasions when things are done in this ministry that I know I could do better. But if I did that, I would destroy my lead-ers' sense of ownership and responsibility. . . . I heard someone once say, 'The responsibility of a leader is to catch a vision, share the vision, find a lead-er, and then say thank you.' I have to remind myself of this now and then."

behavior or make the choice to leave.

The reason a lot of leaders are so busy policing their people is because they've been more focused on programs and behavior than on relationships and the natural accountability that grows out of community.

A CASE STUDY:
Following the Successful Singles Pastor

with a suggested solution from Terry Hershey
Director of Christian Focus, Inc., Seattle, Washington

The Problem

"The single adult pastor before me was very successful and popular. I'm finding it hard to fill his shoes. And the singles here are comparing me to him. How can I establish my own identity, and stop being intimidated by the 'ghost' of the previous pastor, with what God has for me to do here?"

A Possible Solution

This frustration is common. What happens when you enter a ministry where your predecessor has left a legacy of success? You feel uncomfortable, guilty, inadequate. "Maybe I'm not cut out for this position," you might say. "Or for singles ministry at all."

You often hear comments like, "John never did it that way"; "We sure grew when Bill was here"; "You're sure different from Susan." People resist change and wonder whether the new pastor will be able to "keep a good thing going."

How can you overcome this intimidation? Let me offer two don'ts (attitudes to avoid) and three do's (action steps to take).

Attitudes to Avoid

1. Don't measure your success by your predecessor's standards. You are not, and never will be, just like your predecessor. Whatever success he or she accomplished (and, by the way, things always look sweeter in hindsight) should not affect your self-esteem. When someone praises the former pastor, sincerely agree with his or her opinion, or at least make a positive comment. Avoid rivalry, and the single adults will soon see that you are not competing with the past leader.

2. Don't try to prove your worth with immediate success. One wrong way to counter insecurity is to "make a big wave"—that is, to prematurely plan grand new programs. If you do this, you will lose your focus on ministering to people. Your ministry will be reduced to proving a point, to validating your own self-esteem. If you're not trying to prove yourself, you can use your first six-to-eight months to listen, watch, and be available to people.

Action Steps to Take

1. Do join a covenant group. People in isolation are more susceptible to personal decay from envy, criticism, pressure to perform, and insecurity. All problems are intensified by isolation. We need objective feedback from others.

A covenant group is from three to eight persons meeting together regularly to support, exhort, and be accountable to each other. I have discovered that this group should be made up of persons outside your ministry. The measurement of success in ministry is subjective at best, and my covenant group helps me stay objective. Isolation is a killer.

2. Do live within your limits. This is good advice. The question, however, is How do you do that? I recently asked a friend who gracefully followed a successful pastor. He said, "I sat down and figured out what I do best, and focused on those areas of ministry. I realized I couldn't imitate the former pastor."

Have you ever taken inventory of your abilities? Does your ministry emphasize your strengths? After taking inventory, ask for help in your areas of weakness. You are not called to minister alone. You are a member of the Body of Christ.

3. Do build bridges with the past. Don't burn your bridges; it only serves to fuel the fire of comparison and criticism. When I followed a very successful predecessor, my instinct was to make everyone forget him. I'm glad I didn't. Instead, I bought him lunch. (If you can't do this, telephone him.) After talking with him, I saw the ministry through his eyes. We became colaborers in the Body of Christ. We're still good friends.

One thing is clear: There's no easy solution. We all want to be a success and feel like we never work hard enough to please everyone. This feeling is exaggerated when we step into the shoes of a successful predecessor. You can wear those shoes if you want to, but don't complain when you get blisters.

For Those Who Have Moved from Youth Ministry to Singles Ministry: BEWARE OF THE YOUTH-MINISTRY SYNDROME

by Rob Suggs
Minister with singles at Second Ponce de Leon Baptist Church, Atlanta, Georgia

As ministry with single adults continues to grow across North America, an increasing number of youth pastors are moving into singles ministry leadership roles. In my opinion, there are some critical differences between these two areas of ministry that former youth pastors should keep in mind. But first, let's look at some of the advantages.

Moving from Youth Ministry to Singles Ministry— What's Good About It?

Former youth pastors are helping to fill a growing need for singles ministry staff. Based on what I see—at least in Southern Baptist circles—there is a tremendous, growing need for singles ministry, and many churches are beginning to address that need.

They are beginning to realize that this is no longer a "husband-wife-two-children-and-two-cars-in-the-garage" world. And, if they're going to reach the people in all those condominiums, town homes, and apartments out there, they're going to have to reach single adults. Consequently, there are more and more churches looking for singles ministry staff people. A good number of youth pastors are beginning to make "career changes" and are filling many of these positions.

It can be a natural transition for youth ministry workers. Many youth pastors in their thirties and forties are looking for a change. They want to maintain a specialized ministry area, but they also want to spend more time with adults, people closer to their own age. Moving into singles ministry can

> "Some people assume that singles are all lonely, miserable people who need to be occupied to avoid the unspeakable sins that we imagine them doing. Therefore, we are supposed to offer a continuous variety of activities to keep them off the streets. That's a cynical, degrading view of singles ministry."

be one way to provide this desired change.

Furthermore, youth ministers are beginning to spend more and more time with broken families. For instance, in Sunday school, the first and third Sundays of each month often have many different kids in attendance than the second and fourth. Whether the kids come to church that particular Sunday is often determined by which parent they're with for the weekend.

Many of the youth pastors I know are finding a greater need to minister with the single parents or stepparents of their teens. This can be excellent training ground for the youth pastor who someday moves to a singles ministry.

Moving from Youth Ministry to Singles—What to Look Out For

Don't be too program oriented. Often youth pastors spend a great deal of effort keeping their teens busy, entertained, and off the streets. This is partly based on the assumption that teens need a lot of direction in how to expend their bounding energy and hormones.

This may or may not be the best model for youth ministry. But the danger is that many former youth pastors tend to program their singles ministry like this youth-ministry model. And it is certainly not the way to build a healthy singles ministry.

Some people assume that singles are all lonely, miserable people who need to be occupied to avoid the unspeakable sins that we imagine them doing. Therefore, we are supposed to

---

IS PROCRASTINATION HURTING YOUR EFFECTIVENESS?

Check the following statements that tend to be true for you. Find out how serious a problem procrastination is in your life.

Most Procrastinators
- ☐ Won't get started without a large block of time.
- ☐ Value only the finished product.
- ☐ Focus more on what is left to do than on what has already been done.
- ☐ Set high standards and expect to achieve them easily.
- ☐ Tend to feel dumb or inadequate if they have to work hard on a project.
- ☐ Define their self-worth by what they produce, and have a diminished self-worth when they have a product that is not "perfect."
- ☐ Have low self-acceptance and are self-defeated because they never meet their unrealistically high standards for themselves.

"Perfectionists often become bad procrastinators. They can't find the middle ground between 'I must be perfect' and 'I am nothing.'"

"A perfectionist tends to not go anywhere on a project for fear of doing it 'less than perfect.' It would be better for him to shoot for a C grade and get it done than an A grade and never complete it."

"When they are afraid of failing to meet their own high standards, they procrastinate."[17]

---

offer a continuous variety of activities to keep them off the streets. That's a cynical, degrading view of singles ministry.

I'm guilty too. Sometimes programming is easier than spending time with our people, really getting to know them, their needs, hurts, talents, and dreams. Normally, when I go home at the end of the day, I know that my work is not finished. Sometimes I can feel like it's complete if I have it on paper as a program. I have to constantly resist this temptation. This is not what true ministry is all about.

Remember that you are not their chaperone. Possibly one of the biggest challenges to face when moving from teens to single adults is to remember that you are no longer in a "parent-figure," authoritarian role. You are now a peer, in a "brother" or "sister" role. This may also effect the way you talk to—and with—them.

Don't try to do it all: Give singles ownership of the ministry. As a youth pastor, you are expected to run your program—really run it. You come up with most of the ideas and the format, and then you hand them down to your teens from Mount Sinai on a stone tablet.

As a singles pastor, if you try to totally run the program, you will fail, and the singles will rebel. Your title can even make a statement about this area of singles ministry. For example, our Southern Baptist Sunday School Board encourages the concept of ministering *with* singles rather than *to* them. It encourages us to use the title "Ministers with Singles." Ask yourself if your mind-set is to do something *to* them or to partner *with* them.

Recognize the vast span of ages

represented in most singles ministries. Many church leaders tend to think all singles are twenty-two years old (or younger). I hear people talking about singles and young people interchangeably—assuming that they are all just out of college. Or still in college. Where a youth minister will usually work with people representing an age span of from five to ten years, a singles pastor might work with adults from ages twenty-two to ninety.

Dealing with this vast age span is possibly one of the biggest challenges in singles ministry. It requires extra effort and sensitivity to stay tuned to the wide spectrum of needs represented in a group that includes everyone from the younger, carefree, never-married single to the single parent to the older widowed person.

Furthermore, as a singles pastor you are suddenly dealing with people who are older than you. They may have had many experiences that you have not had, know more about life than you, and have tapped into emotional wells that you have never tapped. You have to let go of your youth ministry days' father-figure image and become a brother or sister.

Conclusion

In my opinion, one of the best ways to overcome the "youth-ministry syndrome" in singles ministry is to spend time with your single adults. In many ways, this is easier to do with your singles than it was with your teens. You couldn't just hang around with or cruise the mall with the teens. They would hide somewhere, or think you

were the biggest jerk in the world.

But with your single adults, you are generally not out of place. They are much more likely to love having your company. They want to be touched, appreciated, valued. They're not all trying to escape from you as the teens sometimes were. They enjoy getting together for lunch. In fact, you can do some of your best ministry during lunchtime. Spend time with them. Go to a movie together. Get involved in their lives. Listen to them. Find out what their lives are like. Get to know them as they really are, and you will begin to develop a healthy ministry with your single adults—and overcome the youth-ministry syndrome.

How Big Is Your Group? Keeping the Size Question in Proportion

by Cliff Graves
Associate pastor at Christ Community Church, Carmichael, California

How big is your group? This question seems to haunt singles workers everywhere, especially those in more modest ministries. As an avid student of church growth, I am wholeheartedly committed to ministering in such a way that the Great Commission is honored and the full potential for numerical growth can occur in any given situation.

But, I believe that in many circles this focus has become the "question that ate Saint Louis"—a question that eats up other important questions and concerns. I am also aware that if this question is entertained in an unbalanced fashion it leads directly to discouragement and self-recrimination on the part of singles workers in legitimate but modest ministries.

Let me suggest some other questions singles workers need to keep in mind in order to bring the "size question" into balance.

How Big Is Your Pond?

All things being equal, singles ministries tend to be proportionate to the churches they inhabit. They also tend to grow as their home church grows.

John Wimber, leader of the Vineyard Church of Anaheim, California, has seen his church explode with growth. Yet he cautions his staff against believing they are the singular cause of growth.

Many churches are so progressive and dynamic that just about anything could grow well there. People come on staff and start ministries that grow rapidly and think they are the sole cause of it. They don't realize they are fishing in a stocked pond. Fishing technique, bait, and feeding schedules are less critical in those situations.

When I first started singles ministry, I called up the most successful singles leader in the area and arranged a lunch appointment. He described what he did to expand his group from thirty singles to 600 in six months. I was impressed. He was impressed. Neither of us noticed his context, however. He was fishing in a church of 5,000 that was growing so rapidly that it had to relocate to a larger church facility. Once transplanted, it quickly swelled to 7,000. This is not to diminish his considerable skills as a communicator and motivator.

> "There are leaders who will never have large ministries but who year in and year out will impact singles to go on for Christ."

Rather, it is to say that there was more to his group's rapid growth than can be accounted for by his own capabilities.

How Big Is Your Insecurity?

Somewhere I got the message, "If you just do these fifty-five things, your group will grow, and you will feel so much better about yourself." As a result, I used to go through a weekly emotional ritual familiar to the misfocused. Thirty people would be present as the meeting began. My heart would sink. Over the next twenty minutes, fifteen more people would walk in. I would feel a whole lot better.

Why?

Did I change? Did I go up or down in God's eyes? Was I a better leader after those fifteen people walked in than before? Did I love God more? No. I was exactly the same, and God's opinion of me was exactly the same before and after those fifteen people walked in. It was simply a matter of having my self-esteem tied too tightly to the turnout.

I have since learned that if you feel better about yourself solely because your group grows, you may have a serious problem. That problem involves a confusion of identity. You are probably overidentified with the circumstantial fluctuations of your group. You will start feeling secure or insecure for the wrong reasons.

You are not a mere reflection of today's attendance figures. God relates to you and discerns your heart apart from all that. It is imperative that we receive God's love and affirmation quite apart from these and other oscillating circumstances.

How Big Is Your Real Impact?

Howard Hendricks has said, "You can impress people from afar, but you can only impact lives up close." Jesus' strategy was wholeheartedly impact-oriented. His success at group building was measured in terms of the eleven men who went on to change the face of the Mediterranean in their lifetime. Never mind the thousands who were impressed.

The great equalizer among leaders is not the opportunity one has to impress large audiences but the opportunity one has to impact the few who are ready to be guided into a deeper Christian walk. Whether your group is twenty or five hundred, the important question is, "Are you being responsible with the people who are ready and willing to go deeper in their faith?"

How Big Are Your Footprints?

Who will still be doing what after you're long gone? This is a question that is usually asked when it's too late. You will not always be ministering to the group you are with. When you stop, what you leave behind is not a set of attendance figures but people who either go on to serve Christ or do not. What they go on to do is also a measure of your ministry.

There are leaders who will never have large ministries but who year in and year out will impact singles to go on for Christ. The size of the group from which the few are discipled does not necessarily determine the number or spiritual longevity of those discipled.

How Big Is Your Heart?

Here again, the size of your group is not the determining factor. The issue is not mustering people but ministering to them. There is no necessary relationship between the number of people you somehow rally and the number of people you are burdened for, personally involved with, have compassion for, rejoice with, or cry with.

How Big Is Your Group's Heart?

The size of a group does not automatically tell you much about the loving web of interaction that takes place behind the scenes. However, there are immeasurable elements in any group that form the heartbeat of the group and give meaning to Christ's commandment to "love one another."

How many people engaged how many people for breakfast, lunch, or dinner? How many people were invited for coffee after the main meeting? How many people have helped move how many people? How many friendly phone calls occur weekly? How many people felt comfortable enough by what they encountered at your group to engage a leader in deeper conversation? How many people took how many people aside when they needed words of encouragement? How is your group regarded in the community?

It's amazing how people visiting any function form an automatic opinion about the warmth or coolness of a singles group, regardless of its size. The relational glue of any group is how its members treat one another. Neither large groups nor small groups have a necessary advantage in this area. It is not something that can be forced upon the group from the front, although it can at times be encouraged or facilitated. But that sense of genuine fellowship is the very aroma of grace that your group will or will not have.

What Motives Stand Behind the Size Question?

Why are we so insistent about asking this question? What would a singles conference be like if not one person was permitted to ask the "size question" or venture that information? How would we treat speakers whose biographies were blank in this regard?

At a singles leadership training conference I attended years ago, a singles worker startled the entire audience two days into the conference by saying, "If one more person asks me how big my group is or offers to tell me how big theirs is, I'm going to cut the conversation off right there. I came here to learn about singles ministry, not strut like a peacock or watch other peacocks strut." A knowing silence fell over the room, then light laughter and applause.

May I suggest a way to inject loving confrontation into this area. The next time another singles worker asks you how big your group is, ask the worker why he or she wants to know. Then press for the real reason. Sometimes the answer is simply that the person asking wants to know what you're doing right or wrong. Well and good.

But often the true motive is (a) I want to know if you're significant or insignificant, (b) I want to know if your ministry is significant or insignificant, (c) I need to compare myself or my group to you in these terms because I have no other criteria with which to orient myself, or (d) I want to play "let's compare ourselves to ourselves."

No one conquers the world for Christ. We each get our half acre to assault and hold until He returns. Let's continue to hold ourselves accountable concerning the question of group size and growth rate. It is an important indication of how the battle is going with our half acre.

But let's not be tortured by the size question or fooled into thinking that it's the only question that needs to be entertained as we evaluate what or how

> **"If one more person asks me how big my group is or offers to tell me how big theirs is, I'm going to cut the conversation off right there. I came here to learn about singles ministry, not strut like a peacock or watch other peacocks strut."**

we are doing. A ministry's ultimate question will always have to do with its integrity before God. These questions will seldom be answered by a quick glance at the attendance record.

Can a Woman Be an Effective Singles Pastor?

by Mary G. Graves
Associate pastor and minister of singles at Solana Beach Presbyterian Church, Solana Beach, California

Male leadership is crucial to the success of any singles group. If men aren't leading, people of either sex in the group won't feel comfortable and won't be interested in staying for long. All leadership training conferences for singles ministries stress this point. The survival of your ministry depends on male leadership.

The lay leader in our church (a woman), who founded and organized the singles ministry, discovered this reality. After she worked hard to involve men as lay leaders, the ministry took shape and the church decided to have a half-time singles' minister. As the applications began to roll in, this pioneering lay leader—also a member of the pastoral seeking committee—insisted that the singles pastor be a man. But after much prayer and several interviews with prospective candidates, the committee selected a woman for the position.

So, if male leadership is crucial to singles ministry, can a woman successfully serve as a singles pastor? Many churches understand Scripture to decree that women should not be in positions of authority. But for others, the issue is not as clear. So the question remains: Should women be included as leaders in singles ministries?

I suggest that in order to answer this question, we must step back and answer two other questions first:
• Who should be leaders in the Church?
• Should women be leaders in the Church?

Who Should Be Leaders in the Church?

The specifications for leadership in the church are numerous and rigorous (see the Pastoral Epistles). But the biblical accounts also remind us that God often chooses the most unlikely leaders. Gideon was hardly leadership material. The disciples weren't exactly first-round draft picks, and even Jesus was not what people were looking for in a leader. The point? God raises up and calls leaders. The person God has raised up and called is the person to fill any position of leadership in the Church. Ultimately, having the proper credentials doesn't make a good leader; the Spirit of God makes a good leader (Zechariah 4:6).

But proper credentials are also important. When I'm looking for a small-group leader in our singles ministry, I look for a person committed to Christ, growing in faith, committed to the Church and the singles ministry, and gifted for the particular job description. These guidelines help me to see God's selection for the job. And I pray and ask that person to pray too. I ask God to confirm His choice, and He does. Sometimes I'm not surprised at God's choice, but just as often it is someone I never even dreamed of.

Guidelines are good. They are God-given. But in the end we do not follow guidelines as much as we seek to follow the call of God. And God's Word tells us to be ready for surprises, as the Apostle Paul notes in 1 Corinthians 1:26-29 (RSV): "For consider your call . . . not many of you were wise according to worldly standards, not many were powerful, not many were of noble birth; but God chose what is foolish in the world to shame the wise, God chose what is weak in the world to shame the strong, God chose what is low and despised in the world . . . so that no human being might boast in the presence of God." Who should lead in the Church? The person God raises up.

Should Women Be Leaders in the Church at All?

Much has been written about whether women should be leaders in

---

MALE AND FEMALE LEADERSHIP—THE DIFFERENCES
an interview with Jim Smoke
Founder and director of The Center for Divorce Recovery,
Phoenix, Arizona

As you travel around visiting different singles ministries, what—if any—differences do you find when men are in leadership instead of women?

It doesn't matter whether leaders are professional or lay people, men or women. If the leader is strong, your group is going to be strong. And vice versa. Leadership attracts leadership. If you have strong leaders—men or women—you will have men involved because men respect strength of leadership. However, I think it's important to remember that men will not come if the ministry is mostly run by women. There must be men in visible areas of leadership. I personally think that having men in leadership is best, but there are many capable women who make great leaders, too.

If the tables were turned and it was almost all men in leadership, would you then recruit women for leadership roles?

First of all, that won't happen. Men in leadership will always attract both men and women. Women in leadership tend to attract only other women. To me that's a sociological thing.

I think another important reason to have men active in your group is because many divorced women need a man at least somewhat identifiable in a leadership role. They are suddenly without male leadership in their home. That's why so many women say to me, "How do I just find a man who's a friend with whom I can talk? I don't want to marry him or chase him. I just want to be able to have a cup of coffee with him and say, 'Boy, I just need to talk with you to get a man's point of view about some problems and struggles I'm having.'" That's so important to single women.[18]

the Church. The most commonly held view says that women should not. I, as an ordained female pastor, believe that women should be leaders. Our most reliable sources agree.

Jesus Christ says yes. In a time when the woman's place was only in the home and her status was right down there with slaves and dogs, Jesus welcomed women as His followers and as learners of the things of God (Luke 10:38-42). He not only called women to Him, He sent them out with the good news (John 4:7-42). The very first people commissioned with the resurrection gospel were women. No one believed in them because they were *only* women. But Jesus did.

The Holy Spirit says yes. God pours out His Spirit on His "menservants and . . . maidservants" (Acts 2:18, RSV). The same Spirit is given to both men and women alike—God is not partial. And both men and women have access to the same gifts. If there is

a "higher gift" of the Spirit, it is prophesy (1 Corinthians 14:1), a gift shared by both men and women in the New Testament. The Spirit gifts people for leadership, including women.

Even Paul says yes. The same man who ordered women to be silent in the Church also commended those female leaders who hosted and led house churches, those women who were coworkers with him in establishing the church and spreading the gospel (Priscilla, Cloe, Lydia, Nympha, Phoebe, Euodia, Syntyche, and more).

Should Women Be Leaders in Singles Ministries?

Now we find ourselves at the beginning of our discussion. The perplexing question is this: How can you affirm the call of women as leaders of single adult ministries and also affirm the urgent need for male leadership? It is not difficult if you consider the following.

Male leadership in your singles ministry does not necessarily mean a male singles pastor on your staff, just as being a singles pastor does not necessarily mean being a single person. No matter who the singles pastor is, the need for male leadership must be met by recruiting capable male leaders from among your lay leadership.

But can women recruit, train, disciple, and raise up male leaders? Yes. Priscilla trained Apollos (Acts 18:24-28), Henrietta Mears from Hollywood Presbyterian Church trained a core of male leaders who are major church figures in the country today, and hundreds of women have been on the mission field for hundreds of years

> **"Can women recruit, train, disciple, and raise up male leaders? Yes. Priscilla trained Apollos . . . Henrietta Mears from Hollywood Presbyterian Church trained a core of male leaders who are major church figures in the country today, and hundreds of women have been on the mission field for hundreds of years teaching, training, equipping, and installing male leaders in Christ's Church. It is true that men need male mentors and role models, but women can connect them with the mentors and role models they need."**

teaching, training, equipping, and installing male leaders in Christ's Church. It is true that men need male mentors and role models, but women can connect them with the mentors and role models they need.

Lyle Schaller, a foremost authority on success and failure in church structure and programs, claims that women have been more successful than men in initiating programs for men in the church. His rationale is that men are often more comfortable with women than they are with men.

So, while we have been wondering whether women can and should raise up male leaders, it has been happening. And God has blessed it. In my mind there would be only one reason why a woman should not be singles leader and that would be if there is no support from the church leadership. Just as single ministry in and of itself cannot survive without support from the top, neither can a leader survive, much less succeed, if she is not supported and encouraged from the top.

The Unique Strength of Women as Leaders

The emerging role of women in our society has often been tainted with a jostling for power and a large dose of selfishness. But the blessing in it—for those who have eyes to see—is that there is a trained and competent work force ready to be engaged in the work of the Church. Most women are now working outside the home, and they are discovering that they are not only good at running a home but also an office or a business or even a ministry.

And women bring unique contributions and strengths that have often been underdeveloped in the church. They are often "team players" who do not hunger as much to develop their own superstar status as to develop a team of leaders. Women have strong relational abilities and are very approachable and demonstrative in the expression of emotions and feelings. And they represent the needs and provide role models for the majority of our singles—the women.

Should women be leaders in singles ministries? They already are. Many ministries for singles have been created and sustained by women—and they are bearing much fruit. As Jesus said, "A good tree cannot bear bad fruit, and a bad tree cannot bear good fruit. . . . Thus, by their fruit you will recognize them" (Matthew 7:18,20).

Why I'm Still in Singles Ministry (After Nineteen Years)

by Bill Flanagan
Minister with singles at Saint Andrew's Presbyterian Church, Newport Beach, California

It's not very spectacular how I initially got involved in singles ministry. I didn't get some Macedonian call. I wish I could say that I had this great vision for singles ministry, but I didn't. I just sort of backed into it.

I had been in youth ministry for a long time and began feeling the need to move on to something else. This was in the early seventies, while I was on staff at First Presbyterian Church in Colorado Springs, Colorado. I had been minister with singles for about three years when I discovered that very few others around the country were doing anything similar.

Without my knowing it, I had been one of the first—a pioneer of sorts. One day around 1975, I woke up and discovered, to my surprise, that I was an expert. I'm still in singles ministry today because I like to be a builder; I like to be on the growing edge of something important. I'm not interested in being a maintainer. I like to be constantly plowing new ground.

Second, I'm in singles ministry because of these wonderful single adults. They are the most honest, transparent, open, affirming, caring people that I know. I recently taught a married class for the first time in quite a while. I don't want to be extreme here, but I found that their masks were up more, the transparency wasn't there, nor was the same enthusiasm to learn and grow. Most single adults—especially those going through major transitional times in their lives—are really open to the gospel, open to growth, and open to serving. I find that very challenging.

I also find that being a little part of their healing process is thrilling. One of the reasons I've remained involved in a divorce-recovery ministry for so long without getting bored—even though I'm doing a lot of the same things over and over—is that I always have a new crop of people who really need the touch of Christ. It's thrilling to watch these people coming alive, becoming whole, seeing themselves through redemptive eyes. I don't know of anything in the church more exciting.

Divorced people often come to the church asking, "Can I ever be whole again?" "Is there life after divorce?" "Is there any hope for me?" "Will I ever really smile again?" "Can God ever use me again?"

Thank God that I've had a part in this restoration and forgiveness process; helping people realize that God doesn't reject them, that they are valuable human beings, created in His image, and that they can stand with anyone else in the Body of Christ as redemptive, loved, and gifted people.

The fruit of this ministry is one of the things for which I've been so deeply grateful: having the opportunity to watch people not only in the healing process but seeing them come alive, discovering and using their spiritual gifts, finding a place in the church where they can grow in maturity with Christ, and watching them become the

> **"I'm in singles ministry because of these wonderful single adults. They are the most honest, transparent, open, affirming, caring people that I know. I recently taught a married class for the first time in quite a while. I don't want to be extreme here, but I found that their masks were up more, the transparency wasn't there, nor was the same enthusiasm to learn and grow."**

people that God wants them to be. I can't understand anyone who would get tired of this.

I haven't found anything in the church that compares to this ministry as far as offering a cutting-edge outreach that touches a segment of our society so needing God's touch. I feel privileged to be a part of this growing band of people nationwide who are called "ministers with single adults."

THOUGHTS ON SINGLE ADULT MINISTRY IN THE FUTURE
by Jim Smoke

Greater leadership is needed from our seminaries. There is no place where pastors and students can be trained for ministry with single adults. I know of no seminary in America that teaches something significant in this area on a regular ongoing basis, which means that singles ministry is not being taken very seriously on the upper-educational level. You would think, just by looking at the phenomenal changes in our society over the past decade, that seminaries would be addressing this ministry area much more aggressively. The need to do so is critical.

Denominational leadership is also a must. One of our most critical tasks is to mount an assault on all the various denominational headquarters and challenge them to (1) recognize those single adult ministries already established in their denomination, and (2) put somebody at a national level in charge and provide leadership throughout the denomination in the area of singles ministry.

A few years ago one major denomination had someone in charge of singles ministry at the headquarters level. When that person went to the mission field, they replaced him with someone who had two or three different jobs. Finally, the position was just sort of phased out. That's the kind of thing that happens much too often. Denominational leaders need to take a much more active role in leading the way.

SEVEN

Nurturing the Inner Life of the Leader

Avoiding Ministry Burnout

by Jim Smoke
Founder and director of The Center for Divorce Recovery, Phoenix, Arizona

As I've traveled around the country visiting singles ministries, I've observed over and over the once "going strong" leader who is now burned out, limping, or not going at all. Stress and burnout are two of the most important issues that need to be addressed in single adult ministry.

For the sake of healthy, ongoing ministries, we as leaders must learn to handle our calling in ways that keep us refreshed, vibrant, and growing. To help us be more effective leaders, we should be aware of four common key stress areas that can culminate in ministry burnout.

1. *Spiritual stress.* This results from giving beyond your own depth on an ongoing basis. Con-stant giving with no spiritual intake depletes the giver. People in ministry have the habit of preparing to give rather than preparing to receive. The end result is no strength in the storehouse.

2. *Emotional stress.* This results from the constant submerging of the minister's own emotions and needs in order to help meet the emotional needs of others. A singles ministry involves hours of personal counseling and listening to the emotional unraveling of others. You cannot be a person for others by denying your own emotional needs. We all live on an emotional roller coaster, and we need personal time to attend to our own feelings, struggles, and needs. In short, a minister always needs a nurturing small group or a minister. The "look how strong I am" game seldom goes into extra innings. A cave-in usually comes first.

3. *Physical stress.* A busy schedule usually tires out rather than cares for the human body. Fourteen-hour days are more a monument to stupidity than a shrine to sacrifice and dedication. Most crises can wait twenty-four hours. If your body breaks down physically, sending your mind to the office by United Parcel Service won't help anyone. Exercise has been a key thing in my own life for more than twenty-six years of ministry. Tie this to nutritious food, rest, and weight control and you begin to get your physical body in tune.

4. *Relational stress.* This usually happens when we spend too much time with one kind of person or persons. Youth workers shrivel up and die if they spend all of their time with teens. Singles workers can easily experience the same deterioration, simply because singles demand time.

Somewhere in your life, you need relationships that demand nothing

> **"Youth workers shrivel up and die if they spend all of their time with teens. Singles workers can easily experience the same deterioration, simply because singles demand time."**

from you but can give you something in return. Jesus found that Mary, Martha, and Lazarus could do this for Him. With them, He did not have to be "on." Spending your entire time with "ministry" people can grind down your spirits and reduce your soul to powder.

Eight Ways to Avoid Burnout

1. *Learn to say no!* The word *no* is not spelled s-i-n. There will always be one more "should" to deal with. "Yes" people burn out faster than "no" people.

2. *Realize that you are not "the Messiah."* Many singles workers feel their entire ministry depends on them doing it, saying it, planning it, and picking up after it. But it ain't so.

3. *Run away for a while when you need it.* Peace and quiet can seldom be found in AT&T country. Leave town. It will still be there when you return.

4. *Keep a constant tab on your priorities.* Nonpriorities can bury you. Is your burial worth the expense?

5. *Be good to yourself!* You don't need permission. Do something for yourself once in a while.

6. *Plan a retreat for one!* Take yourself away for a few days to a monastery or a quiet place to realign your life. Things seldom seem as huge when you put distance between them.

7. *Don't take yourself too seriously.* Most of us have fallen into this trap. It is the next step to falling off the ego cliff.

8. *Balance your ministry time with time for the significant other(s) in your life.* (If married, this means your wife and family.) Too many ministers find they have climbed too far out on the ministry limb only to discover someone was sawing it off behind them. It is hard to repair broken limbs.

I also recommend that you read *Ministry Burnout* by John Sanford (Paulist Press, 1982).

A CASE STUDY:
Too Busy for Evangelism— The Plight of a Singles Leader

with a suggested solution from Lawrence W. Kent
Pastor of evangelism and singles at First Presbyterian Church, Flint, Michigan

The Problem

"I've been involved as a single adult pastor for several years. But I've been troubled lately because I seldom lead anyone to Christ. I wonder if I'm so caught up in planning, programming, and counseling that I've lost sight of the most important thing in ministry. How can I be a better steward of the mission God has given me? Should I feel guilty about my lack of involvement in personal evangelism?"

A Suggested Solution

Single adult pastors are often so overwhelmed by the pressing challenges of ministry that they doubt their own faithfulness to God. They become paralyzed by self-imposed guilt and exhaustion. These tired pastors can find comfort in the following principles:

1. *The Holy Spirit does the work of evangelism.* The One who has promised to be our unceasing Friend visits the hearts and lives of others through us in ways we don't recognize. When we rely on the Holy Spirit, "personal evangelism" often takes place in unusual ways. Our very presence is a channel for the Spirit. God will also use our mistakes, our weaknesses, and our laughter.

2. *Our greatest power source is prayer.* Often we crowd Christ out by trying to do too much. We reduce our tools of ministry to our own finite knowledge and strength. Instead, we must pray. To pray is to open our lives to the renewing, directing, and sustaining lifeblood of God who works His divine purpose in and through us.

3. *New strength comes from rest and renewal.* To neglect the Sabbath rest is to compromise our own well-being. To ignore our own limits is to limit God's power in our lives. We must set priorities in our own ministry.

Is it realistic to schedule activities seven nights a week? Can we teach effectively if we don't have time to prepare? A burned-out pastor does not demonstrate the power of God! But a Christian who plays, relaxes, and rests, reflects to others the abundant life God has given us.

4. *Our job is to create an environment conducive to evangelism.* Single adults fear rejection and avoid uncomfortable surroundings. Many are slow to join a singles group and quick to leave. However, when they sense that their lives really matter to other people, they experience the genuine, caring presence of God.

Create an environment where the single adults themselves will reach out and share their faith with newcomers. We are most effective when those we minister to are leading others to Christ.

Although we are occasionally staggered by the work at hand, we are also humbled by the grace and sufficiency of God. Allow the Holy Spirit freedom, pray, live a balanced lifestyle, and create an environment for evangelism. Equip your single adults to be effective evangelists—they have more contacts in the world than you have.

A Retreat for One, Please!

by Jim Smoke
Founder and director of The Center for Divorce Recovery, Phoenix, Arizona

Your office phone is ringing off the wall. You still have four more counseling appointments before dinner and you are running behind. It is Wednesday and you have an executive council meeting this evening with several tough issues on the agenda. You have to teach three times on Sunday and you are way behind in your preparation. You have not been home for the past four nights, and your children keep asking "Who is that man?" when you run in and out the door.

You still have six months to go before your vacation reprieve and on top of everything else, your senior pastor wants you to take on the responsibility for a whole new program he dreamed up on the golf course yesterday.

Sound familiar? It should. Most of us in singles ministry have been there at one time or another. How do you survive and go on?

The Strongest Call
We Need to Hear

In Mark 6:30-31 we read, "The apostles returned to Jesus, and told him all that they had done and taught. And he said to them, 'Come away by yourselves to a lonely place and rest a while.' For many were coming and going, and they had no leisure even to eat" (RSV).

The strongest call we need to hear in ministry today is not the call *to* ministry but the call *apart* from ministry for a time. A place apart is a place for rest and renewal where the seeds of new life and growth can be planted in our spirits. In the place of busyness, Jesus calls us to a center of quiet and calm.

In Matthew 14:23 we read, "And when He had sent [please observe the word *sent*] the multitudes away, He went up to a mountain by Himself to pray" (NASB). Just before Jesus chose His disciples, He "went out to the mountain to pray, and continued all night in prayer to God" (Luke 6:12, KJV). And in Mark's gospel, we read these words: "Now in the morning, having risen a long while before daylight, He went out and departed to a solitary place; and there He prayed" (Mark 1:35).

Jesus knew what you and I still seem to be learning—the importance of getting away from the heat of ministry to rest, renew, and pray. When was the last time you did that? Be honest! Your ministry will not collapse if you leave town for forty-eight hours. If it does, then I would question the foundation it is built upon.

The call to rest and renewal in your life and mine is more important today than ever before. The mountain cabin, a local monastery, a friend's condo, even a quiet hotel can provide a haven for a retreat. Basil Pennington said, "A place apart . . . there are many places apart for each one of us: those we create, those we find and those created for us. Seek and you shall find. Taste and see."

> **"The strongest call we need to hear in ministry today is not the call *to* ministry but the call *apart* from ministry for a time. . . . In the place of busyness, Jesus calls us to a center of quiet and calm."**

Times for Escape

There are two key times to escape to the quiet place. The first is when our stresses and tensions outweigh our graces. The second is when we plan for it well in advance and put it on our calendar. Each will have a different purpose. The first deals with survival, rest, renewal, and quiet listening to God's directions for the days ahead.

And don't forget, if you are married, your *wife* (not your children) needs to share in some of your retreats. You will also need times to be alone.

An excellent format to follow when on retreat is printed in the back pages of *A Guide to Prayer for Ministries and Other Servants* published by Upper Room. If you need a structure to prevent wasting your time, this will help.

Gordon MacDonald cites three ingredients that we all need in our lives: "safe places, still times and special friends." Right now might be a good moment for you to begin with the first two by ordering *"a retreat for one, please."*

MORAL ADVICE FOR LEADERS: Dealing with the Pressures of a Single Adult Pastor

by Dan Chun
Minister with singles at Menlo Park Presbyterian Church, Menlo Park, California

Singles pastors and leaders work with a higher percentage of vulnerable people than perhaps any of their ministry peers. There are many women who, because of rejection, are starving to hear someone affirm them, to have someone just listen. As the pastor, you are the authority figure who understands them and represents spiritual authority. There is fun, passion, and excitement in your voice when you talk about Christ. This can make you very attractive in the eyes of some of your single adults but it can also make for potential dangers in your ministry.

Some Safety Checkpoints to Consider

1. Remember that an accusation can be ruinous to your ministry. Just the appearance of inappropriate behavior can have a devastating effect. Stay miles away from even the appearance of inappropriate or immoral behavior. For example, I have a female associate director. When she first joined the staff, we would sometimes drive each other to our monthly evening leadership meeting because she lives near me. We would arrive at the meeting together and leave together. I think that is fine to do on occasion. But I don't think it's something we should do on a regular basis because of appearances. It might not look good, if at 10:00 p.m. at the end of every meeting, the male and female staff (lay or clergy) jump into the car and drive off into the night.

2. Don't take night counseling appointments. My first reason is I need that time with my family. I have enough night meetings. If people can take time off work during nine to five to see their doctor, dentist, or auto mechanic, they can usually find a way to take time off to see me, and they do it willingly! I'm pretty firm about this, although I will occasionally make a counseling appointment on Saturday morning for those who simply can't come any other time.

I do not go so far as to keep my door open during counseling sessions or have windows put in my door as some colleagues in other churches have. I believe that would be a violation of confidentiality and overly paranoid. But I do maintain my counseling sessions in an environment that minimizes potential dangers, one in which appearances are least likely to be misrepresented and there are people around.

3. If I'm on a retreat and a woman comes to my room to speak to me, I leave both the door and the blinds open. Actually, at retreats I prefer to talk to people outside, though this may be hard for a person who is emotionally upset and crying.

4. If I'm having a private lunch or meeting with a woman, I always tell my wife with whom I will be and where I'll be. I do this even if it's during business hours in a public restaurant. I want her to hear it from me, not others who might say, "I saw Dan eating with a pretty blonde the other day at . . . ."

5. When I was single and on a previous church staff, I made it a policy not to date any of the single women in my church. I felt it might potentially compromise me or my ministry. I don't know of anyone else who has done this so I suppose you need to feel led to do it. But I did it for the following reasons:

- If the relationship failed, it could become a divisive issue in the group, causing people to take sides as to whose fault it was.
- If everyone knows that the pastor is not going to date any of the women,

then the guys have no reason to view him as competition. A pastor has an advantage over others in gaining access to women because he's more visible and in a position of authority. I think it is natural and easy for single male leaders to attract women because of their exposure and because they are supposed to be spiritual and emotionally together (we know better, don't we?).

- Women who want counseling know the pastor would never consider them for a possible date. Hence, they would be less likely to use counseling sessions to get to know him.

God has given us an important role as leader of a flock. We must do everything possible to uphold the honor of the office. When a pastor falls from grace, it makes it even harder for people to trust and believe other pastors.

We always live in grace. Precautions help keep us in grace.

> **"If I'm having a private lunch or meeting with a woman, I always tell my wife with whom I will be and where I'll be. I do this even if it's during business hours in a public restaurant. I want her to hear it from me, not others who might say, 'I saw Dan eating with a pretty blonde the other day at . . . .' "**

Reading: The Key to Spiritual Growth

by Jim Smoke
Founder and director of The Center for Divorce Recovery, Phoenix, Arizona

When summer comes, much of our singles ministry programming falls into "park" for a few short months. And if we are not careful, we do the same thing.

Summer can be a time to put your life into "grow" by setting aside time and energy for spiritual reading. If you're not reading, you will simply shrivel up and drift through those "lazy, hazy, crazy days of summer." Let me share how I go about setting up my summer reading program.

1. *Read from need.* The first big decision is deciding what to read. You don't have barrels of money, and the bookstores are piled high with a lot of good stuff. Your first purchases should be centered around personal need. What are your personal needs right now? What books will address those needs best?

2. *Read to grow and know.* What do you want to know more *about* right now—prayer, healing, silence, the Gospel of John? List the areas before you buy the books or you will buy on impulse and miss the target.

3. *Specialize.* Single out an area to specialize in for the next year. Acquire a book or two on this topic and read it throughout the year. You will be amazed at the knowledge you can acquire when you focus on a particular subject.

4. *Read to teach better.* Read books that will add to the topics you will teach in the fall. Some churches require their pastoral staff to take study leaves of two weeks a year to do this.

5. *Read to be lifted and personally inspired.* Biographies of great Christian leaders of the past and present will challenge and inspire. I am amazed at how few Christians seem to be acquainted with our heroes of the faith.

6. *Read for fun and for the sole purpose of enjoying yourself.* I confess that I don't do as much of this as I need to, but I'm getting better. I have discovered Louis L'Amour in the past couple of years. He helps me get into another world once in a while and forget everything that is swirling around me. (Of course, you have to like Westerns to appreciate him.)

There are two other keys for me in reading. I set apart the time for it just as I calendar in personal appointments. If I don't schedule it, it won't get done. Reading was never meant to be a "leftover pursuit." If you don't give it priority, it will never happen (or you won't ever read past page three before it's time to move on to something else).

Along with time comes place. I know that one can read anywhere, but certain kinds of reading take concentration. All of us get caught going back over something we just read because our attention was diverted or our mind wandered. Find a place where you can really zero in on your reading without interruption. Devoting a whole evening to reading seems like a luxury for some, while for others it is a weekly necessity.

You can always tell who around you is reading and growing; they usually seem to know something you don't.

So what books are you piling up on your desk for summer reading? Your people will know by Christmas.

Overcoming Spiritual Dryness

by Jim Smoke

The greatest enemy of the Christian worker today is spiritual dryness. The pressure to be spiritually productive in our ministries tends to leave us spiritually empty in our spirits. Too many of us only "prepare to present" material for others. We tend to do little that will build and strengthen our own inner spiritual life.

The words of the Apostle Paul beat upon us with convicting clarity: "Don't let the world around you squeeze you into its mold, but let God remold your minds from within so that you may prove in practice that the plan of God for you is good, meets all his demands and moves toward the goal of true maturity" (Romans 12:2, PH). Our challenge is to find ways for God to remold us starting on the inside—inner growth—so that we can be better equipped to live on the outside.

Inner growth is a process adventure that requires exploring topics such as prayer, silence, solitude, meditation, contemplation, reading, study, service, and journal-keeping. As we spiritually stretch ourselves, we must pray that God will do some inside work resulting in inner growth.

Because so many Christians are unfamiliar with the resources available for reading about the inner growth or inner journey, I offer the list on the following page. The books are listed in the order you should consider reading them. If you will take a year to purchase and work through the list, you will be a vastly different person on the inside—through inner growth—than you are today. Let's begin to read and grow together.

Our Need for Spiritual Friends

by Jim Smoke

In order to survive in our journey through life, we need friends. Friends are people with whom we share the celebrations and defeats of life. They are there for us in the good times as well as the bad times. To be a friend means to be a person for others.

We Need Spiritual Friends

As spiritual people, we need spiritual friends. Too many of us try to live out

A READING LIST FOR RENEWAL AND SPIRITUAL GROWTH
(listed in recommend reading order)

- Henri Nouwen, *Making All Things New*, Harper and Row, 1981
- Henri Nouwen, *The Way of the Heart*, Ballantine Books, 1983
- Henri Nouwen, *The Wounded Healer*, Image Books, 1979
- Gordon MacDonald, *Ordering Your Private World*, Moody Press, 1985
- Gordon MacDonald, *Restoring Your Spiritual Passion,* Thomas Nelson, 1986
- Basil Pennington, *A Place Apart*, Image Books, n.d.
- Basil Pennington, *Centering Prayer*, Image Books, 1982
- Basil Pennington, *Centered Living*, Doubleday Books, 1988
- Susan Muto, *Pathways of Spiritual Living*, Image Books, 1988
- Richard Foster, *Celebration of Discipline*, Harper and Row, 1978
- Robert Webber, *Evangelicals on the Canterbury Trail*, Jarrel Books, 1989
- Thomas Merton, *Spiritual Direction and Meditation*, Liturgical Press, 1961
- Campbell McAlpine, *Alone with God*, Bethany House, 1981
- Evelyn Underhill, *The Spiritual Life*, Morehouse Baily, 1984
- Tilden Edwards, *Living Simply Through the Day*, Paulist Press, 1978
- Carlo Caretto, *Letters from the Desert*, Orbis Books, 1972
- Alan Jones, *SoulMaking*, Harper and Row, 1985
- Pennington, Booth, and Jones, *The Living Testament*, Harper and Row, 1985
- *A Guide to Prayer for Ministers and Other Servants*, Upper Room, 1983
  (a must-buy book)

our Christian faith behind the mask of a spiritual Lone Ranger. We often cannot talk about spiritual matters to others freely. If we converse at this level at all, we do so cautiously, lest we be misunderstood or deemed "superspiritual." This spiritual isolationism often leads to lack of spiritual maturity, accountability, and productivity. The age-old idea that faith in God is a private matter may be the reason for our inability to build solid Christian communities through a network of vital spiritual friendships.

Looking for Spiritual Friends

What should we look for in a "friend of the soul"? Allen Jones, in *Exploring Spiritual Directions: An Essay on Christian Friendship*, lists four qualities a spiritual friend should possess:

- love—an openness and readiness to accept another into one's heart;
- discernment—the heart of spiritual direction;
- patience—sitting and waiting rather than making quick judgments; and
- utter frankness and honesty—a naked trust that sets the tone of a relationship.

According to Urban T. Holmes, in his book *Spirituality for Ministry*, people seek spiritual friends who display

- greater spiritual maturity,
- the presence of the Spirit,
- a willingness to listen,

- a liberal amount of holiness,
- compassion,
- a total commitment to their needs,
- an inability to be shocked,
- compatibility,
- honesty,
- confidentiality, and
- kindness.

Most of us would count it a high privilege to have a spiritual friend with these qualifications. We all need someone who is a little farther down the spiritual road than we are, tugging on our spiritual coat sleeves to bring us along. Too often we find ourselves being bulldozed, steamrolled, divebombed, and blitzed into spiritual growth by our well-meaning Christian friends. Seldom are we nudged, loved, and encouraged to spiritual growth in an atmosphere of understanding.

Building Spiritual Friendship Foundations

The following guidelines will help us build foundations that encourage the formation of spiritually friendly relationships:

1. We must sense the need for spiritual friendship.
2. We must pray for the Lord to send the right person into our lives.
3. We must be willing to ask for and receive direction.
4. We must be willing to be spiritually accountable to another person.
5. We must give the relationship time to form and grow.
6. We must spend time with our spiritual friend. This time will include talking about the inner things of our hearts and spirits, praying, and developing long-term plans of action for our continued spiritual growth.

Passing on Spiritual Friendship

As ministers, we frequently talk about church work but seldom discuss matters of the heart and spirit. If such hesitancy exists among those who lead, how widespread must it be among those who follow? Having a spiritual friend and being a spiritual friend means bringing God into the open space between our lives and allowing Him to do His work through each of us. By having and being spiritual friends, we encourage those who receive help and direction from us to share that same friendship with others.

> **"As ministers, we frequently talk about church work but seldom discuss matters of the heart and spirit. If such hesitancy exists among those who lead, how widespread must it be among those who follow?"**

Suggestions for Programming Your Singles Ministry

ABOUT PART THREE

The most important part of your singles ministry
is not your "program," but your people.

Nevertheless, your program is a necessary part
of your total ministry. The "what, when and where"
aspects of your time together require
prayer, thought, and planning.

When is the best time for your group to meet?
How important is humor in your ministry?
How can you minimize turnover and increase commitment?
What makes a singles Sunday school class successful?

These and other questions are addressed in this section
by several experienced singles ministry leaders.

Some Ingredients for a Balanced Program

Planning Guide: A Year-Round Approach To Singles Ministry

by William Van Loan
and Gary Henderson
William Van Loan is minister with single adults, Arcadia Presbyterian Church, Arcadia, California.
Gary Henderson is a licensed marriage, family, and child therapist in Monrovia, California.

Over several years of ministry we have observed that many single adults pass through a sequence of identifiable challenges in the course of a year. The following chart outlines some of the more apparent seasonal changes, briefly describes psychological observations for each, and offers a few ministry and program ideas.

This chart is not intended to be all-inclusive. There will always be a need for a variety of nurturing program elements in any healthy single adult ministry. Nevertheless, we believe consideration of certain thrusts throughout the year to be especially appropriate.

Consider using this chart as a guide to help you plan your yearly teaching and program calendar.

		ISSUES AND CONCERNS THAT MANY SINGLE ADULTS SEEM TO FACE DURING THIS SEASON
	Winter	**JANUARY**—Sense of hope, optimism, goal setting, fresh start. **FEBRUARY**—Getting life under control; stress management. **MARCH**—Developing and/or attempting a new try at relationships.
	Spring	**APRIL**—Increasing interest in friendship skills. **MAY**—Seeking refreshment and relaxation. **JUNE**—Making vacation plans; thinking about a change of pace for the summer; trying something different.
	Summer	**JULY**—Generally more relaxed; may be good book reading time. **AUGUST**—Outdoor recreation and enjoyment; summer child-care anxieties. **SEPTEMBER**—Gathering clouds of concern; anxieties about change; for some, ambivalence.
	Fall	**OCTOBER**—Apprehension about upcoming family gatherings; relationship break-ups and difficulties increase. **NOVEMBER**—Increased questioning about the meaning of life; stress over work and/or school; depression. **DECEMBER**—Hope that next year will be better.

FOCUS, INTERESTS, AND PRIORITIES	PROGRAMMING IDEAS AND POSSIBILITIES	KEY BUZZ WORDS	RELATED SCRIPTURE
THE SELF—Focus on self as opposed to relationship with community. Interest in self-help and self-management. Time for decisions regarding personal growth.	• Seminars and retreats on the meaning of success, goal setting, becoming the best person you can be. • Bible studies on overcoming, life-planning, why we exist, hope. • Begin support groups.	Goals. Fresh start. Make life count! Get going!	Gen. 2; Psalm 139; Prov. 13:16; John 3, 17:11: 2 Cor. 5:17; Gal. 6:4-5; Phil. 4:8-13; 1 John 5:1-5.
INTIMACY—Establishing and developing significant relation-ships. High interest in one-to-one relationships and in defining self in terms of the "other." Self-disclo-sure and assertiveness issues have high interest.	• Workshops, seminars, or retreats on friendship/relationship skills. Offer help in evaluating relationships. • Opportunities for children and adults to do things together. • Socials for meeting new people.	Warmth. Join us! Let's do it. New life!	Ecc. 4:10; Matt. 22:37-40, 28:19-20; John 13:31-35; Rom. 5:7-11; 1 Cor. 6:19-20; Eph. 2:11-22.
COMMUNITY—(Friendships and family). Broadening intimacy search into the larger community. Taking known intimacy skills and applying them to productivity, building general friendships, and nurturing social skills	• Stimulating growth topics for discussion/study. • Explore group vacation/recreation planning ideas. • Topics dealing with changes, transition, and what lies ahead. • Prayer, focusing on the inner life.	Kick back. Celebrate! Mix. Be pre-pared.	Matt. 7:1, 6:9-13; Luke 17:12-19; Rom. 12:1; 1 Cor. 12; Heb. 4:1-13.
SELF-EVALUATION — (Productivity and usefulness). How's my life doing? My kids? My career? Feelings about usefulness and value, not so much in terms of output but life direction, meaning, accomplishment, and achievement. Perhaps there is also a sense of despair versus a sense of value and integrity about decisions.	• Teaching communication and conflict-managment skills. • Handling holiday stress. • Seminars and teaching on tough issues such as depression, anger, and sex. • Support groups (care and share). • Parties and socials for parents and children together. • Spiritual growth issues.	Give thanks. Hope. Search for meaning. Tired.	Matt. 16:26; Mark 9:24; Luke 12:16-21; 2 Tim. 4:7; Heb. 12:5-6, 11.

BASED ON THE RESULTS OF ONE SURVEY, HERE ARE THE . . . Twelve Key Ingredients for a Successful Singles Sunday School Class

by Randy Hageman
Associate pastor of First United Methodist Church, Lufkin, Texas

While in seminary, I conducted a small research project to discover what made some single adult Sunday school classes so successful. My goal was to apply what I learned to help strengthen the single adult classes in my church, as well as to help other churches and newer programs.

Fourteen different churches were surveyed, each with a large, ongoing ministry with single adults. The fourteen churches represented Disciples of Christ, Presbyterian, Southern Baptist, and United Methodist denominations, primarily from Texas and the Southwest. (I didn't initially survey nondenominational and Bible churches, but have since talked to a number of these pastors to gain additional insight from their perspective.) My goal was to determine what the single adult minister/directors in those churches believed made their singles Sunday school classes successful.

Based on my research, the purpose of the successful class is to come together for two primary purposes: *spiritual growth* and *fellowship*. Each of the twelve key ingredients listed here fulfill these two purposes.

GOALS FOR A HEALTHY CLASS

1. Centered on Jesus Christ

This is the most important single element in a successful single adult Sunday school. This sometimes goes unsaid, but that is a mistake. Christ separates a Sunday school class from a singles club. This centering establishes the kind of programming and fellowship the class will have, the way visitors and members alike will be treated, how the class will put its faith into action, the values upheld by the class and its leadership, and the kind of healing that can occur in hurting and broken lives, among other things. The centrality of Jesus Christ is the cohesive element that holds the many elements of a class and ministry together in a healthy way.

2. Meaningful Sunday School Lesson

Spiritual growth is very important to single adults. Most single adults who come to Sunday school have some expectation of being spiritually fed, though they may not always be able to put that into words. But, the lesson must be relevant and timely. There are three basic types of lessons:

1. *Bible study:* Bible study for single adults might be a chapter by chapter study of a particular book or it might be more of a topical study, such as the parables, or the Beatitudes. Generally, the Bible study begins with the Bible and asks what it has to say to life today.

2. *Christian perspectives on current issues:* This type of lesson begins with a particular issue or concern and relies on the Bible and Christian tradition to develop and understand how the Christian single adult would approach the issue or concern. Lessons might be on dating, intimacy, ethics in the work place, or forgiveness, among others.

3. *Book study:* This is the study of a particular book that addresses an issue or concern for single adults. It is related to the previous lesson type. Books studied might include ones on prayer, intimacy, spiritual disciplines, emotional issues, or a number of other topics.

In addition to using the Bible and a person's professional experience, some kind of curriculum is often used in the first two lesson types. At least half the classes, in all age ranges and in all but the very largest classes, used curriculum often or all the time.

3. Quality Teaching and Teachers

In almost every case a successful class has consistent, quality teaching by a competent, skilled teacher. This is more significant than the type of lesson used. A good teacher can use poor material and still present a meaningful lesson. But, *even the best curriculum and resources can seldom overcome a poor teacher.* This is a key area where single adult ministries and churches can interact and work together to improve the overall quality of teaching throughout the church.

Types of Teacher Resources

1. *Permanent teacher:* Many churches rely on a permanent teacher who teaches for specified periods of time (for instance, a year). The permanent teacher is found most often with the youngest classes and the oldest classes. In many cases this may be the single adult pastor. The permanent teacher serves as a good role model for single adults, particularly in the younger single adult classes. Being married or being single doesn't seem to make a difference in the quality of teaching, provided the married teacher can relate to issues and concerns of the single adult.

2. *Teacher's pool:* A teacher's pool consists of members or ministers within the church who have developed lessons or a series that are for a set number of Sundays and are available to all classes, single or otherwise.

3. *Outside professionals/speakers:* Many classes use professionals from a particular field, often related to some

> "In almost every case a successful class has consistent, quality teaching by a competent, skilled teacher. This is more significant than the type of lesson used. A good teacher can use poor material and still present a meaningful lesson. But, even the best curriculum and resources can seldom overcome a poor teacher."

area of ministry or the mental health profession, to teach their classes. These professionals may or may not be members of that church. Particularly outside speakers may need to be screened to be sure their message is consistent with the Christian faith.

The teacher's pool and outside professional/speaker were found in every age group, but were most common in the middle-aged single adult classes. Most large classes, with average attendance of 100 or more, used either the pool or an outside professional.

Teaching Styles

There are three basic teaching styles used by teachers: lecture, discussion, small groups, or some combination of these. Overall, single adults prefer, in order, discussion, then small groups, and finally lecture. It's obvious that most single adults want opportunities to talk and discuss, and to interact with the speaker, the material, and other single adults. But, discussion and small groups won't meet the needs of every group:

1. *Discussion:* In classes with twenty-

WHEN IS THE BEST TIME FOR A SUNDAY SCHOOL CLASS TO MEET ... PLUS OTHER FACTORS TO CONSIDER
by Randy Hageman

- **Meeting Time:** Most Sunday school classes meet around 9:30 because that's the "standard" hour. However, *classes meeting around 11:00 a.m. are often larger than those at the earlier hour.* These later classes give single adults a chance to sleep later on Sunday morning. They also tend to attract more nominal Christians and unchurched single adults. However, single adults attending these classes are less likely to attend a worship service.

- **The Herd Mentality:** Most single adults prefer to be around groups of single adults. Some singles like larger groups because it is easier for them to get lost in the crowd. Some singles like larger groups because there is a better chance to meet new people. And, some single adults like larger groups because there are more activities, and the activities are better managed and attended.

- **Classes by Age Ranges:** A class that tries to reach everyone often reaches no one. Target your age range (i.e., twenties, or thirties, etc.) and plan your class to meet the needs of that age group.

- **Room Spacing:** A somewhat crowded room makes a class seem more appealing because it implies the group is growing. Some classes intentionally under-set the number of chairs so that they have to bring more out as the class begins.

- **Class Agenda:** Begin with fellowship time. Many classes, particularly larger ones, have music, either specials and/or group singing. Many classes have devotionals, prayer requests, and a time to express joys and concerns. Most classes discover they have from thirty to forty-five minutes for their teaching. End with prayer or a benediction.

- **Class Officers:** Set up class officer positions by function, such as service or social or treasurer. The larger the class, the more officers a class needs. Larger classes often have several committees in addition to the officers. Be flexible!

five or more present discussion becomes difficult. Discussion classes often sit around a large table or in a circle. They are more common in middle-aged classes.

2. *Small groups:* This is a great way to allow single adults to discuss in a more intimate setting. However, many groups have chosen to avoid them because it can be difficult to move in and out of groups, and it takes time, which is usually precious during Sunday school. Also, space can be a limitation. Where space is available, the use of round tables allows for built-in small groups without taking time to move. Small groups are often used in conjunction with lecture.

3. *Lecture:* Lecture, by itself, is often the least effective way that adults learn, but in many cases, such as very large classes, there aren't many good alternatives. Many older classes prefer using only lecture, while younger and middle-aged classes tend to use it in combination with either discussion or small groups.

4. Fellowship

Successful classes allow some time for fellowship. It may be an informal time of talking to friends and meeting visitors. Coffee and snack foods are available. Most groups sit together in worship and go to lunch as a group.

Activities outside Sunday morning are fundamental for fellowship in almost every group. Fellowship in these many activities offers single adults a family unit, a community to belong to and give to, a place of acceptance and nurture.

5. Single Adult Leadership

A single adult class is an *adult* class, not an overgrown youth group! They have to feel ownership of their program. There will be little or no dedication and commitment to a class that is not led by its members. That means the single adults establish the direction of the class. They are responsible for class activities. In many churches they choose how they will be taught and by whom. Single adults can decide everything from who sets up the room to who the officers will be. The class and its ministry must be their class and their ministry.

Try to include men in your leadership team. Many men are uncomfortable walking into a group when it is composed largely of women, unless they can identify with another man. The easiest way for this to happen is to have one or more men in visible leadership positions.

> "There are three basic teaching styles used by teachers: lecture, discussion, small groups, or some combination of these. Overall, single adults prefer, in order, discussion, then small groups, and finally lecture. It's obvious that most single adults want opportunities to talk and discuss, and to interact with the speaker, the material, and other single adults."

6. Intentional Leadership Development and Training

Leaders don't grow on trees. Some leadership will rise on its own, but it will generally not be enough to sustain a class over a significant period of time.

CHARACTERISTICS OF A SINGLES MEGA-CLASS
(Those with 200+ Average Attendance)
by Randy Hageman

Based on my research, here are some of the common characteristics I found:
- Meeting time is later on Sunday morning, typically around 11:00 a.m.
- There is always music/singing.
- Will typically use outside speakers or the single adult pastor to present lessons.
- Lesson topics are more often Christian perspectives on current issues and self-help, with occasional Bible study. *Many of these classes intentionally target the unchurched and nonChristian single adult.*
- High quality is expected in the teaching.
- There are many social activities during the week.
- They are most likely to be labeled as a "meat market."
- Many small group fellowships are provided outside of Sunday morning.
- Class is completely, or almost completely, self-run by class members.
- Found in all age ranges: does not seem to be age specific.
- Class is often more important than worship to its members.
- Ecumenical: single adults from many different denominations and churches in attendance.
- Relatively short time for lesson: twenty to thirty minutes.
- Class has a history and a tradition.
- Classes tends to be either ten years old or older, or very new. Older classes are often found in denominational churches, while newer classes are often found in non-denominational churches
- Class was often started with little or no staff help, particularly in the older classes.
- Known as a place to meet other single adults.
- Does not use curriculum.
- Presentation is given lecture style. (A few classes have enough room to set up at round tables to have some small group discussion.)
- Members do an excellent job of welcoming visitors.
- Class has healthy, positive self-esteem.
- There are many church hoppers "passing through."
- People who want to get lost (hide) in the group are more comfortable here.

Many classes experience a 50 percent turnover in a single adult class within a six month period. And it never fails that many of these will be class leaders. Therefore, single adult leadership must be constantly developed and trained. Well-trained single adult leadership will keep the class focused properly, will better understand the purpose of the class, will work toward meeting the needs of the class membership, will be well organized for the Sunday morning session, and will convey confidence to members and visitors alike that this class is in good hands and is intentional about what it is doing.

7. A Single Adult Minister/Director/Lay Leader

A single adult class meets more needs of its adults than other adult classes, and therefore requires more effort. Not every church is big enough to need a full-time staff person, but every church can provide someone, paid or volunteer, who can help with this ministry. This leader or pastor performs several important functions:

- Recruitment, development, and training of single adult leadership—A single adult minister once told me that 50 percent of a single adult minister's time should be spent in the area of leadership development and training. If the program is to survive, much less grow, leadership has to be grown and encouraged. The leader is responsible for "empowering the saints" to do their own ministry through intentional training and role modeling.

- Provide guidance to the program and class—The leader guides the class in healthy directions so that it will continue to meet its purposes and grow.

- Counseling—Divorce, death of a spouse, break-up of a relationship, fears regarding intimacy, and sexual relations are just some of the issues a leader has to face in counseling situations.

- Teaching—Leaders, especially those with appropriate training, can become a resource for helping single adults grow in their faith by teaching in the class as well as in other settings.

- Problem-solver—It is very common for single adult classes to experience ups and downs in its programming and membership. The leader is in a position to see the big picture and serve as a consultant or advisor—but not as the person responsible for "fixing" the problem.

8. Opportunities to Put Faith into Action

This is a healthy sign that the class is succeeding in providing spiritual growth for its members. It is a significant part of the motivation of healthy single adult leadership. One of the most common reasons single adults choose to serve in a leadership position is to give back to God what God has given to them through the class. Successful single adult classes generally support many different service and mission projects, both with their time and money.

> "Classes that move too much in any one direction to the exclusion of the other two will suffer problems. Too many social activities will lead the group into being nothing more than a social club. . . . Too much spiritual growth emphasis may intimidate many single adults, particularly the nonChristian, and drive them away. Too much service/mission can become an end in itself strictly for humanitarian reasons rather than as a response to the love of Christ."

9. Healthy Balance of Spiritual Growth, Fellowship, and Service/Mission

Classes that move too much in any one direction to the exclusion of the other two will suffer problems. Too much fellowship in the form of too many social activities will lead the group into being nothing more than a social club or "meat market." Too much spiritual growth emphasis may intimidate many single adults, particularly the nonChristian, and drive them away. Too much service/mission can become an end in itself strictly for humanitarian reasons rather than as a response to the love of Christ. The healthy class maintains a balance of these three areas.

> "When people feel welcome and wanted, they are much more likely to return and become a part of that class. Successful classes have members who make a conscious effort to look for and greet visitors."

10. Consistent Methods for Welcoming Visitors

When people feel welcome and wanted, they are much more likely to return and become a part of that class. Successful classes have members who make a conscious effort to look for and greet visitors.

Many classes have committees set up to make sure visitors are welcomed using greeters at the doors, handing out information about the class, providing name tags, and often pairing them up with a "buddy" for the day. Visitors are often introduced in the class, sit with other class members in worship, and accompany class members to lunch. Visitors are then contacted by phone, card, and personal visit. Often the visitor is invited to some activity that week, with the caller being available to transport or meet the visitor there. Some groups sponsor visitor/new member dinners or lunches once a month or once a quarter. All of these activities are more successful when done by class leaders and members, versus the single adult minister or leader.

11. Positive Self-Esteem

This ingredient and the next are more intangible, but still very important. How does a class feel about itself? If the class is negative and has a defeatist attitude, few new people will be attracted to it and effective ministry will be difficult. Healthy classes are classes where members want to invite their friends, where exciting things are happening, and where people are growing in their faith and in their relationships with others. Members will be more dedicated and committed. Programs and activities will be better attended. If a class feels good about itself, it will be more aggressive in everything it does without being desperate.

Self-esteem comes from knowing who we are, and whose we are. True self-esteem comes from developing a healthy relationship with God through Jesus Christ, and leaders need to always be striving to help members develop or grow in that relationship. In addition, a class can develop self-esteem by being successful in its ministry. It is important that the class leadership help build self-esteem by providing opportunities for the class to succeed. Start with little things, where the chance for success is good. As the class grows in self-esteem, seek new challenges that encourage the class to stretch.

12. Vision

One of the biggest difficulties facing new programs and classes is not seeing what they can be. They don't know what is possible in a single adult class. Classes may tend to think too small and restricted. They limit themselves to "the way we've always done it before." The class lacks vision!

Vision opens the doors for creative ministry and outreach in a single adult class. Vision calls a class forward in its relationship with God and challenges it to go beyond the status quo. Vision sees what is possible, not what is impossible.

Leaders grow in vision as they are encouraged to dream. Planning retreats are great ways to open up the horizon. Visiting other single adult ministries, attending leadership conferences, and reading the latest literature all help to open eyes to what is possible in the name of Jesus Christ. Vision brings excitement to a class. Members begin to grasp the bigger picture and see God's hand at work in many areas.

Are We Being Deceived About Our Primary Mission?
GETTING SINGLES INTERESTED IN SPIRITUAL THINGS

by Barry Palser
Pastor with singles at Happy Church, Denver, Colorado

I'm concerned that many singles ministry leaders are being deceived. Let me explain.

On occasion, when I've been the guest speaker at another singles ministry function, I've been asked not to talk much about Jesus or spiritual things because "we are trying to reach the unchurched." I've also observed this attitude and thinking in the programming and leadership of several singles ministries across the country.

Where does this thinking come from? Is it enemy-inspired or God-inspired? As I study Scripture, I can't find any examples of a person trying to reach the unchurched without relying on the gospel of Jesus Christ.

Many singles leaders have believed the lie that if you let the program get too spiritual you will scare singles away. It's interesting that Jesus was never cautious about being too spiritual. He always encouraged people to

SPIRITUAL HUNGER MAY BE ON THE RISE
by Jim Smoke
Founder and director of The Center for Divorce Recovery, Phoenix, Arizona

One significant thing I've noticed in my travels across the country is that the fun-and-games concept of a singles ministry—the mate-date-and-relate kind of thing—is on the wane. What I'm hearing more and more is that singles want to deal with life-significant issues. They don't want to just be entertained. They don't want groups where you just go to meet whoever else is there, but they want a ministry that speaks to their needs and offers something that is life-changing.

I've even noticed a change in the requests I get to do seminars across the country. When someone calls, I usually say, "What are your needs and what are the main issues you would like me to address?" For the first several years the response was, "Oh, anything to do with singles, dating and mating, sexuality, and this and that." But now I get a pause, and people will say, "We've got a serious-minded group, and they really want to talk about heavier issues such as faith and life and trusting God." There has been a very significant turning away from the "pop" singles topics—the heavy psychology stuff—of a few years ago. It's the "deepening one's walk with God" that I see as the growing trend. There's an honest quest for facing the lasting issues of life—the "meat of the Word" as opposed to the "milk of the Word."

I think this is very healthy. But I also think it's going to demand a lot more from our leadership in singles ministries. I don't think we can settle for rah-rah entertainers to lead our groups anymore. We need leaders who are well read, people who can really address the deeper issues of life.

seek first the Kingdom of God.

Maybe I'm overlooking something, but it seems to me that if the gospel is not being boldly preached, and people are not being saved and encouraged to obey Jesus' commandments, it is not a Jesus-led ministry. Instead, it is primarily a social gathering.

And this is where I believe many of us are being deceived. We have forgotten our first call. Rather than boldly proclaiming the gospel of Jesus Christ, too often we have become just another organization that is empty of God's life-changing power.

We have placed so much emphasis on numbers being the sign of our success that we have let the social events take priority. But Jesus calls us to be concerned first about encouraging and nurturing the singles' need for a personal, intimate, and eternal relationship with God. Was it not Jesus who said, "Seek ye first the kingdom of God, and all these things will be added unto you"? We need to let God worry about our numbers.

Commands for Our Ministries

Being a singles leader in a church fellowship is really being a representative of the Lord Jesus Christ. Even though we are in a position of leadership, it is still God's church, and God's people; and we are to be doing His will in every situation. Jesus said in Matthew 28:19-20 that we should do two things: (1) "Go and make disciples," and (2) "teach them to do all things whatsoever that I have commanded you."

For singles ministries and singles leaders to be on the cutting edge of what God is doing, we must cling to these two commands. Singles must be at the forefront of all that we do and at the heart of our vision for ministry.

The Greatest Need Is Spiritual

Singles have many different needs in their lives, but the greatest, deepest need of all is spiritual. The only way we can address that need is to help them establish their personal, intimate, and eternal relationship with God. Everything else is meant to flow out of this relationship.

Leadership styles and personalities will vary. Leaders will use a variety of effective methods to reach out to their singles and to "make disciples." But the underlying purpose and message should always be the same: God is the answer to all our needs. We are complete in Him.

As leaders, we can have a strong vision of our single adults totally surrendering their lives to Jesus Christ . . . and have an exciting, vibrant, growing singles ministry that is on the cutting edge.

Focusing on Spiritual Things

My desire as a singles pastor is to raise up singles to be effective leaders in the Body of Christ; victorious warriors in the spiritual battles. And I know I'm not alone in this desire. I've heard many singles leaders say, "How do we get our singles involved in spiritual things? We've tried this or that and

nothing has really caught hold."

I don't profess to have all the answers. Nor do I mean to imply that this is as easy as one-two-three. But the following are some of the practical ways I've found to help get my singles headed more clearly in God's direction:

1. *Publicly seek and acknowledge God's presence in your ministry's vision and purpose.* Keep this in front of your group as a reminder for your regulars. Also, first-time visitors will immediately sense the focus of your ministry. (This distinguishes you from just another social interaction group.)

> **"Maybe I'm overlooking something, but it seems to me that if the gospel is not being boldly preached, and people are not being saved and encouraged to obey Jesus' commandments, it is not a Jesus-led ministry. Instead, it is primarily a social gathering."**

2. *Challenge and encourage your singles toward a deeper, personal prayer life.* Be excited about prayer and be a person of prayer yourself. If you don't have a vibrant, intimate, one-on-one communication with God, start with yourself. Diligently seek this as a top priority in your own life. It will bear fruit for you personally as well as for your ministry.

3. *Constantly challenge your singles to seek and live God's call on their lives.*

4. *Emphasize through your teaching and activities that true, lasting fulfillment and satisfaction come only as people daily give themselves to God for Him to use.*

5. *Schedule specific times each week for your singles to pray personally and as a group.* Have set-aside times to pray for one another and for important events, such as mission trips, conferences, or retreats. Through these special, corporate times of prayer your singles become caught up with the awareness that God is working in other's lives, that their singles ministry is a tool that God uses to reach others, and that they are instruments God uses to make His plans and His purposes a reality. When your people begin to see God at work in miraculous ways, it has a powerful effect on their lives.

"I cannot fully express what I feel when I walk into a room packed wall to wall with single adults at 8:00 a.m. on a Sunday morning when the temperature outside is 10 degrees. Something inside of me says, 'Yes! This is what singles ministry is all about. Seeking first the kingdom with all our heart!' "

The best antidote for loneliness is to take the focus off ourselves and to set our sights on the big picture of what God is doing in this world. As singles reach out to others, they receive. And as they receive, they give back. This is the lifestyle God has commanded for each of us.

But I believe it must all begin with challenging singles to pray . . . then they will hear from God the answer to their innermost needs and desires.

A Room Packed with Praying Singles

At the beginning of this past year, as I sought the Lord's direction for our ministry, I felt that everyone in our singles group needed a time of prayer to seek from God a fresh anointing and direction for their own personal lives, as well as for our singles ministry.

I challenged them to come to an intercessory prayer time at 8:00 a.m. each Sunday for seven weeks. In our prayer meeting we started with praise and worship, then we prayed. Sometimes we would all join hands or get into circle groups and pray for specific needs in the group. Other times we would pray corporately for an upcoming event, all the while seeking guidance and direction from the Lord as to how He wanted to use each of us individually and corporately as a ministry throughout the year.

I cannot fully express what I feel when I walk into a room packed wall to wall with single adults at 8:00 a.m. on a Sunday morning when the temperature outside is 10 degrees. Something inside of me says, "Yes! This is what singles ministry is all about. Seeking first the kingdom with all our heart! Yes! This is the beginning of a singles ministry that is on the cutting edge of the gospel of Jesus Christ."

The Importance of Laughter in Your Ministry

by Rob Suggs
Minister with singles at Second Ponce de Leon Baptist Church, Atlanta, Georgia

Humor is a vital and necessary ingredient in a healthy singles ministry. Think about your group for a minute. Many single adults come with serious needs and questions. If you don't believe me, look at the kinds of seminars we present to our singles: divorce recovery, stress, self-esteem, surviving as a single parent, loneliness, broken relationships. These are not light, laughable issues. This is serious stuff.

Singles Need Humor

I'm convinced that to create a warm, caring, inviting atmosphere in your group—plus to help improve their self-esteem—you must help singles take themselves less seriously, to lighten up and see the humor in their lives and circumstances.

One of the top things singles look for in others is a sense of humor. That says to me that they already acknowledge their need for laughter. They realize they have a need for more of the lighter side in their lives, and they look for it in others.

Humor helps break down walls and creates a sense of sharing—we can all laugh in this together, and in so doing,

---

HUMOR: AN ATTRACTIVE QUALITY IN SINGLES

Nationwide research conducted by Jacqueline Simenauer and David Carroll, authors of the book *Singles: The New Americans*, reveals the qualities that single adults consider "very important" in one another. We list them here in order of importance:

1. Integrity, sensitivity, kindness, understanding—Men: 65 percent; Women: 81 percent.

2. Sense of humor—Men: 60 percent; Women: 65 percent.

3. Intelligence, perceptivity—Men: 39 percent; Women: 52 percent.

4. Common interests, talents, backgrounds—Men: 26 percent; Women: 32 percent.

5. Skill as a lover—Men: 28 percent; Women: 30 percent.

6. Physical attractiveness—Men: 29 percent; Women: 17 percent.

7. Money, status, position—Men: 10 percent; Women: 15 percent.

Simenauer and Carroll state, "On the list of most important attractions—above physical appearance, above intelligence, above money or expertise in the bedroom, above all priorities but one—comes sense of humor. Among singles of all ages there is little variation of opinion on this issue . . . [they] claim sense of humor to be a very important or at least a somewhat important attraction."[19]

at least for a moment we stop being a lone entity. Humor implies some level of intimacy. It pulls us together.

Theologically, we can and should laugh because we are redeemed. We're broken and fallen, yet we see hope, we see a light at the end of the tunnel, we see ourselves slowly being conformed into the image of Christ. Therefore, we can learn to have joy even when things are broken. It seems to me that we Christians are really the only ones who have the right to have a sense of humor.

C. S. Lewis, in *The Screwtape Letters*, talks about two kinds of laughter. The first is a bitter, sarcastic laughter. The second is healthy and affirming. Rather than casting people down, it pulls them up. People laugh out of either desperation and madness, or because they truly believe that things will ultimately work out all right. The latter is a happy, healthy kind of laughter. It's a Romans 8:28 kind of laugh.

The dangerous side to laughter—especially in our ministries—is that we can sometimes be insensitive. There are times when people should be able to laugh about their situation, but they're not there yet. It may still be a very painful matter to them. Thus those of us in leadership must be constantly sensitive to the real feelings of our people.

Put Laughter into Your Group

Find the people in your ministry who have a natural gift, a healthy sense of humor. In some ways, I believe this is as important as the other spiritual gifts within the Body of Christ. That gift needs to be nurtured and encouraged. Allow those people to participate in making announcements or doing something in an up-front position.

Another idea would be to develop a "humor index" for your ministry. Ask yourself if there is enough good, healthy laughter in your group. Discuss it as a leadership team. And make sure there are at least one or two people on your team who have—and are exercising—the gift of humor.

Your Singles Ministry: "Meet Market" or "Meat Market"?

by Paul M. Petersen
Minister with singles at Highland Park Presbyterian Church, Dallas, Texas

There is probably not a single adult ministry (SAM) in the world that has not at some time been accused of being a "meat market." Most SAMs provide a premier location for finding opposite-sex friendships.

In a letter I recently received from one of our singles, the writer described the scenario well: "They file in every Sunday, many hoping to leave with a date. Yet what they really need to leave with is a personal understanding of Christ. They come hoping to leave with

Sally's phone number when they need to leave with John 3:16."

Advantages of a Meat Market

Although having your SAM labeled as a meat market is not particularly appealing, it can have its good points. In fact, it is one tension-causing label I gladly live and minister with. Why? Because the church groups in my area that are accused of being meat markets are those groups that are most actively reaching the local, unchurched singles community with the gospel of Jesus Christ!

On any given Sunday morning, from 40 to 50 percent of those attending one of our larger groups are either not from our church or are unchurched. They are there because they have heard that we have a fun group and that many attractive people of the opposite sex attend.

If you ask our present leadership (all committed Christians) how they started in the class, 75 percent would tell you they originally came for the social activities and to meet the opposite sex. But as they got involved and met people, they discovered what a real commitment to Christ meant, and they made that commitment. Although they initially came to find some "meat," they ended up "meeting" Christ and other single adults who are following Him.

Moving from "Meat" to "Meet"

How do you turn a detrimental situation into one that emphasizes wholesome relationships with others and strengthens a relationship with Christ? The following are three keys that have proven effective in our ministry:

1. *Emphasize up front at all activities that your purpose, even at social events, is spiritual.* For example, in each week's printed program, one of our groups includes a column entitled "What We Believe." The column explains what being a Christian means in everyday language.

What We Believe

Many people feel that a happy and meaningful life consists of good friends, a good job, a lot of money, or doing something worthwhile. All these things make sense, but we all know people who have these things and still feel empty.

Many people feel they are "Christians" because they were born into a religious home, go to church regularly or try to be "good people." However, the Bible teaches that you are not truly a Christian until you have a personal relationship with God. You can become a Christian simply by taking these three steps:

• First, acknowledge that you (along with all people) have sinned, and are therefore separated from the Holy God (Romans 3:23).

• Second, believe in your heart that Jesus Christ died to save you from your sins, and rose again (Romans 5:18).

• Third, pray to God and personally invite Jesus Christ into your heart as your Savior and Lord (John 1:12, Revelation 3:20).

2. *The leadership of your SAM must be committed to Christ and to the ma-*

turing of His people. Part of being mature in Christ is a willingness to reach others wherever they may be spiritually. As we are called to be salt, we should cause others to become spiritually thirsty. It is not necessary that the leaders be extroverted evangelists, only that they be comfortable with their faith.

3. *A proper balance of social and spiritual programming is necessary.* Don't schedule only potlucks, sporting events, and parties. Include Bible studies, prayer meetings, and service projects in your calendar as well. Make sure the spiritual growth opportunities receive equal billing with the social programs.

The three most popular singles hangouts are bars, health clubs, and churches. Guess which one is the healthiest for meeting Christ and meeting people?

Reducing Turnover

by Dan Chun
Minister with singles at Menlo Park Presbyterian Church, Menlo Park, California

High turnover is one of the biggest challenges in singles ministry. Some churches experience a 50 percent or higher turnover in single adults every six months.

I can't determine all the reasons for it, but since 1985, we have experienced a general trend toward a lower turnover rate in our ministry. We are also finding that our singles are becoming more involved in the worship services. Why is this happening? Here are a few thoughts:

1. This positive trend began about the same time that we started requiring a one-year commitment (rather than six months) for our leadership teams. I'd hesitate to say that the longer-term leadership requirement is the primary reason for this lower turnover, but it's clear that we are now experiencing a longer-term involvement rate in the singles group overall. This provides more continuity.

2. Another possible factor is the stability of my presence. We used to have guest speakers teach some of the classes. But since my associate has joined our staff, she and I do nearly all the teaching. We now have more consistency in our teaching and topics, and more regular weekly contact with the singles.

3. We have also started a small-group system, which has helped us encourage our singles to be involved in building a deeper sense of community. As relationships are established and nurtured, people are much less likely to leave.

Except for a couple of blips, our general direction in turnover rates has been down, and I'm excited about that.

NINE

Scheduling Your Meeting Times

Sunday Night Is Singles Night: How We Doubled Our Attendance

by Dan Chun
Minister with singles at Menlo Park Presbyterian Church, Menlo Park, California

For several years, our young single adult group met from 8 to 9 a.m. on Sunday mornings and averaged 100-150 in attendance. Limited to one hour by facilities and scheduling problems at our busy church, many of them expressed frustration. They wanted an extended meeting time: longer, more in-depth teaching with more time for discussion, singing, praise, and prayer. As an alternative, a group of them began meeting informally (not as a part of our singles ministry program) on Sunday night in someone's home. Following the "ACTS" format (adoration, confession, thanksgiving, and supplication), someone led a short devotional. They sang for thirty minutes. They loved it. This group eventually grew to about seventy people.

In the meantime, our Sunday morning group was growing and running out of space. And the singles continued to express the desire for my associate and me to teach thirty minutes instead of twenty; they wanted to sing for thirty minutes instead of ten or fifteen; and some wanted small-group discussions like that of the Sunday night group. So we decided to move everything to Sunday night, combine with the house meeting, and make it one large group. (Our church does not have a Sunday evening congregational service.)

This transition took several months and a lot of negotiation in which our singles leadership team was vitally involved. We considered all the options—holding the meetings on Friday or Saturday nights instead of Sunday, having it on campus or off. We made it clear from the beginning that everyone would not get everything he or she wanted. The singing people wanted sixty minutes for music but had to settle for thirty; the small-group leaders wanted thirty minutes but had to settle for twenty; the announcement people wanted fifteen minutes (this is always a battle in a singles group) but had to settle for five. But when we made the change, it was unanimously accepted.

This transition was successful because we had taken the time to slowly "ramp up"—a popular term at our church. When we ramp up, it prohibits us from making hasty decisions and allows everyone to be on board and be part of the ownership.

The format of our Sunday night meeting is as follows:
• Open with music
• Teaching—thirty minutes
• Short break
• Small-group discussions related to the evening's teaching led by trained leaders—twenty minutes
• Worship through singing—twenty

minutes
- ACTS—adoration, confession, thanksgiving, and supplication
- Song to close

The evening lasts about two hours.

The week we went from Sunday morning to Sunday night, we nearly doubled our attendance—from 150 to 290. It has continued to grow since.

Advantages to This New Format

1. If our people are gone for a long weekend, most of them are back by Sunday night for Monday morning work. We would have missed many of our singles by meeting on Friday or Saturday night—or even Sunday morning.

2. Meeting from 6:00 to 8:00 p.m., the evening ends early enough for people to go to a movie or dinner as a group or with a date. Those who were not dating have a comfortable, casual way to socialize. This meeting time has facilitated and encouraged the socialization process among our singles in a less anxious, more healthy way. Half of our group goes out to nearby restaurants for dinner together.

3. The small group provides a more intimate family within the large group. People stay with the same group for ten weeks, then rotate. This builds trust and friendship. Everyone wears a name tag with a small group number on it.

Advice for Making a Major Transition

1. Don't make major changes quickly—"ramp up." We actually spent from five to six months in meetings and re-

search before we made the change.

2. Constantly remind your people that one of the primary reasons for making a change is for the good of the church body and to be more successful in scratching people where they itch. We simply want to find a way to be more effective for a greater number of people, meeting the needs and desires of our group and those we are trying to reach.

3. Remind the people that when making changes, everyone is not going to get everything he or she wants. Everyone has special interests, but a transition requires give and take, accepting less of some things for the good of the whole group.

4. Have patience; don't take an alarmist attitude. Remind yourself and everyone else that it will take time to work out the bugs. Don't expect everything to work perfectly at first.

5. Encourage your staff and lay leaders to go out and have large ears—to listen to the people and find out how it's going so you can make proper changes as you go along.

6. Remember that the change is not set in concrete. It's not the end of the world. You are still in the discovery process. You can always junk the plan after a few months or a year if you find that it really does not work.

> **"Constantly remind your people that one of the primary reasons for making a change is for the good of the church body and to be more successful in scratching people where they itch."**

A CASE STUDY:
How to Start a New Class ... and Not Break Up the Old Gang

with a suggested solution from Jim Smoke
Founder and director of The Center for Divorce Recovery, Phoenix, Arizona

The Problem

"At our church we have two different singles classes. One is for people who are in their twenties and thirties. The other is for those forty and up. These two classes have been going for several years. The problem we are having is that as the years march along, the twenties-and-thirties class keeps getting older. Rather than moving on to the forty-and-over group, many have chosen to stay in 'their class.' Consequently, a lot of the younger singles coming into the church feel like it's not a place for them because the group tends to be older than they are. So we are losing them.

"What's the best way to go about dealing with these class changes over time? It's understandable that people don't want to leave their class because that's where their relationships are. Should we try to enforce the age perimeters, or should we just begin a new class?"

A Possible Solution

1. *Nurture an established group's sense of community.* When you force adults to leave their class, you may destroy their sense of community. I learned this while I was on staff at Garden Grove Community Church (now Crystal Cathedral). I tried to make some class changes, and the singles said, "Why are you doing this to us? We like each other—can't we stay together?" They were strong classes because they'd grown together, been through life's storms and tempests together, and they were sort of like family—which is the way it should be. That's what community is all about.

When we come in and say, "Okay, let's break it up," what we're doing is divorcing people relationally from one another. We need to encourage more—not less—of this kind of community-building within the church, especially in our transitory world.

2. *Keep starting new classes.* Depending on the size of your church, you may need to make it a part of your master plan to begin a new class every three or four years. This encourages you to stay fresh and always aware of new needs or groups around which you can build a ministry. There is something exciting in the life of a ministry that has new beginnings. People enjoy being part of something new. Some great bonding can take place in these situations. It also helps you constantly provide new opportunities for leadership.

3. *Stay flexible when forming new classes.* I used to think there was only one way to form new groups. That

was by age, and the age groups should be twenty-one to thirty-three, thirty-four to forty, and so on. I used to even preach that. But after years in singles ministry, I don't preach that anymore. I think there are only two distinct groupings to consider: the never-married and the single-again. But even then, there is not just one way to do it.

So much depends on the leadership, the church, and the particular needs and opportunities within the community. My philosophy still is, "If it works, work it and let it fly. If it doesn't work, try something else." We make a mistake when we decide that everything has to fit into a predetermined structure. Stay flexible.

Some groups will work wonderfully when formed around ages. Others will form around interests or life situations. Some classes will even be built around a particular image or distinction. For example, one of the classes we started was big into outdoor sports. Members were always going sailing, jogging, or skiing together. Some of my other classes had quite different interests. Each class did certain kinds of things, and they were known for that activity. There are many ways to begin healthy classes. Don't limit the possibilities.

4. *It's okay if a class dies.* It's important to remember that classes—like the Body of Christ—are primarily organ-isms, not organizations. They live and breath. Classes are born and they die. So if a class doesn't go forever, that's okay. Maybe it provided a vital function during its life, but new needs and opportunities are always around the corner. Learn to tune into the various needs of your people. Build classes from the bottom up, not the top down.

5. *Be cautious when building a class around a particular individual.* I get nervous when a class is built primarily around one person. I know that some classes are built around a person who is charismatic and has wonderful leadership skills. And many times these classes work out very well. But I think it's the weaker way to go. I've found that when you build around a sense of people drawn together because of mutual needs, love, and concern—rather than an individual person—you've got a better base. Again, build from the bottom up.

> **"It's important to remember that classes—like the Body of Christ—are primarily organisms, not organizations. They live and breath. Classes are born and they die. So if a class doesn't go forever, that's okay. Maybe it provided a vital function during its life, but new needs and opportunities are always around the corner."**

Speakers and Conference Planning

Planning a Successful Singles Conference

by Jim Smoke
Founder and director of The Center for Divorce Recovery, Phoenix, Arizona

Many singles conferences are being held across the country each year. This is exciting, as more and more leaders realize the potential growth and outreach that a local conference can have in their ministry. I believe there are five essential keys to having a successful singles conference in your city or area.

1. *Content.* What do you want to say to the singles who will attend your conference? Singles have different needs, and it's wrong to simply let any speaker come to your group and speak on anything he or she desires. Get a reading on your people. Ask them what topics they would like to hear covered in your conference. Many conference planners never think of the content. They simply book a speaker, find a place, think up a catchy slogan, and let it happen. Content is the key to a good, growth-producing conference.

2. *Staffing.* Who do you want to communicate the content you have chosen? There are two kinds of staff in any singles conference—local and im-

ported. Often, the specialists who live in your own city can do a super job at your conference. You don't always have to fly a person in from the far ends of the earth. A nationally known speaker or writer can add snap and appeal to any conference, but it is not always a necessity.

When you look for speakers, look for the ones who are warm, loving, and sensitive to the areas you want covered. Have they worked with singles? Do they understand them? Will they speak in a language your singles understand?

3. *Promotion.* How will you tell the world about your conference? Many groups just seem to hope it will happen. Promotion has to be planned and carefully prepared *well in advance.* Flyers, brochures, posters, news releases, radio, and TV coverage have to be planned. Based on my own travels across the country, I have come to the conclusion that only about 20 percent of the conferences I address have done an effective job of promotion.

Much of the publicity material floating around the country looks like it was done by a third-grade artist. Have your major promotional pieces done by a professional. Your flyers can either breathe quality and content or be second class and amateurish.

4. *Finances.* How will you pay for your conference? Many groups are afraid to plan a major conference because they fear they won't meet their financial goals. *Plan a budget and stick to it.* A careful, prayerful budget will make for a good conference that finishes in the black. Make room for the un-

expected in your budget. It usually happens. Get all your costs down, set a *realistic* attendance figure, and set a per-head fee. Many groups will raise a lump sum in advance, aside from what they need for specific fees. Conferences do cost money! Speakers and talent cost money. There are a million details and all of them seem to have a dollar sign in front of them, so *be realistic.*

5. *The place.* Where will you hold your conference? In your church? At a school? At a church camp? At a hotel complex? Plan well in advance and find the right place. Ask yourself, "If we put 400 singles in this place for three days, would this place hold up?" Decide the kind of facility you want, then go find it. Check the rates and possible package deals. Some motels in the off-season will be cheaper than some church-owned facilities. The place you choose can often make or break the spirit of your conference. Good housing and good food add a great deal to a well-programmed singles conference.

One last word. Don't try to do it all your first time. Start small and grow big. Don't watch all the conference ads and try to outdo everyone. Most conferences billed as "national" won't attract any more people than yours will. And start at least eight to ten months in advance in your planning!

So You Want to Schedule a Speaker?

by Jim Smoke

Your program committee has just run out of creative ideas and you are three days away from your next singles function. Someone suggests a solution: "Let's get a speaker!"

Who?

Good question.

Who would you trust to effectively and lovingly communicate relevant truths to your group for forty-five minutes?

Speakers come and speakers go, but your singles stay in your program. It's an important responsibility to choose someone to communicate with your group. Here are some helpful guidelines for selecting a speaker:

1. *Get a recommendation from someone you trust.* Always check the quality of your speaker with someone who has used that person. Just using a speaker because he or she puts out a good news release or brochure is unwise.

2. *Find out how much the speaker charges.* Even before that, find out how much you can afford. If the two don't match, keep looking and consider using the person at a later date. A few speakers depend on speaking for their sole income. They have to charge more than the person who has a

paying job and speaks on the side.

3. *Don't be afraid to suggest a topic to your speaker.* Remember, you know what your group's needs are.

4. *Give your speaker all the details of the meeting.* Assign one person to meet the speaker and serve as host before, during, and after the meeting.

5. *Pay your speaker before he or she leaves your meeting.* A check sent out three months later gives little inspiration for a speaker to return.

6. *Always ask the speaker what equipment he or she needs* (i.e., PA system, blackboard, podium, overhead projector, etc.).

7. *Give your speaker an idea of what your group is all about before he or she speaks to them.* This will help the speaker prepare more adequately.

8. *Be kind to all your speakers, workshop leaders, and retreat speakers.* Communicating is a demanding and tiring craft. Kindness makes a speaker feel appreciated and is one way in which you can minister to your special guest.

The Care and Feeding of Traveling Speakers

by Jim Smoke

During the past sixteen years of singles ministry, I have been host to numerous traveling speakers. For twelve of those sixteen years, I have criss-crossed America as a traveling speaker myself and have been hosted by many wonderful people.

The following things that I have learned (often the hard way) are being shared to help you be a better host to those travel-weary seminar and retreat speakers who come your way.

1. *Always ask what a speaker charges for his or her services.* Even if he or she doesn't talk about it, you should. Then get it in writing. Many speakers make a major portion of their income from a traveling ministry. Their fee is just like your weekly paycheck.

2. *Get the travel details straight.* Arrival and departure should fit your conference schedule. Do you do the flight bookings and send a ticket, or does the speaker make the travel arrangements and bring you a bill? Make sure your speaker gets to your city in plenty of time for your program.

3. *When your speaker is to be picked up at the airport, make sure your driver is there when the flight ar-*

rives. It is rather lonely flying to a strange city and having no one there to meet you.

4. *Check your speaker into the motel, allowing time for freshening up before driving him or her to the conference center.* Always check out the facility before you make reservations. Ask yourself, "Would I like to spend the night here?" If it's your responsibility to pay for the room, do it in advance when you make the reservation. It is embarrassing to have your speaker asked, "And how do you intend to pay for your room?" when it's your responsibility.

5. *Meals!* If you agree to pay for your speaker's meals, do it. When it's convenient, allow your speaker to charge meals to his or her motel room. If not, give the speaker cash for meals on his or her own.

6. *"Your check will be in the mail on Monday!"* These are not kind words to a traveling speaker. Give the honorarium to the speaker before he or she leaves your city. There may be a house payment due the following week!

7. *Give your speaker a room or quiet place where he or she can relax between speaking sessions.* Speakers need to collect their thoughts, too.

8. *Allow some alone-time in the schedule.* Every group has a few people who simply want to chew a speaker's ear to the bone. Protect your speaker from these dear folk. Allow time for your speaker to mingle, but don't forget that even Jesus got "mingled out" and needed time alone.

9. *Appropriate attire!* Most speakers don't carry their whole closet when they travel, so let them know what the attire will be for the event. Is dress to be casual, sport, tails, or early Goodwill?

10. *Don't arrive unnecessarily early.* Few speakers need to be at the event an hour before they are on the program. This is often "dead time" for them and sometimes allows people to drain them conversationally before they speak. Respect the speaker's time. An hour of rest at the motel will better equip him or her to communicate with your people.

11. *A bowl of fruit in a motel room lets a speaker know that you care about him or her.* Motel rooms are lonely enough. A friendly gesture of fruit and cheese is most thoughtful.

12. *Don't expect your speakers to stay in private homes unless they tell you they want to.* Speakers need privacy, and motels and hotels allow that best.

13. *You will never spoil a speaker with too much hospitality!* In over ten years of traveling, I have had the best and the worst. The best always makes me want to return. Your added touches will make a speaker's ministry much more memorable. Your follow-up thank you letter will seal the good memory.

14. *When your speaker arrives, give him or her a printout of the weekend schedule and the times of the events.* It will help him or her get a clear picture of the weekend or day.

And finally, don't ask "How was your flight?" They are all good as long as they go up in the right place and come down in the right place!

Single Adults: The Role They Play in Today's Church

Singles Ministry and Its Relationship with the Church **169**

ABOUT PART FOUR

One of the biggest challenges
for the local church, in relation to a singles ministry,
is how to integrate single adults into
the body and life of the church.

A singles ministry cannot be truly healthy
if it is a separate group, off in the corner,
doing its own thing.

In this section, two leaders discuss the new,
changing role that single adults are playing
in the church today, and give suggestions
for how they can—and should—be
involved in the church body.

Singles Ministry and Its Relationship with the Church

Singles— A New Force in Today's Church

by Frank Tillapaugh
Senior pastor at Bear Valley Baptist Church, Denver, Colorado

S ingle adults are slowly becoming a new power base. But how is this newfound power being used? Will it be used for good in the church of the future?

Those with the Power Control the Church

In the past, churches have not been particularly interested in using their resources to minister to people different from those holding power. In most churches in America, the power people are the married middle class. They have literally taken our churches captive. Everything churches do relates to them, or it isn't emphasized. Every major ministry that we have come to expect in the church has serviced the middle class, whose primary focus is on raising kids, making their place in suburbia, and finding the ladder of success.

Second-Class Singles

Singles have often been treated like second-class citizens by the church. In many places, singles ministries are nonexistent. Because the church doesn't see singles as a part of its mainstream population, they are not formally recognized within its structure. This is especially true of pastors who take a hard-nosed position on remarriage and hesitate to allow divorced or remarried people to hold leadership positions. In some cases, divorcees are not even welcomed in the church.

Pressure: The Historical Path to Change

The church does not move or change except under pressure. In Acts, Jesus tells His disciples to go into Judea, Samaria, and the uttermost parts of the earth. But they didn't hear that at all. They were very happy and content in Jerusalem, as long as things were going well. But God forced them out through persecution; forced them into the rest of Judea; forced them into Samaria; and forced them to witness to Cornelius. Throughout human history, the only way society has moved is when it felt pressure.

Single Adults: Now 50 Percent of Big-City Populations

For example, in the fifties, things were safe, secure, and affluent. The church settled pretty much into the role of a commissary, with a steady flow of customers from the thousands of new and growing "traditional" nuclear families. Problems such as prison conditions, illiteracy, the homeless, and the increasing number of singles were not visible. Today is different. Society has changed, and the churches are feeling the pressure.

When the singles population rose to 50 percent of major cities, the church simply could not ignore singles any longer. It realized that if it didn't develop a strong ministry among singles, it would be ignoring things that were vital to the operation of a successful church: increased attendance, bigger budgets (more money to work with for ministry), more people to do ministry. The general singles population is educated and affluent. Those were enormous powers to be tapped.

Kicking the Door Down

Because the church has been pressured to change, the formerly disenfranchised group called singles has "freshly kicked the church door down" and is moving into the mainstream of the church. Much like the minority who leave the ghetto and make it, singles are becoming a recognized part of the church. But in spite of the progress, it remains very difficult to move from separation to integration.

Integrating into the Mainstream

The church itself needs to make provision for integrating singles into the mainstream church body. There is no ingenious way to achieve this. Our own culture is still very segregated. The church needs to provide Sunday school classes that are topical or age-oriented rather than marital-status-oriented. It needs to provide opportunities for singles to do ministry in target areas alongside married people. The best way to integrate is out of common commitment to ministry.

Integration with a Difference

But there must be a difference in the way singles become integrated in the church. If they set up shop in the church like married couples have done, the church will continue to bask in its segregated indifference to other disenfranchised groups. By simply joining the church's forces, singles will become part of its original problem and will make it more difficult than ever to penetrate. Unless singles develop an insatiable passion to become change agents themselves, the pressure for change in the church will not be sustained.

Using the New Power

Singles must use their new power in church circles to bring other disenfranchised groups, such as the elderly, the foreigners, the homeless, and the functionally illiterate, into the church with them. Denver alone, where I live, adds 4,000 abused children to its social-service rolls every year. If 4,000 single Christians were to give three hours a week to those kids, they would make a dynamic statement to the rest of the church about the desperate need for integration, healing, and wholeness.

The Unique Opportunity Facing Us

The solution to breaking down the church's power barriers lies in having the mind of Christ: being interested in others, paying the price of reaching

> **"When the singles population rose to 50 percent of major cities, the church simply could not ignore singles any longer. It realized that if it didn't develop a strong ministry among singles, it would be ignoring things that were vital to the operation of a successful church."**

out, breaking out of the comfort and security of the status quo. Singles and single adult leaders have a unique and historic opportunity to do just that. The power people of the church, the ones toward whom its programs and money are directed, are no longer exclusively the married middle class. Single leaders and single people must direct their newfound power and influence in the church toward breaking down the many barriers that still exist.

Integrating Your Singles into the Life of the Church:
DON'T LET YOUR MINISTRY BECOME A SINGLES "GHETTO"

by Jim Dyke
Minister with singles at
Grace Church of Edina,
Edina, Minnesota

Specialized ministries—such as single adult ministries (SAMs)—are sometimes shunned by churches because they tend to be "separatistic" and "dis"-integrated.

We even occasionally hear the word *ghetto* applied to singles ministries, implying that they detrimentally segregate singles into an artificially disconnected "church-within-the-church." Unfortunately, these characteristics are descriptive of some singles ministries across the country.

But the most effective, successful SAMs are invariably solidly attached to a strong local church and are operating as a healthy, contributing part of the body.

The issue of integration is critical—a lot is at stake! If your SAM does not have a strong tie to its parent congregation, you will struggle more with the "mobility" of your singles—they will be more likely to move on or shop around at other churches.

You will also lose the advantage of ministry continuity. When singles move on (especially after marriage), you will forfeit the opportunity to have a long-term impact on their lives, and on the lives of their children, as well.

Your church will suffer, too. Without strong integration, the congregation will be in danger of becoming a "married ghetto" in an increasingly single adult culture. This can signal the loss of cutting-edge growth for the future.

The church will also lose the long-term contribution of singles who have much to offer in the way of talents, abilities, gifts, and finances. The truth is that a SAM can make an invaluable contribution to the ministry of a local church (and vice versa) but only if it is meaningfully integrated into the life of its parent congregation.

The challenge is how to accomplish this and avoid the damaging separatism that can so easily develop. So, where do we start? Here are ten suggestions that can help you effectively integrate your singles ministry into the life of your congregation.

Make Sure the Senior Pastor Is on Your Side

The single most important factor is the attitude of the senior pastor. The pastor of your church must share your vision for single adult ministry and really believe in the worth and value of single adults.

If he understands the unique circumstances of single adults, and appreciates the potential impact of singles in the local church, then your ministry is off to a good start.

But if he has any misgivings about single adults as valuable, contributing members of the church, your SAM may never be effectively integrated.

Have a Positive Attitude Toward Your Church

The second most important factor in successfully integrating your singles ministry is your attitude toward the church. If you don't believe in the importance of the local church in general, and your own local congregation in particular, then maybe you're ministering in the wrong location.

The people you are leading will resonate your attitudes, whatever they are. If you're critical of the pastor or church leaders, it will come out sooner or later —usually in conversation.

If you're indifferent to the congregation as a whole, you'll probably demonstrate it with poor participation in church functions, and in lackluster promotion of key church events. The single adults you minister to will emulate your attitudes and behavior; make sure you really believe in your own church.

Promote Church Membership Among Your Singles

The next step is to make sure your singles know about the various ministries of your church. Help them recognize the value of being a part of your church body. For example, if your church has a good children's program or youth ministry, then you have an excellent "draw" for single parents.

But beyond that, encourage your singles to take an active part in the life of the total church—and the best place to begin this is with church membership. When your singles officially join the church, they are affirming the theology of "body life," which teaches that each person has an important part to play in the life of the congregation.

There are emotional payoffs in church membership as well—your singles will feel a greater sense of identity and belonging. The result, as pointed out earlier, will be less mobility among your singles as well as the opportunity for a longer period of impact on their lives.

Practically speaking, since most churches require membership status for major leadership roles in ministry and administration, church membership means more clout for your singles in church polity and decision-making.

Also, when the pastor and other

> **"Without strong integration, the congregation will be in danger of becoming a 'married ghetto' in an increasingly single adult culture. This can signal the loss of cutting-edge growth for the future."**

leaders see your singles joining the church, they will give your ministry more credibility and feel a greater sense of ownership and identity for your SAM; they will begin to think and talk about "our singles" and "our ministry." That means more loyalty and support from the church—two valuable assets to your ministry that you can't do without!

> **"Challenge and encourage your singles to attend the worship services of your church. Don't let your midweek or Sunday singles meeting become their only place of visible involvement."**

Encourage Worship Attendance and Giving

Challenge and encourage your singles to attend the worship services of your church. Don't let your Sunday or midweek singles meeting become their only place of visible involvement.

Additionally, encourage your singles to be "givers of record." In my church, we have a computerized envelope giving system. I always invite our singles to call the church office and ask to be assigned an envelope number, so they can begin systematic giving.

Keep track of how much your singles are contributing (we collect their tithes in their Sunday school classes, so we can measure their giving). This kind of information comes in handy when you approach the church board for an increase in your SAM budget!

Encourage Your Singles to Seek Opportunities for Service

Next, get singles involved in personal ministry. Encourage them to seek opportunities for service in your church as well as in your SAM.

For example, in my church a significant percentage of the youth-ministry staff are single adults. Our "Pioneer Boys and Girls" program for junior-age children also has a number of singles in staff positions. And many of our single adults serve in the youth and children's Sunday school program as teachers, teacher-aides, and department coordinators.

Believe me, your singles will be more than welcome in these areas of ministry, where recruitment of staff is a constant challenge!

Don't forget the importance of adult ministries as well—encourage singles to serve as ushers, choir members, musicians, altar counselors, and even deacons (if your church will allow them to serve in this capacity).

Single adult participation in these areas sends a strong message to the rest of the church: Singles are an active part of our fellowship.

Get Your Singles Involved in Key Leadership Positions

Of course, the most important arena of single adult influence and participation is in leadership and administration. You should be looking for qualified singles to serve as officers in your church, and as members of the policy-making boards and committees.

For example, we have a single adult on our board of finance—his participation in that key group of leaders gives invaluable support and credibility to our singles ministry.

Promote Your
Singles in the Church

The key to promoting your singles in the church is visibility. As the leader, be personally available for platform assistance in the worship services. The congregation needs to see you up front, where your participation reinforces your loyalty to the entire church and reminds them of the presence of an effective SAM in "our church."

Don't be afraid to toot your own horn a little! When in a position to inform the pastor, the staff, the boards, or the congregation, point out where singles are having an impact in the church and let it be a point of pride for the entire congregation.

Single adult participation in church leadership is also strategic for good public relations. The presence of singles on various boards and committees ensures a flow of information that will communicate the importance and loyalty of the members of your SAM to the church.

Include Your Singles
in Church Missions Projects

Recruit single adults to participate in adult missions projects sponsored by your local church or denomination, especially those projects that get them out on the field where the action is.

And don't close the door to recruiting singles for career missions. We have two full-time missionaries on the field that have come right out of our own singles ministry—one is a never-married single adult, the other is a divorced, "empty-nester" parent.

Involve Singles in Major Church-
Wide Events and Programs

Another important arena for integrating singles involves having them participate in church-wide events or projects. Promote single adult support and participation in your church's fund-raisers, missions weeks, outreach projects, and retreats/conferences. Above all, don't schedule conflicting singles activities during these important events.

In addition to the ongoing activities, there are occasional high-visibility ways you can reinforce the tie your singles ministry has with your church.

Our group occasionally sponsors a special event for the whole congregation. Last year, for example, we provided the manpower to bring a "Walk-Through-The-Bible" seminar to our church. Because we organized it, we were able to attach our name as the sponsoring group. It was a great success, and people came away from it impressed with the "really good things our single adults do for our church."

It can also be great PR for your SAM to make a special donation of supplies, equipment, or furnishings to the church. These become constant reminders to the congregation of the presence and the support of your single adults.

> **"Is your single adult ministry a sociological ghetto or a meaningful and effective part of the greater ministry whole? The choice may very well be up to you! Choose a strategy for ministry that says to your singles and to your whole church: 'We're a part of this family!'"**

Help Assimilate Newly Married Couples into the Church

Finally, make sure that singles who marry in the church are effectively assimilated into couples groups and Sunday school classes. It really doesn't make very good sense to invest time and energy ministering to singles who disappear after marriage because there is no meaningful place for them to fellowship in your church. And really, this is what true integration ultimately means: a place for people in your church from start to finish, cradle to grave.

So, is your single adult ministry a sociological ghetto or a meaningful and effective part of the greater ministry whole? The choice may very well be up to you! Choose a strategy for ministry that says to your singles and to your whole church: "We're a part of this family!"

Making Small Groups Work in Your Ministry

Nurturing Healthy Relationships with Your Single Adults **179**

ABOUT PART FIVE

Most single adults are looking
for a sense of family, of community.
We all have a need to belong.

One of the most effective ways to meet this need
is through small-group ministries.

Small groups also play a vital role
in nurturing relationships,
involving people in the lives of one another
in healthy ways, and building a level of commitment
to the ministry and to each other.

The writers in this section provide
some foundational principles and offer suggestions
to help you build a healthy small-group ministry
with your single adults.

Nurturing Healthy Relationships with Your Single Adults

Building Community in Your Singles Ministry

an interview with Denny Rydberg
Director of University Ministries
at University Presbyterian Church,
Seattle, Washington

What does "building community" mean to you?

A collection of individuals is often called a group when it is not. When I talk about building community, it means taking those individuals and really helping them become a group, a family, a community where they care for each other, listen to each other, support one another. A healthy group is much more than individuals who've gathered together.

What can a single adult pastor do to help build community in the group?

The first thing is to understand that it's a gradual sort of thing. You're not going to get instant community.

Second, from a philosophical point of view, I think it's vital that we understand that only the Holy Spirit can really create the kind of community we need in our ministries. Our responsibility as leaders is to help provide the environment where community can happen more easily. It's a lot like evangelism. The Holy Spirit calls people to repen-

tance, but we can create a climate where people can be more open and willing to hear.

What are some specific steps necessary to build community? As I see it, there are five steps:
1. Bond building
2. Opening up
3. Affirming
4. Stretching
5. Deeper sharing and goal setting
Let's explore each of these five steps.

Step 1: Bond Building

This is where you get people working together in a nonthreatening situation. They're trying to solve a problem, they're having some fun, they're laughing. It's not a heavy deal or very revealing personally.

I can easily see bond building working in a youth group where there is a tendency to be "less adult," to have more fun and games. But how do you handle it when you are dealing with a group of single adults who may be more formal than teenagers?

First, I would probably not do a lot of bond-building exercises in a normal Sunday morning or Sunday evening class. I'd introduce them at a retreat where people are more informal. I might start with an exercise called "Tied Up." You get these little forty-inch strings, tie each other up, then try to get untied. Do it just before lunch. If they can't get untied, they have to eat lunch in whatever way they are tied together.

There are also some less physically active bond builders. For example, there are those murder-mystery games where you give away a few clues, then sit around trying to guess who did it. Because the people are not allowed to write down the clues, they have to rely on each other, working together to solve the mystery. I've seen these bond-building exercises work very well with adults.

So one of the things you're saying is that retreats are an important part of the community-building process?

Yes, but I don't think bond building is limited to retreats. For instance, it can also happen with some nonthreatening small-group questions. But retreats are especially helpful if you have a group where community doesn't exist, where people still remain by themselves a little bit, if not physically, at least emotionally. So a great place to begin bond building is at a retreat or a social event.

What about the group that has no retreats? Or let's say they have only one retreat a year and less than a third or a fourth of their single adults are able to attend. Can bond building ever take place in a Sunday school setting?

Yes. But certainly not if the teaching is strictly lecture. We can't build community by having only one-way communication. Every single adult Sunday school class should have some sort of interaction or small-group activity if it's interested in building community.

But small-group activities need not be boring. This is where a leader's creativity comes in. Small groups can discuss the lesson, deal with a particular topic, or answer questions posed by the leader.

You can also do something physical. For example, the "Blind Line-Up" is where each member of the group is blindfolded (or closes his or her eyes). Then the group is asked to line up from shortest to tallest by voice recognition only. There are many quick and easy things like this that can be done in a Sunday school small-group setting when the leader uses a little creativity.

> **"We can't build community by having only one-way communication. Every single adult Sunday school class should have some sort of interaction or small-group activity if it's interested in building community."**

It's important to remember that, regardless of where you do it, the keys to bond building are laughter, a team effort, and a common goal where people are pulling together.

Step 2: Opening Up

This is where people begin to share their life a little bit but still in a non-threatening way. One opening-up exercise I use is called "Fantasy Island." I ask the following questions:
- If you could change who you are, who would you like to be?
- When would you like to live in history?
- What would your personality be like?
- What would be your occupation?
- Describe this imaginary person you would like to be.

Allow people to be as flip as they want. If, however, the singles are really talking to each other and exploring why they want to change, then real relationship building may begin. For example, "I don't like who I am because of this and that's why I want to change." How vulnerable the people get is totally up to them.

Another exercise is called "If I Were to Die," in which I ask,

- If you were to die tonight, what would have been the highlight of your life?
- Who would have been the person who influenced you the most?
- What would have been the best compliment you ever received while you were living?
- What would be one low point of your life?
- What is one of the nicest or most significant things someone ever did for you while you were living?

These hypothetical situations get people talking about issues they usually don't discuss. (They work equally well in a Sunday school or retreat setting.)

What if the group leader is not wonderfully creative or confident in coming up with the right questions for a small group?

That's why writers write resources —to help people who feel uncomfortable leading. There are excellent resources available. (See recommended books at the end of the interview.)

When dealing with these "opening-up" questions, what can a leader do to help the small-group members open up and share, to be less inhibited and more responsive?

THE BENEFITS OF BUILDING COMMUNITY
by Denny Rydberg

1. *Building community fulfills a biblical mandate.* Jesus wants us to be the family, the body. If we're really serious about that, we'll work at building community. It's a matter of being what God has called us to be.

2. *It creates a home for singles.* In our impersonal society—especially for single adults—we need a home, a place where we can come and be who we are and know we are accepted and loved.

3. *It models that Christianity is not a religion* but a relationship. I think that is important.

4. *People begin to see their gifts* and use them. I'm convinced that when we're afraid to fail, we can't really experiment with our gifts. If people are going to laugh at me or misunderstand me, I'm not as likely to try anything that might fail. It helps group members discover their gifts, which means it also provides a greater pool of leadership within your group.

5. *Building community enables people to be more sensitive* to and better listeners of others. It also increases motivation. Folks want to be part of a group like this. When people are taking risks, and really getting to know one another, they are more fired up. It takes away the boredom that I see in some groups.

The best thing I know of is to be a good model. One thing I do is answer the first question or two in front of the group. In other words, I say, "Hey, we want to get a little better acquainted with each other, and the first question I'm going to throw out is, What was life like for you in the fifth grade?" Then I tell them what life was like for me in the fifth grade. That way I can show that it's kind of a fun question, and I reveal a little of myself.

The leader is crucial. How much fun your group will have depends on how honest and how vulnerable you are and how much fun you have in answering the question.

Step 3: Affirming

Anytime people share things about their life, they should be affirmed. You don't just let a person share something meaningful and then move on to the next exercise or send them out the door. For example, if someone shares that he just found out he has cancer, you wouldn't say, "Okay, wow, that's great. Let's go play volleyball." Make sure that people who have shared something get affirmed in some way. Tell them that you appreciate them and why.

What about those times when you're not well acquainted with the people in your small group and feel like you have to come up with something "affirming"—even when you don't feel very sincere?

Your question is a good one. I had to model these community-building steps for a group of leaders two weeks ago.

When we came to the affirming time I said, "Hey, you don't know each other very well, so your affirmations are going to be really shallow; they're going to be like, 'Gee, I really appreciate your personality.' "

It's stupid to do affirmations if people don't know each other, if they haven't experienced anything together. But it's surprising how quickly sincere affirmation can take place once bond building has occurred. For example, five minutes after a "Trust Walk" (where a blindfolded person trusts someone to lead him or her through an obstacle course), people are saying, "I felt insecure at first because I didn't know you, but within minutes I was able to trust you. Thanks for leading me." That is affirmation. But I really agree, affirming can be empty and insincere. My guideline is that if people don't know each other, if they haven't experienced bond building and some opening up, then don't force the affirming.

> **"I recommend that a small group stay together for six to eight weeks, allowing for some flexibility. For instance, if a person brings a friend, I think that friend should be allowed to come into the small group, even though it may break up the group's dynamics. . . . For new people who come by themselves, I would have small groups designed specifically for newcomers."**

Should group members rotate every week or stay together for several weeks?

I recommend that a small group stay together for six to eight weeks, allowing for some flexibility. For instance, if a person brings a friend, I think that friend should be allowed to come into the small group, even though it may break up the group's dynamics. But I think you need to be flexible. For new people who come by themselves, I would have small groups designed specifically for newcomers. These would form every week or however often was needed.

Step 4: Stretching

After the group members have worked together, grown to know each other a little, and have experienced affirmation, they begin to feel safe with one another. Now it's time for stretching. That's where we force people into situations they've never been in before—to make them take some risks. Risks are hard to take if you don't feel like the community is with you. The risks—the stretching exercises that I'm talking about—really cannot be done in an hour on Sunday morning.

Real stretching is something like a white-water rafting trip or rappelling down a mountain. It could also be going out on a prison ministry team or a Mexico mission work project, or participating in a community evangelistic outreach. Community begins when people experience risk-taking together.

So one way a singles ministry builds community is by planning into the yearly calendar various group activities such as white-water rafting, mission projects, and evangelistic outreach opportunities?

Right. These activities can include physical risks, spiritual risks, or both. The important thing is that people are moving out of their normal comfort zones. And this seldom happens in a Sunday school setting.

Step 5: Deeper Sharing and Goal Setting

This is where you really level with people about how you want to change. Deeper sharing/goal setting usually happens best at the close of a year or at the end of a good community-building retreat. One of the things I dislike about small-group sharing is spilling your guts at the end of a one-day session. That's unrealistic. For deeper sharing/goal setting to really happen, your single adults need to have worked through the previous four steps.

One of the exercises I use here is called "Faces of Me." It's where group members talk about the masks that they've been wearing, and answer questions like,

• What does "real" mean?
• What mask do you want to drop?
• What price will you pay to remove it?

Another exercise is called "Overcoming Adversity." This involves people talking about

• The two biggest current problems in their life,
• How they are contributing to the problems, and
• Who they think can help them overcome these problems.

This is where the group members begin to develop a healthy level of accountability to one another.

What about those times when the small groups start becoming monotonous and dull? Or when the sharing starts feeling forced or routine?

When that happens you should discontinue the small groups for a while. After a period of time, unless the group is sharing more deeply and more honestly, it can become stagnant. To me that's the time to consider changing groups. But another thing to watch for is this: If a group is constantly at the first stage and not going deeper, it's a good sign that they need some stretching exercises. These do wonders in keeping your small groups alive. Give them new challenges.

What are some books you recommend for further reading on the subject of building community?

Building Power by David Williamson (Prentice Hall). This guy, a pastor in Minnesota, really understands the dynamics of small groups.

Serendipity Group Bible Study New Testament by Lyman Coleman, Denny Rydberg, and Dick Peace (Zondervan). This excellent resource provides small-group discussion-starters and questions for content and reflection on every section of the New Testament.

Building Community in Youth Groups by Denny Rydberg (Group Books). Although this book was written for youth groups, the truths are transferable. If leaders read it through the eyes of a single adult ministry, they can apply it to their situation.[20]

Making Your Singles Ministry More Than Just a Stopping-Off Place

an interview with Andy Morgan
Director of Single Point Ministries at Ward Presbyterian Church, Livonia, Michigan

How can a leader build community within a singles group?

First, let me comment on some harmful things I've heard said about singles ministry that greatly affect this whole concept of community. I've read that some leaders think single adults should not stay in a singles ministry more than two or three years; that it is just a transition place, a stopping-off place on the way to another stage in life; or maybe a place to meet someone and then get married. I think this is possibly some of the worst teaching and thinking in singles ministry.

Here's why. We say that being single is a viable lifestyle, one that is accepted, encouraged, and modeled, even in Scripture. Consequently, a ministry with singles should not be one primarily built around transition but around community and continued growth. For many single adults, the singles ministry may, in fact, be their primary support community. And I can find nothing wrong with that. In fact, we should be so intentional on building solid, healthy relationships in our ministries that even after one of our people gets married, the relationships that were established will continue.

On the other hand, if a ministry is more concerned about establishing programs than community, then it probably is unhealthy for singles to stay for a long time in any particular program. But I react when I hear someone say that singles should not stay in community. Many of our singles have stayed here for years, and that has given them the support base, the encouragement, and the freedom to move into the total church body. Many of our singles are elders, teachers, choir members, and deacons, but they remain actively involved in our community of single adults.

"I've read that some leaders think single adults should not stay in a singles ministry more than two or three years; that it is just a transition place, a stopping-off place on the way to another stage in life; or maybe a place to meet someone and then get married. I think this is possibly some of the worst teaching and thinking in singles ministry."

Would you encourage single adults to stay involved in your singles ministry for a long period of time without being involved in some significant way?

We don't do anything in our ministry that will make it easy for people to just hang out. Everything we do is designed around challenging people to grow—in their relationships, commitments, and involvement. Every single adult that comes here is challenged with a relationship—a relationship with God, a relationship with themselves, and a relationship with one another. Our singles ministry has a very high percentage of leaders because of the expectations and requirements we have established. Real ministry is not developing just another program so that people can hang out.

What are the specific things that you have found helpful in community building?

Everything we do is aimed at a small group. When we go on retreat, we always take buses. We don't let people drive by themselves. Getting to the event may take a four-hour bus ride, and people have already started developing a relationship when we get there. When we do "Talk It Overs" on the second and fourth Friday nights, there is a seminar teacher. We then divide into small groups for discussion.

How much are small groups a part of your community building?

Small groups are vitally important in our ministry. In fact, we do everything we can to get our singles involved in some type of small group.

At any one time, we have at least fifteen or sixteen small home groups meeting on a weekly basis. In addition, we have other small-group experiences such as divorce recovery, drama team, and others. All together, I would say at least 50 percent of our total ministry is involved in some type of small-group experience.

Overcoming "Single-Cell Anemia":
WHY HEALTHY SMALL GROUPS ARE VITAL

by Jim Dyke
Minister with singles at
Grace Church of Edina,
Edina, Minnesota

How Healthy Is Your Single Adult Ministry (SAM)?

1. Does your group number less than fifty or sixty? ❑ Yes ❑ No
2. Do all the members of your group know one another? ❑ Yes ❑ No
3. Do the singles who visit your group seldom "stick" and become "regulars"? ❑ Yes ❑ No
4. Is your SAM one of those groups that is frustratingly stable—it seems to survive over time with a core of die-hard "regulars," but it never seems to grow? ❑ Yes ❑ No

If you answered yes to any of these questions, your singles ministry, like many others, is probably suffering from a disease that church-growth experts call "single-cell anemia." [21]

Social scientists have a name for a group like this. They call it a "primary social group." It may number anywhere from twelve to sixty or seventy and has some very specific characteristics: it is hardy (it can survive over time) and fairly close-knit (everyone knows everyone else). But a primary social group has some real problems that hinder the work of the church.

Problems with a "Primary Social Group"

1. *It is not a fellowship of true personal intimacy.* It's a group of "familiar strangers." (Members know one another, but they don't share intimate, accountable relationships.) This lack of intimacy hinders the process of spiritual renewal and revival in your ministry.

2. *This kind of group is extremely resistant to change.* This immutability looks like stability to the untrained eye, but it can be a barrier to growth. Why? Let me remind you—*change is fundamental to growth!* It's only a matter of time until you have to make changes in your singles ministry in order to keep up with changes in people, the church, and the culture. If your ministry is inflexible, your programming efforts will fail.

3. *A primary social group is also resistant to new people.* Once you're "in" you're really "in," but the process required to get there prohibits all but the hardiest and most determined newcomers.

These three basic characteristics produce a predictably stable but frustrating singles ministry—a group that never dies, but also never grows.

Some Solutions to Consider

So what's the solution? You need more groups in your singles ministry. More small groups within your SAM will dilute the resistance of the primary group effect.

What kinds of groups will break up the resistant unity of the primary group? There are really only two fundamental types of groups—relational or task. Church-growth researcher Lyle Schaller explains: People visit churches for a lot of reasons, but they decide to stay at a particular church for only two:

• They know someone in the church (relationship), or

• They have a job to do (role or task).[22]

All groups fall into one of these two categories—they are either organized around relational goals, or around task accomplishment.

You could design relational groups to promote spiritual growth and mutual caring (like home Bible study groups, or discipleship groups, or four-member "covenant" groups). Or you could organize task-related groups (like a social committee, a Christmas party committee, a musical ensemble, a missions project team, or a convalescent home visitations group). Ad-hoc task committees are particularly effective in assimilating new people, because they create new jobs, new spots for incoming leadership to fill. Task committees also provide a great opportunity to mix the people and relationships in your group, so don't hesitate to organize a task-oriented team that may only be together a short time.[23]

Don't be afraid to organize a group based on a distinctive element of the

---

RELATIONAL AND TASK—THE SMALL GROUPS THAT WORK
by Jim Dyke

A healthy singles ministry will have a wide variety of groups. When thinking about what kind of groups to start, keep tuned in to the needs, interests, and talents represented in your group and community. Again, keep in mind that all groups basically fall into one of two categories: relational and task.

Ideas for Relational Groups

1. *Home Bible study.* This is probably the most common type of group. In our ministry we have a wide diversity of home study groups. Our leaders are given considerable freedom to pick the study topic and intensity level of study. For example, some of these groups are more social, alternating each week of study with a potluck or event (beach barbecue, dinner together at a local restaurant, a night out at the movies, etc.). Other groups are much more intense, assigning weekly reading or homework and saving social activities for other times.

2. *Discipleship and covenant groups.* These are vital for new Christians and those seeking to deepen their spiritual walk. We offer studies for beginners as well as for those seeking accountability for their own personal study, devotional life, and daily lifestyle.

3. *Common interest groups.* We had a cooking group recently (with mostly guys) that featured a dinner every meeting, with each course prepared by a different group member. These groups help build community.

4. *Support groups.* Some of our groups are built around specialized support needs. For example, one is built around the twelve-step principles for recovering from chemical dependence. Other support needs include divorce recovery, single parents, weight loss, sexual abuse/violence, and relationship addictions.

members' lifestyle. A single-parent group can be very attractive to other single parents. Age-related groups can also help your singles ministry grow.

In our ministry, we have an adult Sunday school class for singles in their sixties and seventies. In the relatively short time it has been in existence, it has become a warm, encouraging, and thriving "family" for many senior singles. (We have seen three marriages within the group already!)

Some people may see these distinctive groups as isolating or disunifying, but don't let that philosophy pervade your ministry—you need to "bless" these groups and keep telling your people how important it is to be able to meet specific needs in this way!

Where to Begin

But, you may ask, where can I begin in my small-group ministry? The easiest place to begin organizing new groups is with your leadership core. Turn your leadership meetings into discipleship or leadership training. Invite new people with leadership potential to the meetings and model the kind of acceptance you want your leadership to practice.

Another easy place to begin is with home Bible studies. Start with at least two study groups running at the same time. (Force people to make a choice, otherwise your home study will turn

---

Ideas for Task Groups

1. *Primary leadership teams.*

2. *Ad-hoc committees.* These committees, responsible for a one-time special event, require a short-term commitment. Consequently, they are an excellent way to begin assimilating new people into leadership in your ministry. Recruit committee members from a mix of old-timers and newcomers. This is also an excellent way to test the leadership skills of new people and to help them make friends with your current leaders.

3. *Missions groups.* Whether involved in the inner city or with an overseas project, these groups provide some of the best opportunities to build close friendships through the intensive bonding experience that the projects provide. One of our most popular groups supports a Mexican orphanage right across the border. This team's regular visits deploy a host of diversely skilled and gifted singles, including professionals in the building trades (plumbers, carpenters, concrete workers, and painters).

4. *Ministry teams.* We have a group that hosts a fellowship lunch for newcomers. Twice a month, they provide a delicious meal right after our Sunday worship hour. Visitors to our singles classes can stay for a free lunch, meet some of our leaders, and learn more about our overall singles ministry. Another group of guys sponsors a once-a-month outing for kids of single parents. A few of the guys do the planning, and the rest of the men just come to spend time with the kids, providing companionship and supervision.

So what groups do you need? Look over your singles ministry and do some creative thinking. The place to serve is always the best place to begin.

into just another meeting of the same primary social group!) Handpick key people to be a part of each group. Use good curriculum and make sure the members realize they are expected to duplicate the experience for others down the road.

> "Instead of trying to inject new life into old, resistant groups, start new groups on a regular basis. (New groups assimilate new people much faster than old groups!) Another word of advice: It is usually much better to start a new group than to divide a group that is already well established."

How Many Groups Should Your Singles Ministry Have?

Schaller estimates that you need six or seven groups ("different, but overlapping") for each hundred people currently involved in your ministry.[24] Don't let the number of groups that you may need scare you—just remember the variety of groups that can exist, then start thinking and brainstorming more creatively with your leadership team.

Finally, be sure to plan regular times when the "whole group" can be together. (For example, rallies, retreats, major social events, times with special speakers, seminars, conferences, concerts, and possibly your regular Sunday school class.)

Grow Your Ministry with "Groups"

1. *Take charge!* As the leader, be the initiator-organizer-developer of groups in your singles ministry.

2. *Start seeing and developing your SAM as a "group of groups,"* and look for opportunities to develop new groups.

3. *Start new groups.* Instead of trying to inject new life into old, resistant groups, start new groups on a regular basis. (New groups assimilate new people much faster than old groups!) Another word of advice: It is usually much better to start a new group than to divide a group that is already well established.

4. *Allow groups to establish their own identity*—even their own treasury! Encourage the groups to have their own get-togethers and social activities. Allow them to have a sense of autonomy and responsibility.

5. *Challenge each group to get involved in occasional tasks or ongoing projects.* This keeps the focus of the group from becoming self-centered.

6. *Provide both teaching and fellowship.* If you develop adult Sunday school classes, be sure to have good teaching, but always allow plenty of time for fellowship as part of the class schedule (i.e., refreshments, mixing, sharing, and meeting visitors).

PART SIX:

Outreach and Evangelism in Your Ministry with Single Adults

ABOUT PART SIX

One of the unhealthiest places
for any of us to be is where we are primarily focusing
on ourselves, on our needs, problems, and hurts.

There is a time to care for ourselves,
to stop the bleeding,
but reaching out to others is a vital part
of the healing process.

In this section, several leaders look
at ways to reach unchurched singles adults,
as well as how to challenge singles to be involved
in giving of themselves to others.

THIRTEEN

Reaching Young Single Adults

(Ages Twenty to Thirty-Two)

193

Why Today's Young Singles Avoid the Church

by Terry Hershey
Director of Christian Focus, Inc.,
Seattle, Washington

Young adults (those in their twenties and early thirties) continue to express their attitudes toward the church most conspicuously by their absence. In an article in the *Orange County Register* (a southern California newspaper), a reporter offered this sobering conclusion to a nationwide Gallup poll on religion: "Religion's importance in everyday life increases with age—the strongest believers are fifty-five and older."

We must understand the relevance of this fact if we are to embark on an effective ministry with young adults—a population that mostly avoids and ignores church. In 1958 almost 50 percent of adults under thirty attended church. By 1980, the number dropped to thirty percent.

Why the dropout rate? Why the decline in overall involvement?

1. *The church avoids intellectual struggle.* Our culture is rapidly changing, and organized religion is paying a price in members. Young adults as a whole are more educated and sophisticated. Fearing the ultimate questioning of church doctrine and convictions of moral practice, the church avoids encouraging young adults to use their intellectual capacities. The result? Young adults who have no time for what they see as nonrelevant religious platitudes and easy answers.

2. *Increased affluence.* Martin Marty observed that "lifestyle is the main factor in determining who goes to church, and the country's 'yuppie' lifestyle isn't a church going lifestyle."[29]

Marty is not suggesting that all single adults are "yuppies." But thanks to the pervasive presence of media, we live in a culture saturated with values that say we need to consume, achieve, and "have it all."

3. *Increased mobility.* Almost 50 percent of young adults move on an average of once per year. It's no wonder they're reluctant to sink roots into a church community that may be available for only a year. I often hear young adults refer to the time when they "hope to settle into a church that they enjoy." In the meantime, with little time available and "things" that need to get done, church becomes an occasional experience.

Unfortunately, churches have traditionally not positioned themselves to be helpful to people in transition. Consequently, we've not only missed the boat, we've missed it long after it has left the port for open seas. Perhaps we have contributed to the phenomenon of young-adult mobility. Can the church learn to touch young adults in the midst of mobility?

4. *The church's attitude regarding evangelism.* There are two unhealthy extremes. One is the laissez-faire "We have what you need. Come and get it."

With such an attitude, it's easy to criticize young adults for never seeming to show the commitment to "take us up on our great offer." Those who do come are the visibly needy, and we can find no neutral ground.

The other extreme is to join the ranks of the majority of social institutions and become a merchandiser. "Step right up. We've got what you need here. And the first ten receive a free. . . ." Can evangelism be reduced to a better brand of entertainment? Is hype necessary to build a singles ministry?

5. *Our own self-fulfilling prophecy.* Our stereotypes only reinforce themselves and promote distance. Far too many church leaders attribute lack of church attendance to laziness, unbelief, self-centered behavior, or a failure of parents to inculcate a sense of duty in their children. We reap what we sow.

6. *The church's unwillingness to give young single adults a sense of ownership.* I have found that their lack of involvement or responsibility in the church is not necessarily due to a lack of commitment (as is usually assumed). When I ask young adults why they are not involved in their church, they usually answer, "No one asked me," "I don't know what I can do in the church," "People think I'm too young."

Churches that are developing strong singles and young adult ministries have this philosophy in common: They don't ask for responsibility; they give it away. There is a significant difference. The first approach assumes that young adults are not committed; the second assumes that they are, but simply need encouragement, and an opportunity for expression.

I'm convinced that many young adults refrain from involvement in the church (and also have their tremendous enthusiasm stifled) because they haven't been asked, because the leadership has not intentionally sought out young adults for service. (Remember Jesus' example. He didn't wait for volunteers to come to Him. He intentionally and specifically sought and invited twelve men to be His disciples!) Look at young adults as givers instead of takers and you may be pleasantly surprised with their response.

> "I'm convinced that many young adults refrain from involvement in the church (and also have their tremendous enthusiasm stifled) because they haven't been asked, because the leadership has not intentionally sought out young adults for service."

Giving away responsibility begins by getting to know your young adults, allowing them to dream and actively participate in the conceptualizing and planning. Then use their input and ideas by making sure they are involved on planning committees for the church at large.

It is time for us to take an inventory. Based upon what you've just read, are you hopeful for the opportunities of ministry with your young single adults? Are you excited about what the next year holds for you and your ministry opportunities?

Many people respond with discouragement. Still others, who don't see statistics and trends as particularly relevant, hope to find a cure-all program that will magically remedy the decline of interest. They have missed the point.

Rather than discouragement or apathy, I see hope. Never before has there been such a vast resource of untapped leadership ability. Young adults are not only tomorrow's church; young adults are today's church. The potential is unlimited.

Our Need for New Wineskins

an interview with Jack Sims
President of B.O.O.M.E.R.S., Inc.,
Consulting, Placentia, California

Why do today's young single adults avoid the church?

Look at the religious jargon. Many churches today still use the King James English with the different tones of voice. Nowhere on earth do you hear this kind of speaking except in a church. It's not something you can prepare for except by being in a church. You walk in off the street and hear an otherwise normal individual talking in a strange tone of voice—and using strange words.

Theological buzzwords are a second example. It's a different language: "saved, sanctified, Holy Ghost."

A third example is the music. Most churches still rely primarily on two-hundred-to-four-hundred-year-old hymns. And the organ is still the focal musical instrument. One young adult, after hearing church organ music, told me, "I had a strange urge to go skating when I'd go to a worship service." He was making a point. As far as the baby-boomers are concerned, the only place you hear these sounds are at a skating rink and possibly a ball game. Look at the hymn that goes, "Here I raise my Ebenezer." I've been a Christian for more than eighteen years and I still don't know what an Ebenezer is.

Another example would be the role of women. The Church—particularly the more conservative side of it—is out of step in not offering women roles of meaningful leadership. Again, it's a reflection of the culture and leadership of an older generation. It's the Harry Truman Generation versus the Pepsi Generation.

Are you saying that one of the problems is that most of today's church leaders are older and out of touch with today's adults?

Yes. Most local churches, particularly those based in a denomination, were founded before 1960. The people who support them are between forty and sixty-five years old. The people at the helm are men either near or past retirement age. It's a simple matter of economics and culture. Those churches and denominations can't do anything over the long run that forty-five-to-sixty-year-old donors won't pay for and that sixty-year-old men won't allow. By definition, they won't be funding activities that will effectively reach those in their twenties and thirties. Too many "sacred cows" stand in the way.

It's the kind of problem faced in Matthew 9, where you have new wine being poured into old wineskins. Just what Jesus predicted would happen generally happens. The old wineskins burst, so you hurt the old wineskin (the church), but you also lose the new wine (young single adults). So the only way to prevent that is to pour new wine into new wineskins. That's why many of the younger-minded, less-denominational type churches are more effective in reaching young adults.

Describe the ideal or model church that you believe would be most effective in reaching today's young single adults.

Specifically, churches that will be most effective in developing a healthy ministry with young adults will exhibit five basic traits.

1. *Sensitivity to experience.* Every church need not be Pentecostal or charismatic, although many young adults tend to be more receptive to these kinds of churches. This generation of singles has been raised on the social sciences and knows that man is more than intellect. He's also emotion and will. So a church that is open to a total experience with Christ—involving intellect, will, and emotion—will be more appealing. Young adults seek to

---

BRINGING BOOMERS BACK TO CHURCH
by Jack Sims

Churches must change their approach if they want to bring baby-boomers back to church. Churches that are effective at this share these ten characteristics:

1. **An openness to experience.** Boomers are interested in more than churches that feed the mind; they need to experience God. Things like praying for the sick—or the Pentecostal experience where culturally appropriate—are very appealing.

2. **Bible teaching that focuses on practical living.** Baby-boomers are more interested in what happens at the end of the month than at the end of the age.

3. **An emphasis on developing relationships.** At this stage in life, the boomers—especially the ones giving birth to the echo boom—have a strong need to build relationships.

4. **Evangelism in word and deed,** but not just in remote parts of the world. Baby-boomers expect to see things being done in their own neighborhoods and cities.

5. **Fewer titles and less formality.** Pastor Jones should be known to his congregation and everyone else as Bill.

6. **Recognition of the ability of women to serve and to teach.** Women don't want to go from the boardroom on Monday to the nursery on Sunday.

7. **Understanding of the new American lifestyle** in the context of two career families, divorce, and the reconstituted family.

8. **An emphasis on worship.**

9. **A tolerance for diversity.**

10. **An action orientation.**

be experiential.

2. *Bible teaching on practical living.* They're not interested in pie-in-the-sky theology. They've got to pay bills, keep their job, find someone to love them, or whatever it may be, depending on a person's station in life. Young singles in our culture are dealing with horrendous pressures of economics, loneliness, temptation. It doesn't make a whole lot of difference what's going to happen at the end of the age. It's what happens at the end of the party that gets a lot of us in trouble. Our theology may be just fine, but if we don't have practical in-the-trenches teaching from the Scriptures, we'll really be in serious trouble.

> "An opportunity to build healthy relationships is essential. But, when you realize that most churches are built around a worship setting that presupposes the use of fixed pews, it's not so easy to do. For forty-five minutes to an hour you're seated in a row, looking at the back of someone's head, which gives little opportunity to build any kind of meaningful relationship."

3. *Healthy relationships.* An opportunity to build healthy relationships is essential. But, when you realize that most churches are built around a worship setting that presupposes the use of fixed pews, it's not so easy to do. For forty-five minutes to an hour you're seated in a row, looking at the back of someone's head, which gives little opportunity to build any kind of meaningful relationship. Plus, you're being talked "at" and ministered "to." For the most part, you're not able to engage in personal ministry yourself. The setting has a lot to do with this.

Young adults want to be building relationships, probably more than any other segment of society. Once you're married and your children begin to come along, your need for relationships beyond the family begins to diminish. But when you're single, you have little or no family commitment other than to your parents. (And in many cases today, they are distant geographically.) So, the need to build relationships is important.

4. *Churches and religious organizations that share their faith by what they say and do.* This relates to the integrity aspect. Young adults want to be a part of groups whose walk matches their talk. It's not just what is said, it's what is done that's important. Unfortunately, sometimes they hear a lot more talk than they observe action. In this sense "do-gooders" might be a positive term.

Are you talking about social action?

Yes. It isn't enough just to tell someone about the gospel, they also have to see it worked out. But it doesn't necessarily have to be in the same breath. It's a matter of balance. Sure there may be evangelism teams involved in beach evangelism, door-to-door witnessing, or a gospel concert outreach series. These are run by people with a special heart for evangelism.

But within the same church there could also be a welcome wagon taking food to the elderly, a tutoring program for children, and people providing clothing for the underprivileged or homeless. When you look at the overall activities of the church, you should see a balance rather than just an "evangelistic" center.

5. *Less formality.* This generation of young adults has a healthy disrespect for authority. I don't see it as rebellion. They've grown up in the critical period of Vietnam and Watergate. They've been lied to by political and religious leaders. Over the years they've gained a media sophistication and a critical eye that make them wary of worshiping men and women.

One of the ways this is manifested is in their tendency to be a lot less formal relating to people. I personally think many churches will soon be calling pastors by their first name. Instead of Dr. so-and-so, it'll be Fred. People will command respect based upon their leadership, not a title.

In addition to less formal titles, I think we're going to see a decline in the "classroom church," where all the communication is one-way, from preacher to parishioner. There will always be the very gifted person—a Chuck Swindoll for example—who makes his teaching come alive. But I think to reach young adults there's going to have to be more two-way participation and visual involvement than the traditional "classroom" worship experience offers.

Why Young Singles Are Often Unresponsive to Our Ministries

an interview with Terry Hershey
Director of Christian Focus, Inc., Seattle, Washington

Most singles ministries today seem to be reaching those in their thirties, forties, and fifties. But we are not doing so well in reaching those in their twenties and early thirties. Why do you think we are not more effective in reaching the younger single adults?

Unfortunately, many churches build their ministry on the assumption that a singles ministry includes everyone from twenty on up. But younger singles—those from ages twenty-two to thirty-five—generally will not respond to this "singles" approach.

One reason young single adults aren't beating a path to the church door is because we're trying to lump them, even though they don't feel single, in with the older singles who do feel single. For example, if I had a group of twenty-five-year-olds in a church, I would never lecture them on "Happiness is being single" or "One is a whole number." Most of them are not going to tune it in.

Singles ministry—by its very name—

is where singleness is an issue. Divorce makes singleness an issue; death of a mate makes singleness an issue; being over thirty-five and unmarried often makes singleness an issue. But for most twenty-five to twenty-eight year olds, singleness is not an issue.

> **"Singles ministry—by its very name—is where single-ness is an issue. Divorce makes singleness an issue; death of a mate makes singleness an issue; being over thirty-five and unmarried often makes singleness an issue. But for most twenty-five to twenty-eight year olds, singleness is not an issue."**

It's been my experience that if a church wants "young adults" of any kind, it must specifically target that group, whether it targets them as the "young singles" group, or as the "young adult" group. But it has to target that population specifically. You will not effectively draw young single adults just by announcing your singles ministry.

Another factor of our effectiveness has to do with the negative tone that many singles ministry leaders have emphasized. By that I mean that most often the focus for a singles ministry has been on wounded, hurting people. Addressing these painful issues is often a necessary focus for the older single adult. But that image just doesn't cut it with the majority of single adults under thirty-five. Consequently, many younger singles have been turned off to active participation in a singles ministry. And yet there is seldom any other place in the church where they feel at home.

When do people begin to identify with being "single"?

It varies, of course. But in our culture today, most people don't begin to feel single until their early to mid-thirties. (This is a significant change from the previous generation.) If you were to survey young (especially never-married) singles in their twenties today, my guess is that the majority of them would say they feel uncomfortable being called single. Consequently, most young singles don't want to be in a "singles group." They are more drawn to words like *adult* and *career*.

It's not until they hit their early to midthirties that "single" becomes a part of their identity. Then they begin to lay their cards on the table, to acknowledge their marital status. But up until then, the marital options are still open. Whether they are single or married is usually not a major concern.

If you want to reach those from ages twenty-four through their early thirties, you will probably need to do so with a specific young adult ministry. In my opinion, the "singles ministry"—labeled as such—will reach primarily those in their mid-thirties and up.

It would seem that singleness becomes an issue earlier than age thirty-five, especially for women. Don't many begin to feel single around age twenty-six or twenty-eight?

Perhaps so. But I'm not convinced that they necessarily feel "single." Rather, I think they begin to feel the call of motherhood. It may magnify their marital state, but I think often even then the marital status issue is secondary. (The exception may be in the more conservative churches, where a greater emphasis is placed on traditional marriage and family roles.)

How is singles ministry different from young adult ministry?

They are distinctively different. Young adult ministry is more similar to youth ministry in that it is a ministry of transition, of lifestyle, of a "time of life."

Single adult ministry is also a ministry of transition, but moreover, it is a ministry of crisis, of decisions, of choices. It begins as a ministry of identity confusion. The crisis elements—single parenting, divorce, widowhood, unmarried and childless—are significant.

It's almost as if the singles ministry in the church is targeted around very specific needs, whereas the young adult ministry is targeted around a stage in life or a lifestyle. Young adult ministry is specifically targeted to young adults, married or single, up to age thirty-five or so.

How would you divide age groups?

If I were a pastor responsible for the young adult ministry, I would do an eighteen-to-twenty-two age group. This would be college and career. Then I would have a ten-year age span from around twenty-two-to-thirty-two that would be the young adult ministry.

A major concern about having a young adult ministry is that most people think of high school or college when they hear the words "young adult." For example, when you advertise a young adult ministry function in a newspaper ad, how can you make sure that people will understand what you mean?

You've got to define what you mean in your advertising. If you're going to use "young adults," define it as "adults in their twenties and thirties." I think it behooves a church to take on the job of public relations. (You need to define your singles ministry, too.) Never assume that the public will read your mind. They may not define something the way you do. I recommend that you always overdefine your message so that it is clearly understood by your intended audience.

In fact, I'm convinced that one of our primary responsibilities as leaders is to reeducate. Helping people better understand our many misunderstood subcultures is a significant part of ministry. I think more would be accomplished if I spent a greater portion of my time doing reeducation than doing programming.

For example, we need to help the church realize that young adults have creativity, energy, and vitality to offer in a variety of ministries. And we need to

> **"If you were to survey young (especially never-married) singles in their twenties today, my guess is that the majority of them would say they feel uncomfortable being called single. Consequently, most young singles don't want to be in a 'singles group.' They are more drawn to words like *adult* and *career.*"**

help the church realize that young adults don't need to be mated. It's not our primary job to be a dating service.

We also need to reeducate the church about single adults. Being over thirty-five and unmarried does not make one a half person. A healthy church will be a place of healing, grace, restoration, and the giving of authority so that singles can feel welcomed and involved as full members in the Body of Christ.

Based on your earlier descriptions of single adult and young adult ministry, it would seem that you feel single adult ministry is intended to be more short-term. Is that correct?

Yes. This is where I disagree with a lot of people. I believe the goal should be to keep your people in a singles ministry for as short a period as possible. View singles ministry as an open door into the church. It's not a destination point; it's a hallway. Singles ministry programming often focuses more on a particular "short-term" crisis or need. Young adult ministry, on the other hand, focuses on a stage in life. And that stage may continue for up to ten years.

MARRIEDS AND SINGLES: SHOULD THEY BE TOGETHER?
an interview with Terry Hershey

You have suggested that a young adult ministry should include both singles and marrieds? Why?

First, let me say that most attendees of this group in any church will be single. But I would avoid using the word *single* because I don't think it's healthy to force young marrieds to graduate out of the group. The connection between young marrieds and young singles needs to be encouraged.

Would you encourage the newly married couples to remain involved in the young adult group for an extended period?

It's not that you encourage them to stay. It's just that you don't encourage them to leave just because they're now married.

My experience is that, usually within six months, they'll move on to another class anyway. The point is that they shouldn't feel forced out from a group that has become their Christian community. They need time to develop another place in the church to move to—if they so choose—and the transition must be done at their own pace. They've established a support base in the young singles group. Don't divorce them from that just because they get married. Besides, I think the two groups have much to learn from each other.

That may sound nice on paper. But there seem to be few, if any, ministries across the country that have effectively blended young married couples and young singles together for any long-term period.

I never said that it would necessarily be long-term. I only said there need not be a "graduation date" for young couples as soon as they are married. There needs to be a period for making the transition. When couples get married, they should not automatically be forced out. If they happen to be in one of the small

In fact, I don't think people should be in a singles ministry program for more than about two-and-a-half years. I use two-and-a-half as a healing framework for divorce and grief. That's approximately how long it takes to recover from a personal crisis.

The primary focus of the singles ministry should not be to collect a bunch of singles in a room, but instead, to channel them into other ministries within the church, to mainstream them. (The one exception to remaining longer than two-and-a-half years is if someone is actively involved in a singles leadership position.)

One wonderful thing about a healthy singles ministry is that it provides a caring, healing community where people receive support, affirmation, and renewal. But that cannot be the end result of our ministry. That's not where we want to leave our single adults (or our married adults for that matter). We want to take them to a place where they are vitally involved in some ministry in the church, where they are using their gifts and abilities. That's what the end result must be.

How can you build a large singles ministry if one of your goals is to

study groups in the young adult ministry, they need to be allowed and encouraged to continue even after they're married. Your people need to hear, "When you get married, you don't need to feel like an alien in this group."

I admit that this model may not work for everyone. But if you're not going to have an integrated ministry, then make sure you at least have a very good transitional one.

What are some of the advantages of allowing young marrieds to remain involved in the ministry?

One big advantage has to do with your leadership team. Oftentimes it is your high-quality leadership folks who get married first. They tend to be more visible in the group, more outgoing, more involved, and consequently, often more "attractive."

But when they get married—and when your policy is "married folks get out"— all of a sudden you've just eliminated some of your high-quality leaders. When they're allowed and encouraged to stay, it helps keep your leadership team together. And if they happen to get married in the middle of the year, they're able to complete their term of office without feeling uncomfortable.

Do you also see young married couples with children fitting into this group?

No, that is where I draw the line. It is a natural line. When children come along, the needs and issues are drastically different. The child now becomes the primary focus. On the other hand, young childless couples and young singles share many of the same interests and concerns.

Would you also encourage singles in their thirties, forties, and fifties—once they get married or remarried—to stay in the singles ministry?

No. The goal should be to keep people involved in a ministry with older singles for as short a period as possible. *(See accompanying interview).*

keep single adults in the group for as short a period as possible?

First, I would never measure success by the number of people who are in the group. I would measure success in terms of the way my singles are being involved church-wide, and by how effectively I have funneled them into small groups. (I would always have a link with small groups because I don't think they're an optional ministry within the church. They're a necessity.)

> **"This is where I disagree with a lot of people. I believe the goal should be to keep your people in a singles ministry for as short a period as possible. View singles ministry as an open door into the church. It's not a destination point; it's a hallway."**

When people tell me their numbers aren't growing, I say fine. They don't have to always be growing. Sometimes just holding steady is okay. You don't need 700 singles in your group after three years to show that you're a success. We need to scale down our expectations for what we can—and should—do with a singles ministry. It's not meant to be the biggest collection of single adults in town. If you're a singles pastor operating with the same mentality of building a church that many senior pastors have, then you're going to get disillusioned and discouraged.

Success in singles ministry is enabling your people to take their new-found strength, healing, and knowledge and mainstream it—put it to work in their church or community. We need to challenge our singles to ask, "How can I give my particular, unique gifts as a single person back to the church, to God?" Both the church and the singles lose if single adults remain isolated in a singles group. They have tremendous gifts and abilities that need to be funneled into ministry.

What concerns do you have about single or young adult ministries across the country?

One is that I see many leaders put more emphasis on entertainment and program than on relational ministry. It is only through relationship—with God and one another—that people's lives will ever change in any significant way. Many SAM leaders place too much emphasis on the "how to" stuff when training leadership. It definitely has its place. There's a need for it. But in the end it's going to kill your ministry if you've assumed that a good program is all you need to make it work. Because it's not.

Reaching the Unchurched Single Adult

Reaching Unchurched Singles in a "Meat Market" World

an interview with Charlie Hedges
Singles pastor at South Coast Community Church, Newport Beach, California

I n this interview pastor Charlie Hedges discusses how getting rid of the "meat market" aspects of a singles ministry may be like throwing the baby out with the bath water. To effectively reach the unchurched, we need to have some "meat market" attitudes in our group.

What would you tell pastors and leaders who are worried about the "meat market" influence that nonChristians (and those less committed to their faith) bring to the church?

I would tell them to get out of their comfort zone. Unfortunately, the comfort zone for too many of us Christians is to get rid of sinners. If they don't get their act cleaned up right away, then it's "one, two, three, you're out." We need to stand back more often and ask what God wants us to be in the world. Does He want us to be "holier than thou" people, or does He want us to live out our faith among sinners?

When you look at the whole ministry of Jesus, there seems to be only one audience He was always down on. It was not the sinners but rather the religious, pious ones in the church.

I have to continually evaluate what I am doing in light of Jesus' example. Who am I going after? Who am I trying to please? Where is the softness of my heart? Jesus' comfort zone included the sinner. I trust that our singles ministries will include them, too.

What are some of the problems or situations to expect when you actively draw nonChristians to your group?

Not too long ago one of our groups sponsored a Halloween social and intentionally invited many nonChristians. One guy came dressed as a super Tampax. Now I'm not thrilled that somebody would come dressed that way, because it's offensive. But on the other hand, I was thrilled because it told me we were drawing people from the outer fringes, people who didn't yet know all the "rules."

And we don't need to beat them up for coming that way. We need to trust the Holy Spirit to deal with the people who come to us. We need to love them, to build bridges and help lead them to Christ. Of course we walk a fine line, but it's always going to be that way when reaching the nonChristian.

Another major issue leaders will face has to do with promiscuity. It will probably become more apparent in your group as nonChristians increase. Yet most surveys I've seen show sexual activity among single adults to be basically the same for those in the church as for those outside. The only difference is that—because nonChristians usually don't try to hide it—it will be more noticeable. But it's a whole lot easier to admit the problem and work with it, than when we deny that it exists, as Christians so often tend to do.

Why is the church not being more effective in reaching the unchurched single adult?

First, I think we need to look at the church as a whole. My thinking has been heavily influenced by my senior pastor, Tim Timmons. He is first and foremost an evangelist. His primary desire is to bring unsaved people into a relationship with Jesus Christ. One thing that frustrates him most about churches today is the fact that so many of them still view other churches as "competition." The concern about competition only exists when we are afraid that people may leave our church and go to another one. If we were genuinely focused on the unchurched, we'd have so many people to reach that competition wouldn't even be an issue.

A survey taken at many of the large churches here in southern California—many of them nationally known—showed that between 92 and 95 percent of the people attending these churches came from other churches. The churches are not reaching the unchurched. All we seem to be doing is shuffling people from one church to another.

Part of this is due to our seminaries. Don't take me wrong. I'm a big fan of seminary. In fact, three of my best years were spent there. But, unfortunately, seminaries teach men and women to talk to themselves rather than to the unchurched. And so does the church. We teach each other to talk to ourselves. We have our own language. It's almost like we need our own Christian dictionary. In the church we use so many words and phrases that the unchurched do not understand: justification, sanctification, "under the blood." Listen to how people pray in church: "Lord, undergird us," they say. What? I'm tempted to pray back, "Lord, don't do it. I don't know what it is, and I'm not sure I want it."

Another church phrase I hear often is, "Charlie, I want to share something with you." I want to say, "Wait a minute. Don't share it with me. You tell me what it is first, then I'll tell you if I want some of it. I may not want to share whatever it is you've got."

One thing you need to remember is that I didn't become a Christian until I was thirty, and I raised a lot of hell

> "Unfortunately, seminaries teach men and women to talk to themselves rather than to the unchurched. And so does the church. . . . We have our own language. . . . We use so many words and phrases that the un-churched do not understand: justification, sanctification, 'under the blood.' Listen to how people pray in church: 'Lord, undergird us,' they say. What? I'm tempted to pray back, 'Lord, don't do it. I don't know what it is, and I'm not sure I want it.' "

before that. So in many respects, I still think as a nonChristian. And in a very good sense, that is healthy. We've all got to do a better job of communicating with the unchurched, not just to ourselves.

How can we do this in our single adult ministries?

We need to be more effective in recognizing the needs of our audience. What are the singles in your community needing or looking for? In a marketing course you learn how to evaluate two different types of audiences: the one you already have, and the one you don't have yet but want. To be successful, you need to meet the needs of both audiences. This can be done by visiting with your key leaders in the church as well as by getting to know unchurched singles in the community.

> "First and foremost, single people are seeking relationships. If we don't recognize this and do something to facilitate it in every one of our singles meetings, then we are dropping the ball."

What have you found to be some of the main needs of single adults?

I've been in singles ministry now for several years, working both in Portland and here in southern California. I've found that single adults are primarily looking for three things in a church:
- relationships,
- spiritual nourishment, and
- involvement—an opportunity to give, serve, and do something with and for others.

If we are going to effectively reach today's singles, we need to make sure we are gearing each of our meetings and activities around these three needs.

Which of the above three things is most likely to bring an unsaved single adult into the church?

First and foremost, single people are seeking relationships. If we don't recognize this and do something to facilitate it in every one of our singles meetings, then we are dropping the ball. The number one thing singles look for in relationships is a dating partner or mate. I don't have any problem with the church intentionally being a "meet" market. Where else should single adults look for a decent spouse? I get upset when I hear people knock that idea or make it sound unspiritual. I think it's a fine thing, something the church should facilitate in healthy ways.

It is, however, also important for the church to recognize that not every single adult in its group is going to meet a mate. So, part of our ministry is to also focus on the value and importance of building healthy nonromantic relationships with both sexes.

How do you help facilitate relationships in your singles ministry?

On Sunday morning, we sit around tables instead of auditorium style. You don't facilitate relationships by seeing the sides of two faces and the backs of seven heads. The backs of heads do not talk very well. That is not intimate communication.

Before anyone thinks sitting around

tables comes easy for us, let me say that we have to set those tables up ourselves every Sunday morning before the meeting. We set up between thirty and thirty-five tables with eight chairs at each table. It's extra work but well worth it.

Sitting around tables helps break down barriers. You see the faces of others, plus you have something to hide behind. I've found that many people—especially new people—can emotionally hide behind a table. In group therapy that would not be good. But when people come to our group, hiding behind a table helps them feel more comfortable, and that is good. You can also set your coffee on the table and take notes more easily. It provides for a very comfortable setting.

At the beginning of each of our meetings, we have an open session around the table. Sometimes it's serious and sometimes it's fun. For example, I might ask them to tell each other how they squeeze the toothpaste tube. I might ask the question, "When you're lost, do you stop and get directions, or do you continue driving, trying to find the destination yourself?" Sometimes they are just dumb questions. The purpose is to get people talking, interacting, meeting new people.

I also design my teaching to include questions for table discussion. For example, I will stop in the middle of my teaching two or three times and say, "Turn to your neighbor and discuss this or that." Remember that, while many of the people are there to listen, the primary reason most of them come is to get to know other singles. If I'm not facilitating that, I'm failing.

The goal for my questions is not that they come up with an answer but rather that they interact. In fact, sometimes my questions may have nothing to do with my lecture. As long as they're talking to one another, then I win. Because I want to keep them coming until the gospel has a chance to penetrate their minds and hearts.

Learning to Think Like an Unbeliever— and Other Guidelines for an Effective Outreach Strategy

by Johnny Crist
Senior pastor of Vineyard Christian Fellowship, Atlanta, Georgia

Sooner or later the strategy question will arise among the leadership of a singles ministry. Someone will want to know if a swim party or Bible study will attract more nonChristians to the group. How does a Christian singles group effectively reach out to the nonChristian single adult? This is a question of strategy. In my opinion, three guidelines hold particular relevance.

Guideline 1:
Target Your Audience

The leadership of a singles ministry may find that taking an advertising executive to lunch will bring invaluable returns. Advertisers understand well the value of targeting a specific audience. Barbie doll manufacturers buy Saturday morning TV time because their target audience watches at that specific hour.

You need to ask yourself, "Who are we wanting to reach?" I can name at least seven categories of singles, each with its own particular set of felt needs:

1. Young never-married singles
2. Young divorced singles (under twenty-four years old)
3. Single parents with children under six years old
4. Single parents with teenagers
5. Singles who are separated but not divorced
6. Confirmed celibates
7. Single by mate's death (over sixty-five years old).

(Most effective outreach ministry occurs with people who are single by two or more of these categories. They are generally the ones who feel the greatest spiritual need.)

Determine which of these homogeneous units will be your target. It is not wise to consistently mix singles from the seven homogeneous units for ministry. The homogeneous unit that has the greatest number of singles in your church will undoubtedly be the most logical choice for a target group. It will be natural for this core group to win others like them and get them involved in your group.

Singles should be very alert here to evangelize those within their homogeneous unit. This is a major factor in growing a singles ministry—evangelize and concentrate your outreach among your homogeneous unit.

Guideline 2: Learn
to Think Like an Unbeliever

Richard Warren, a church-planting pastor in Orange County, California, coined the interesting phrase, "Learn to think like an unbeliever."

Christians live in the balance between being in the world but not a part of its system. Sometimes we cannot relate to the lifestyle and culture of those we want to win. Engle's Evangelistic Countdown (see next page) has proven to be a helpful tool for singles leadership. It will help you to identify how much "message" your target group is able to receive.

Guideline 3:
Clear Communication

Communication in singles ministry must occur at two levels—among "us" and to "them." Have your leaders chart the present status of those they want to reach on the right side of Engle's scale. Then have them match the appropriate Christian response from the left side of the scale. For example, if your target group is a -9 or -8 (on the top of the scale), your group should offer an activity with little or no preaching.

The problem with many of our outreach ideas is that we plan +4, +5, and +6 activities for -7, -8, and -9 kinds of people. We must learn to "get into the skin" of the nonChristian we want to reach. We must find out how they spend their free time. We must discover their fears about attending a church-related function. In short, we must learn to "think like an unbeliever."

Once you have established your purposes and goals among your ministry leadership, clearly communicate it to your group. What do you want them to do? Inform them of your expectations. For example, if you plan an outreach event, clearly delineate to your group what level of proclamation, if any, is desired. Sometimes the best activity to reach your target audience will include no preaching.

It is equally necessary to send clear communication to your target audience. Don't let your message get trapped in language and symbols known only to Christians. Read the Saturday church page in your local paper. Is it any wonder that nonChristians view Christianity as boring and irrelevant? Try reading the ads from a nonChristian's perspective and ask yourself whether the ads entice you. What appeal would the sermon title "God Forbid that I Should Glory Save in the Cross" have to the nonChristian?

Have you ever read your ads through the eyes of a nonbeliever? You may be surprised! In our advertising we use no religious words or phrases like "Hallelujah," "Expect a miracle," "Receive a blessing," or "Come prepared to receive." These words and phrases communicate certain expectations to one already "Christianized," but have little relevance to our nonChristian target audience.

ENGEL'S EVANGELISTIC "COUNTDOWN"

Presence	**-10** Awareness of Supreme Being
	- 9 No Effective Knowledge of Trinity
	- 8 Initial Awareness of Need
	- 7 Interest— Acceptance of Medium
Proclamation	**- 6** Awareness of Gospel
	- 5 Grasp of Implications
	- 4 Positive Attitude
Persuasion	**- 3** Personal Problem Recognition
	- 2 Challenge/Decision to Act
	- 1 Repentance/Faith in Christ

A NEW DISCIPLE BORN (Matthew 28:19-20)

	+ 1 Post-Decision Evaluation
	+ 2 Incorporation
	+ 3 Personal Fruitfulness
Discipleship	**+ 4** Conceptual Growth
Christian Education	**+ 5** Discovery of Spiritual Gifts
	+ 6 Incarnational (Social) Growth
Body Life	**+ 7** Stewardship
	+ 8 Prayer
Koinonia	**+ 9** Use of Spiritual Gifts
Diakonia	**+10** Witness and Reproduction

Three Keys to Reaching Single Adults

by Ray Larson
Senior pastor at Bethel Assembly of God, Redding, California

Reaching singles is a key issue for the local church in its quest to reach the entire community. Singles must be evangelized and then discipled for the Kingdom of God. The goal of the church should be to fulfill the Great Commission in the single adult community. Here are what I believe to be three keys to accomplishing this goal.

Commitment of the local church

Beginning with the senior pastor, the local church must have a vision to reach singles. It is imperative that the pastor see the single adults of his town as a key ingredient to the success of (a) the church at large, and (b) the local gathering of believers. The entire church, married and single, must be fully committed to reach the single adult community.

Commitment of the singles

Singles must be committed to reaching singles outside their fellowship. How else will the singles in the community know about the exciting group at the local church? The singles pastor or leader must challenge his group, whether it be five or five hundred, to reach out into the community.

Outreach

Effective ways of developing outreach in your single adult group has three major components.

Planning Stage

The first step in the planning stage is to establish reaching singles as a valuable goal for the whole church. That vision must be communicated from the pulpit.

Second, you need to decide what and where the definite single pockets are in your community. Where do singles hang out? Where do they spend their time when they're not at work?

The third step in the planning stage is goal setting. It is important that you not only set goals, but that singles feel a personal and collective responsibility for the accomplishment of those goals. There must be high personal involvement in the task.

In our planning stage of "Singles Alive," we found out where the singles were spending their free time. Then we set goals for effectively reaching those groups. We planned park outreaches with music and drama. We visited single-parenting groups. We invited these people to attend our alternative singles group on Monday nights. It took time for our group to realize our goal of participation, but the success was overwhelming. Hundreds of singles were involved in our park outreaches. They invited their single friends from work to activities and shared their faith one-on-one with singles.

Preparation Stage

First, we must equip people for evangelism. First Corinthians 7:32-35 challenges singles to use their free time ministering to others in the Kingdom of God and to nonChristians. We give our singles ideas for success in sharing their testimony, such as how to move a normal conversation into a natural discussion about Jesus Christ.

The second area of preparation is in the area of discipleship. *You cannot go out and reach other singles for the Kingdom of God unless you are prepared to disciple them as well.* The command of Matthew 28:16-19 is to make disciples of all nations. With that goal in mind, we have developed methods of nurturing the new believer; small groups of singles meet together to grow in the Word, pray, and fellowship.

Propagation Stage

Our goal is to take people from the kingdom of darkness and bring them into the Kingdom of Light—to reproduce spiritually. It's great to have a planning and preparation stage, but the final goal is propagation.

There are two types of evangelism: (a) attracting nonChristians to the local church using programs of interest as evangelistic tools; and (b) launching your people into the nonChristian community.

Attracting NonChristians. We've seen many people come to Jesus Christ through our divorce-recovery workshops. We also have a "Christian Singleness and Relationships" series,

inviting the community to see what the Word of God has to say about how singles handle their relationships with members of the opposite sex. We provide a single-parenting class, taking single parents who are frustrated, without direction or help, and giving them biblical guidelines to live by. We do a series called "Sex and the Single Christian," highly controversial but very effective. We provide financial planning seminars where we help people set up budgets, plan for their retirement, and put together a will. These activities bring in people from the community and expose them to our group.

> "The first step in the planning stage is to establish reaching singles as a valuable goal for the whole church. That vision must be communicated from the pulpit."

We also have Bible studies, home groups, and support groups that are open to everyone. We promote these ministries through advertising and word of mouth. At these special gatherings, the leader introduces people to the other aspects of our singles ministry and invites them to come to our Monday night "Praise Celebration." We see many come to Christ through this highly productive approach.

Launching Out. Our program includes witnessing in singles bars, a highly controversial type of ministry because many think that you shouldn't go near where people are living in sin. I disagree. Jesus went where people were hurting, so we should go there as well. We organize street and park evangelism, where not only singles but often whole families hear our music and drama. We have singles participating in such groups as "Parents Without Partners" and other social groups. *We purpose to be a part of these groups without being obnoxious or obtrusive; available to share our faith when the opportunity comes.* A plan of evangelism through establishing friendships is used in this setting.

Additionally, we minister through involvement in crisis-pregnancy centers, or wherever there are needs and people in crisis. We have singles throughout the community, ready to share Jesus Christ and invite singles to a loving support network through our church and our "Singles Alive" ministry. We reach out to those in hospitals and convalescent homes, we preach Sunday morning services, we visit the elderly and hurting.

One Christmas our singles group "adopted" three needy families and provided them with food, clothing, and gifts; singles reaching outside of themselves, acting in the true Christmas spirit. We have seen tremendous results from our launching out; our group has grown from thirty people in our early days to over 300 in three years' time.

By implementing these stages—planning, preparation, and propagation—in our singles group, we have developed maturity in our people and brought great fruit to the church and our singles ministry.

Our Need to Become More Evangelistically Minded

by Georgia Coates Gonzales
Singles ministry consultant, San Diego, California

O ften I've been asked, "What evangelistic program can we do that will win a lot of singles to Christ and build vision and faith in our members?"

My answer is that sharing Christ on a one-to-one basis is the most effective method I've seen (and the "program" I practice and teach to our singles). But for evangelism to truly be effective in our ministries, this one-on-one sharing must begin with those of us in leadership—you and me. Until and unless this happens, the church will probably not become much more effective in reaching nonChristians around us.

God Provides Our Appointments

Whenever I travel, I pray that God will give me opportunities to share Christ with those I meet. On a recent flight from San Francisco to San Diego, I noticed that the woman in her thirties seated next to me had a self-help book from a cultish self-actualization group.

Even as a "trained, professional Christian" my first response was fear, as I immediately assumed she was an "expert cynic" and could talk circles around my presentation of the gospel. But expecting her to be the divine appointment I'd just prayed for, I took a deep breath and jumped in.

As it turned out, she had been "searching for God for about four years." As our conversation developed, and after I shared my testimony, she accepted Christ. She kept telling me that she couldn't wait to share her newfound faith with her husband. Then she said she wished she would have understood these things during the many lonely years when she was single. She told me she had literally asked friends and colleagues how she could get to know God or be born again, but they couldn't tell her. Finally, she said she had brought along this book, holding up the one in her lap, in hopes of finding some answers on this weekend trip.

When her ride didn't show up at the airport, we had even more time to talk as I took her to my home for dinner and finally to her destination. Excited, she thanked me and left with a Bible in her hand!

Nothing that you or I can do in this world is more important or gratifying than reaching others with the gospel of Jesus Christ—helping others to grow, becoming witnesses for our Savior.

Work of the Spirit

Not once have I ever led anyone to Christ, and I never shall. However, I have had the privilege of praying with hundreds of people who have received Christ as a result of my witness. When a person receives Christ, it is the work of the Holy Spirit. As we sometimes teach our singles: "Witnessing is simply sharing Christ in the power of the Holy Spirit, leaving the results to God."

Equipped to Share Christ

When single Christians realize that this power is available and this message has been entrusted to them, and that people are hungry to know Christ, they get motivated. I personally have seen this happen and have seen a group take their eyes off themselves and begin sharing Christ daily.

I believe singles need training from their pastors and leaders to help them be more effective in sharing their faith. This training should include guidelines for

- telling His story—the gospel (tools like the *Four Spiritual Laws* can be helpful);
- telling my story—my personal testimony (which isn't the gospel but illustrates its power); and
- telling the other person's story— sharing how His story relates to the person with whom we are witnessing.

> "Rebecca Manley Pippert once made this very astute observation: 'Jesus always seemed to be doing two things: Asking questions and telling stories. Christians always seem to be doing two other things: Giving answers and "preaching." ' "

I'll illustrate by referring to my witnessing example. I had caught the attention of my friend on the airplane by telling her of my search for God and how I found Him. She listened intently as I explained how my life had changed and that I had even prayed earlier that I would sit next to someone on the plane with whom I could share this good news (my testimony).

At that point she still had many unanswered questions. But it was clear that she had been tremendously attracted to Jesus. This is what I call the "critical moment," a time when I transition to the other person's particular needs and relate why he or she needs a personal relationship with Christ (the other person's story).

Rebecca Manley Pippert once made this very astute observation: "Jesus always seemed to be doing two things: Asking questions and telling stories. Christians always seem to be doing two other things: Giving answers and 'preaching.' "

Asking questions, even personal ones, is a great way to start or develop a conversation. Telling "our own story," which everyone can become comfortable doing, is a good way to develop our listener's interest in Christ. Most people find it hard to argue with our own personal experience, especially when we tell it briefly with sincerity and compassion (never critically or pridefully).

Why We Do Not Witness

There are two basic reasons why the majority of Christian singles have never introduced anyone to Christ:
- The average Christian single is not living a Spirit-controlled life.
- The average Christian single doesn't know how to effectively communicate his or her faith. (Sometimes Christians lack witnessing opportunities because they snub or fear their nonChristian friends.)

Model What You Teach

Do you have twelve or twelve hundred singles in your group? Do you want to reach other singles in your city? Begin sharing your personal faith regularly under various circumstances.

Enthuse each single adult in your group with the knowledge that people become hungry to know God when they can see who God really is and how He changes lives. As you help them to grow and teach them to share their faith, you can offer some programs or events to which they can bring their nonChristian friends. But beware of the "evangelical trap."

Most Christians only know how to share Christ within the walls of a church—they bring their friends to let the pastor tell 'em! I'm not knocking evangelistic events. Our singles ministry has used many activities, such as dinners, concerts, topical debates, community activities, and fun and wacky parties, to attract new people to our group and to share Christ. But I strongly feel that God uses the individual to share and then follow up with a personal relationship (not just the pastor).

I would like to encourage each of us as leaders to continue having creative evangelistic events, but also to take the next step and share our faith on a regular basis as an overflow of a vital walk with Christ. Let's teach singles by our example and train them to become effective Spirit-filled witnesses to those in their sphere of influence.

Encouraging Singles to Be Missions-Minded

- Short-Term Missions for Single Adults:
  Why and How **218**
  by Chris Eaton

Short-Term Missions for Single Adults:
WHY AND HOW

by **Chris Eaton**
Executive director of Single Purpose Ministries, Tampa Bay/Orlando, Florida

C*hris Eaton has planned and supervised nine short-term mission trips to Haiti, the Dominican Republic, and Honduras. During the past five years he has taken more than 150 single adults on mission trips. Chris discusses in this article the benefits of short-term missions for singles and the first steps for a singles leader interested in leading a short-term missions trip.*

Why Be Involved In Short-Term Missions?

1. *We are called to be "world Christians."* Christ commanded us to go into all the world. We have a responsibility as singles leaders to help our singles fulfill that command. Short-term missions open singles' eyes to the needs in other countries and to the part they might play in meeting some of those needs. A trip overseas helps people realize that God is not just a God of white middle-class America.

2. *Singles who go overseas encounter God in a way they rarely do at home.* They are placed in an unfamiliar environment and culture. They don't have the comforts and conveniences of American life. They're working in close relationship with other believers. As a result, they learn a lot about themselves and about God. They grow spiritually.

Ninety-five percent of our people come back and say that God has taught them more in one or two weeks than they've learned in a long time. They learn about servanthood and living simply. They see nationals whose commitment to God sometimes far exceeds their own. They develop sensitive hearts.

Singles say they go to serve and give, and every year they come back saying, "I couldn't give enough compared to what the people gave me. What I learned far outweighs what I taught."

3. *A short-term missions trip can develop unity in a singles group.* When you take singles who are part of a community—a singles group—on a missions trip, the whole group grows. Recently, we took twenty-two singles to the Dominican Republic to build a school. Even the people who stayed behind got involved. They prayed, they gave, and now there's a school building that belongs not only to the Dominicans but also to a group of singles here. Now our singles care more about what happens in the Dominican Republic—and they care more about each other.

4. *Short-term missions make international news more interesting.* When Duvalier left Haiti, I wanted to go out and celebrate because people I

knew—my Haitian friends—were free from that repressive regime. Last year one of the guys said whenever he saw starving people on television, he'd always change the channel. While he was in a hospital in Haiti, he held a small child, and it was like God said to him, "Now try to change the channel." Today, he thinks in terms of his responsibility to help them.

5. *Singles who go on short-term missions meet needs that otherwise may never be met.* When we built the school in the Dominican Republic, the Dominicans thought we were angels that dropped from heaven. It was worth the trip just to see the looks on people's faces. To them it was a real miracle. A year ago they didn't dream they would have a building, and now it's there.

Also, if people get a burden for a particular country or ministry, they more consistently and faithfully give financially for the rest of their lives because bonding has taken place.

6. *Singles who go on short-term missions become more aware of needs in their own communities.* Singles I've taken to Haiti look around and say, "How can the wealthy live like this with all these slums around them?" Then they say, "Wait a minute—don't we have poor neighborhoods in our community, and don't we just stay away from them?" We've seen an increased interest in local community outreach among singles who have gone overseas.

7. *Singles on short-term missions often see God do the impossible.* For example, we went to build a clinic that a nurse in Haiti had been praying about for three years. The location was on a dirt road three hours outside of Port-au-Prince. The rains had been really bad—the roads were impassable and we couldn't get the materials out to the site. The team had nothing to do.

We said, "This woman has prayed for this; now we're here, and God, You've just got to answer our prayers." We finally began to get the materials to the site, and the team built the clinic in about six days.

Another time we committed to two building projects and raised about $11,000. When the buildings were complete, we had spent $14,000. Everything was paid for. We still don't know where the extra money came from.

Some cases are more dramatic than others, but even when it's not the "we almost all died" experience, people really grow and are stretched and learn to love the nationals. We have a high return rate. People can't wait to go on the next project. Some people have completely dedicated their vacations to going on short-term missions.

> **"Singles say they go to serve and give, and every year they come back saying, 'I couldn't give enough compared to what the people gave me. What I learned far outweighs what I taught.' "**

How To Plan
a Short-Term Missions Trip

1. *Check with your own church missions program.* Talk to the missions pastor or committee chairman in your church. Get the church behind you.

Write the missionaries your church supports and ask them how you and your singles can help the people there.

2. *Talk to people who have organized trips before.* Learn from those who have already made a missions trip—someone in your area, a missions agency, or someone like me. Be teachable. These trips require a lot of planning—if you just pop down to a country, you could have a big disaster. We don't want to destroy a missionary's work, or a church's testimony, or have someone get sick and die because of our foolishness. Most people who have taken short-term trips are more than willing to share ideas and materials they have used. For that matter, you might consider taking a joint trip with your singles and a group that has gone before.

3. *Visit missionaries.* Go to a country, or a couple of countries where you know missionaries. Talk to them. Observe their situation. Through them, make contacts with nationals who might be able to use your help. Or talk to missionaries while they are on furlough in your area.

4. *Decide on a specific project.* As you decide on a mission project, consider these elements:

> "Short-term missions are an adventure—a step of faith. Missions are an integral part of helping people grow in their relationship with God and opening their eyes to needs around them so they can make an impact on the world. As a single adult minister, I just can't imagine not taking singles on short-term missions."

- *The needs.* In Third-World countries, the needs are infinite. Look for the "real" needs, not only what you perceive to be needs. Talk to missionaries and nationals—trust their judgment.

- *Your resources.* How much money do you expect to raise? What skills do the people going on the trip have? How much time do you have? Be realistic about what you can accomplish on a trip.

- *Your goals.* What do you want to accomplish, not only in the country, but in the lives of your singles? Will your goals be better met through a construction project or a teaching or medical project?

It's important to work in partnership with missionaries and nationals. You don't want to take a bunch of Americans somewhere and do something unrelated to the local people. If you don't work with nationals, bonding won't take place between them and your group, and you won't know whether you're really helping the people.

5. *Consider going to the country for a set-up trip.* Unless an agency is making the arrangements for you, you should visit the country to make arrangements and get familiar with the environment before you take your group. And again, before you go, talk to people who have been there. We have developed a four-page checklist that covers all the questions we need to ask on set-up trips.

Once you've decided where to take a group and made the necessary connections, the success of the trip depends on planning the logistics. You must be prepared for the cultural norms of the country, health precautions, customs, food, and dress codes, to mention only a few details. As you plan, talk to someone who has done it before. Don't go off half-cocked. Learn from others' experience.

Short-term missions are an adventure—a step of faith. Missions are an integral part of helping people grow in their relationship with God and open-ing their eyes to needs around them so they can make an impact on the world. As a single adult minister, I just can't imagine not taking singles on short-term missions.

(For more help on leading a short-term team missions trip with your single adults, see the book Vacations with a Purpose—Leader's and Team Member's Manual *by Chris Eaton and Kim Hurst.)*

PART SEVEN:

Counseling Single Adults

ABOUT PART SEVEN

Over recent years,
counseling has played an increasingly
important role for anyone in ministry.

This is especially true in singles ministry.
Many singles are dealing with relational issues,
divorce, single parenting, grief, and other traumas.

It is not possible for a singles pastor or leader
to deal with all of these issues
and expect to maintain his or her sanity.

But here are some guidelines—shared
by both counselors and single adult leaders—
to help you be more effective
in your counseling ministry.

SIXTEEN

Guidelines for Counseling Singles

COUNSELING IN THE GRAY AREAS: How to Give Advice When Everything Isn't Black and White

an interview with Lewis Smedes
*Former professor of theology
and ethics at Fuller Theological
Seminary, Pasadena, California*

What do you do when you have a situation you don't know how to handle? How do you know the wise thing to do in a difficult counseling situation?

First, I generally like to avoid giving specific answers to difficult situations. It's more important to help people become responsible and thoughtful in reaching their own decisions than telling them what I think they should do.

But there are three basic guidelines that each of us can follow when trying to determine the right thing to say or do. I call them my "three Rs": rules, results, and responsibility.

Rules

Rules are like a road map that helps us find our way when we're traveling in a strange country. The map doesn't inhibit our freedom—it helps us reach our destination. The Bible has two absolute moral rules. The first is to always be just and fair. The second is to be loving and helpful. Love and justice are the two most important rules to follow. Make every major life decision—and do all of your counseling—based on love and justice.

Results

Another way to evaluate your counseling is to ask whether it's helpful or not. Does it have good results? However, you have to help your counselee decide what constitutes a good result. And who is it good for? Your counselee? Other people? The majority? And when is it good? Right now? Later? Cocaine may seem great for right now, but it's disastrous over the long haul. You've got to help the person you're counseling have a sense of moral values in order to judge whether or not the results are good.

Responsibility

Being responsible is an important factor in making right choices. Help your counselee ask, "What is likely to happen if I do A or if I do B? How will this affect my commitments to Christ, to my family, to the church?"

I have a catalog of tests for determining the responsible thing to do. I ask myself these questions:

- Have I prayed for and exercised the gift of discernment?
- Do I have all the facts?
- What would a specific person whom I admire do in this situation?
- Is this appropriate to my position as a pastor?

Many times moral decisions are not

simply decisions between right and wrong. They're decisions between the better way and a worse way of doing good things.

What role does community, the church, or one's network of friends play in good counseling and decision making?

I think it's dangerous to be a lone ranger. Discernment of the will of God is a community affair. We need community because none of us is wise enough. We need common wisdom. I think the pastors these days have to be told, "Hey, before you decide what's right and what's wrong, consult your colleagues, or some wise, discerning people in your congregation (without divulging confidentiality). Don't be a lone ranger."

After the person you are counseling has sought advice and wisdom, read the Bible and prayed, what do you say to help the person make the decisions he or she needs to make?

I'd say: Don't presume that God will give you a divine revelation about what's right and wrong in the gray areas of life. Dare to make choices knowing that you might be wrong sometimes. Don't allow the fear of being wrong paralyze you. The last word about choices is not whether they're right or wrong, but that you can be forgiven for making wrong choices. Morality is about making right choices. Faith is about being forgiven for making wrong ones.

Biblical Guidelines for Counseling Singles

by James Richwine
Minister with singles at Coral Ridge Presbyterian Church, Fort Lauderdale, Florida

Counseling—a recent trend in Christian circles—can include everything from a few minutes of encouraging conversation to months of weekly meetings with a person to help him or her overcome difficult personal problems. Unfortunately, the purpose and goals of counseling have become even broader. Many counselors merely help their counselees adjust to society without solving deeper problems.

Counseling Defined

I believe a good definition of counseling is, "That process whereby one person equips another person to
• define and analyze personal problems according to Scripture;
• find principles in Scripture that apply to them;
• map out a plan to apply these principles."

The goal of Christian counseling is to "present every man complete in Christ" (Colossians 1:28, NASB). That means we are to help the counselee become more like Christ in thought, word, and deed—that is, to become sanctified. To do any less is to shortchange the counselee who looks to us for guidance.

Philosophy of Ministry

The following four principles should form the philosophy of a counseling ministry with your singles.

- Your counsel must be biblically based—the truths you teach must be founded in Scripture.
- Your counsel must be practical. Scripture references should be accompanied by practical applications. Every assignment must have measurable objectives.
- You must "wean" your counselees; train them to solve their own problems.
- Your own relationship with God must be growing.

Getting Started

You may have a good philosophy of ministry and biblical goals, but how do you get a counseling ministry started with your singles? Here are some suggestions:

Get training. Becoming an effective counselor takes effort. Seek out the materials and centers for counselor training that will help you become better equipped. If you need more practice or supervision, arrange for an experienced counselor to help you. Start by counseling only a few individuals.

Offer counsel in your Bible teachings. If you teach a singles class every week, teach more than simple knowledge. Address the problems, thoughts, and fears facing your singles, and offer specific solutions. Soon your people will realize that you have answers that really work. (Note: Do not use illustrations describing counselees in your group. This breaks their trust and discourages them from sharing openly with you.)

Develop counseling resources, such as

- a library of books and video and audio tapes;
- contacts with professional counselors to whom you may refer your singles;
- a secretary who can listen to and pray with people and determine (at least in a preliminary way) the need of those who call for counsel;
- small ministry groups to provide fellowship, support, and opportunity for singles to help each other.

Train others to assist you. After your counseling ministry is established, train lay counselors to help carry the load. A lay counselor should

- be applying God's principles in his or her own life;
- show dependence on the Holy Spirit;
- not be a novice in the Christian faith;
- be compassionate, humble, and insightful.

Reminders for Counselors

When counseling singles, keep the following points in mind:

Move beyond the circumstances to the underlying attitudes and beliefs. It's easy to get caught up in the difficulties a single person faces, but remember that everyone—single or married—has the same tendency toward sin. Of course, every situation is different, but don't focus on circumstances.

Focus on the individuals' attitudes and responses.

Learn about the common problems singles face. These include loneliness, single parenting, dating, sexual temptation, drug or alcohol abuse, social adjustment, and self-image.

Find the balance between judgment and compromise. You must not judge the counselee, but neither can you compromise the principles of God's Word. Present the standards of Scripture as absolute, but do so in such a way that shows compassion for the counselee.

Be aware of the dangers in counseling. Don't allow any of your counselees, particularly those of the opposite sex, to become dependent on you. Discourage "hero worship"; it can create some very sticky problems. All of us have a deep need to be appreciated, respected, and listened to. Be aware of these needs in your counselees (and in yourself), and always work to keep your counseling relationships healthy.

In Closing

Here are some of the books and training centers that I recommend. These resources can equip you for a more effective ministry with your single adults.[30]

Inside Out, Larry Crabb
Encouragement, Larry Crabb
Competent to Counsel, Jay Adams
Christian Counselor's Manual, Jay Adams
Meeting Counseling Needs Through the Local Church, Larry Crabb (Textbook for The Institute of Biblical Counseling)

For Further Study

Christian Counseling and Educational Foundation
1790 East Willow Grove Avenue
Laverock, PA 19118
Phone (215) 884-7676

The Institute of Biblical Counseling
16075 West Belleview Avenue
Morrison, CO 80465
Phone (303) 697-5425

We Don't Live in a Pain-Free World

an interview with Larry Crabb
Founder of The Institute of Biblical Counseling, Denver, Colorado

What concerns do you have about what you see happening in single adult ministries?

First, let me say that I believe the church must address single adult needs. The single adult population is not going to wane. It is a fact of life. But one trend that bothers me is this: It seems that many single adult ministries exist primarily to help singles accept their singleness, to help them feel complete and whole and just as worthwhile as a married person. That seems to be the underlying motivation behind many of the efforts to reach single adults.

The truth is that I don't think single adult pastors should be focusing on helping their singles feel better. That is a kind of kid-glove mentality. I don't mean to sound insensitive or antagonistic toward single adult ministry. I would say the same thing to those working with married couples or pregnant teenage girls.

Instead, what we need to focus on is that each of us can face the truth and deal with it, because we live in the strength of the fact that there is a God who is good. That is the only true route to joy.

So you feel that the focus in many single adult ministries is in the wrong place?

Yes. One major mistake many of us in leadership make when dealing with any specific group of people—whether always-single, divorced, widowed, or married—is to essentially say to them that somehow our ministry will relieve the ache in their soul. This seems to be the implicit premise behind singles ministries (and marriage seminars too!). The church tells its people that if they follow its teaching and understanding of the Christian life—be it charismatic, Bible exegesis, or strong discipleship—the ache in their soul will go away. But it isn't going to happen. Because we live in a fallen world, there are pains and heartaches that cannot be relieved. I believe one of the heresies of the evangelical church today is that we are telling our people they can have, here and now, the blessings that are really reserved only for heaven.

WHEN SINGLE COUNSELEES TAKE ADVANTAGE OF YOU
by Timothy Foster
Licensed psychologist in California

Editor's Note: Many times pastors/leaders have the temptation or desire—noble as it may be—to "rescue" single adults in need. But by becoming the rescuer, you inevitably become the victim. Here are some suggestions that can help you maintain healthy counseling relationships with your single adults.

Don't Tell Counselees to Drop By Anytime

That is virtually always a mistake because you will get burned out and end up not being a help to anyone. It is far kinder to everyone to suggest a specific time that is convenient to you. Remember, you are doing counselees a favor by listening to their problems and trying to help. You're probably doing it for free, so don't allow others to take unfair advantage of you.

I'm aware that I probably just offended some dear idealistic people, but once you've made this mistake and left your son's birthday party to listen to somebody tell you the same problem for the third time in a week, *you'll realize that structuring your counseling to have a beginning and an ending is more loving than allowing yourself to be drained.*

I have only thrown one person out of my counseling office in fifteen years. That was a woman I allowed to take advantage of me until I was victimized, and finally I exploded. She would show up for appointments an hour and a half late, expecting to be seen without paying anything toward the agreed-upon charge. (I do counseling as a profession, so I have to charge people.) Finally, after months of this, she

Are you saying that the church or pastor can do little or nothing to help ease the heartaches of life?

Obviously, it's possible to provide relief for some level of a person's pain. But in my opinion it's not the job of the pastor or a requirement of the church to make us pain-free. In fact, I think the single adult has a unique ache that should be "exploited" for the good of the individual rather than be relieved.

What do you mean by "exploiting the ache"?

First, the ache can be exploited by giving perspective. Second, it can be exploited by helping us see the many subtle, unhealthy ways in which we try to relieve the ache. Let me explain.

In Romans 8:23, the Apostle Paul follows the phrase "we groan inwardly" with "we wait eagerly."[32] This is where our aches become an opportunity to get things in perspective, to remind us that we really are strangers and pilgrims living in expectation of something better to come. There's coming a time when the tears and heartache will be gone. But now our primary purpose is to worship and serve God rather than seek personal fulfillment.

Even when I hurt as a married man—for example, when my wife and I aren't getting along—I need to do at least two things. First, I need to work on my marriage and see where I'm failing. Second, I need to remind myself that there is no relationship on earth that is not disappointing at some level.

started blaming me for some problems she had, and I blew up. I am not proud of that, but I have tried to learn from it.

Avoid Being a Rescuer

There is an inevitable series of events that, once set into motion, always progresses toward the same conclusion. It begins when you, the counselor, make yourself a rescuer. *You become a rescuer when you accept the responsibility to fix someone's problems.* Healthy counseling accepts only the responsibility to try to help the counselee fix his or her own problem. There is a major difference between the two approaches.

Once you're the rescuer, you inevitably become the victim. You will be taken advantage of and misused. You see, *when you communicate the message that you are going to be responsible for the rescue, counselees feel they don't have to be responsible anymore.* It's your problem, so they let you do the work.

Avoid Being a Persecutor

The last part of the inevitable series of consequences is that sooner or later you will become the persecutor. When I threw that woman out of my office, I let out all of my frustration and anger on her at once. I ended up persecuting or hurting the very person I started out to rescue. Eventually you have to stop carrying people because they simply become too heavy. And when you stop carrying them, they get hurt.

I didn't discover this pattern of human behavior. Someone showed it to me once, and I have found it to be true many times since then.[31]

It also can be a reminder that I'm living here on the Lord's terms. So by exploiting the ache I can gain perspective.

We also exploit the ache by seeing the subtle, unhealthy things we do to try to get relief. Often, we use others to relieve the ache; this is almost always the opposite of love. When one person proves incapable of totally eliminating our pain, we'll use somebody else. We are living for ourselves rather than for others. This is one reason why there is such a perpetual vicious cycle in the relationship world. Going from mate to mate, from church to church, from singles group to singles group, or from alcohol to cocaine—they're all unhealthy ways to relieve the pain. Somehow we must understand that in this world we can never be pain-free. And we must stop using people in our attempt to be so.

> "The truth is that I don't think single adult pastors should be focusing on helping their singles feel better. That is a kind of kid-glove mentality. I don't mean to sound insensitive or antagonistic toward single adult ministry. I would say the same thing to those working with married couples or pregnant teenage girls."

You mentioned earlier that single adult ministries often focus on the wrong area. Where do you think the focus should be?

Rather than looking at a person's singleness, why they are single, or the pros and cons of being single, let's look at his or her life as a Christian. When we are moving towards God, then whatever His best is for our life will be more easily realized. If it's marriage, fine. If it's effective singleness, fine.

The focus areas that need foremost attention in a singles ministry—or any ministry—should be the things we are doing that are keeping us away from God. When we honestly deal with these, then I think the issues of aloneness, separateness, and "feeling better about being single" become less significant.

What advice do you have for the single adult who struggles with loneliness?

One of the assumptions many single adults make is that they experience more of a sense of loneliness than a married person does. In one sense that is very true. Every night I go home to my wife and I climb into the same bed with her. The single adult does not have that level of companionship.

But I think the single person ought to be aware of the fact that there is a sense of loneliness in living in a fallen world. That loneliness is shared by *everyone* who is honest.

Laying the Foundation for a Counseling Ministry

by Paul M. Petersen
Minister with singles at Highland Park Presbyterian Church, Dallas, Texas

A bortion, abuse, broken hearts, corrupt employers, divorce, homosexual lifestyles, "living together," lost jobs, pregnancies, premarital counseling, postmarital counseling, sexually transmitted diseases, sexual addictions, suicide—I have dealt with all of these in the past twelve months as a single adult minister. What's a leader to do? How can we begin to counsel the singles we minister with?

The Climate of Trust

A climate of trust and openness to receiving counsel must be the foundation of an effective counseling ministry. The following six qualities will build this foundation among your singles:

1. *Availability.* Our singles must know—and feel—that we are always available (except on those important days off—and even then in crises) to listen, to act, and to intervene.

2. *Prayer.* When I began praying for each of my singles by using the class roster, the requests for counseling increased dramatically. Others sense the power of prayer in a Christian's life.

3. *Confidentiality.* Our singles must know that whatever they share will remain confidential (except in cases of child abuse, homicide, and suicide, which we're legally required to report).

4. *Friendship.* Our singles must sense our deep concern for them as friends. If they sense that we are not truly interested, or can't be bothered, then our ministry will be severely limited.

5. *Listening.* The basic skill of good counseling is the ability to listen without interrupting or daydreaming. Singles (and many married people) do not have "built-in listeners," so they need a counselor who listens.

6. *Education.* We must educate our singles that we are willing and available to pray, keep confidences, listen, and befriend them. This education takes place formally in the classroom, but also through the informal network of relationships within the group.

Peer Counseling

A single adult leader can be an effective counselor or friend to only a few individuals, so it's critical that we train lay people to be sensitive to the hurts and needs of others around them. The best counseling is peer counseling, where deep mutual friendship needs are met.

I firmly believe that the best single adult ministries are owned and run by the singles themselves. A single adult minister spends his or her time most effectively by training and advising lay leaders. When you do so, your ministry is multiplied. If you or other staff

members at your church feel unquali-
fied to train lay counselors, other
churches or counseling centers in your
area may have the resources to share
with you.

Referring Counselees

Many of us don't have degrees in
counseling and can very easily get in
over our heads in counseling situations. It's very important to know a
trusted professional counselor to
whom you can refer clients. If you
find yourself counseling in an area
for which you have no training or
experience, refer the counselee to a
professional.

There are other reasons for referring
clients. I try to keep my counseling load
at less than ten hours per week, so it
doesn't dangerously consume my time
and emotions. If you allow it to, counseling can fill your week. I also set a
maximum number of times I counsel
a person before referring him or
her. If you must see someone more
than three or four times (my rule of
thumb is two times), he or she
probably needs the attention of a
trained professional.

It is not only possible, but necessary,
to have an effective counseling ministry
for singles. If you haven't yet established such a ministry, start with the six
basics to establish a climate of trust.
Counseling can become one of the
most sought after—and productive
—areas of your ministry.

A CASE STUDY:
"A Christian Leader Came on to One of My Single Women"

with a suggested solution from
French A. Jones
Counselor in Dallas, Texas

The Problem

"One of the single women in my
group (we'll call her Susan) came to
my office this week and told me the
following: 'I recently served on the hospitality committee for a singles conference in this city. Part of my assignment
was to assist one of the speakers in
town for the conference (we'll call him
Dr. Taylor). During the conference we
had the opportunity to visit several
times. We seemed to sort of click.

" 'Toward the end of the week,
when I dropped Dr. Taylor off at his
hotel, he invited me to come to his
room. While there, he began talking
about how his sexual relationship with
his wife was not good because she had
lupus and seldom felt well enough for
sex. He was lonely, he missed a good
sexual relationship, and asked if I
might be willing to have sex with him. I
suppose a part of me was tempted to
say yes. But I was also quite shocked
and disappointed that he would come
on to me like this. I said no and left,
rather disillusioned about Christian
men.

" 'Since then, I've been struggling with my anger and disappointment with Christian leaders. I tend to be much more suspicious, and I sometimes find myself questioning the truth of the Bible, wondering if there is any real difference between Christian men and nonChristian men.' "

A Possible Solution

Tough problems require courage and convictions—courage to confront the issues and convictions based on biblical principles. Too often, single adult pastors and leaders lack one or the other. Without courage, we fail our people. Without convictions based on God's Word, we fail our Lord.

Confronting Dr. Taylor

To begin with, I would confront Dr. Taylor and his sinful behavior. The following are guidelines I would recommend for confronting such issues.

1. *Make sure your motives are proper.* Galatians 6:1 instructs "you who are spiritual restore such a one [caught in sinful behavior] in the spirit of gentleness, considering yourself, lest you also be tempted" (NKJV). We must confront with a humble attitude.

2. *Make sure you have the facts.* Matthew 18:16 says we should "take one or two others along with you, that every word may be confirmed by the evidence of two or three witnesses" (RSV). What are the facts of the situation? Is the information firsthand? What is the issue to be confronted? We must be clear on each of these points in order to allow for a confession to be made.

3. *Meet in private with the individual to be confronted.* Begin by sharing your feelings. Then share the observed behavior. By sharing your feelings you communicate your frustration or anger. By relating observed behavior instead of accusing the person, you keep communication going in a relatively nonthreatening atmosphere.

This allows the person to either ask forgiveness or work through the issue with you. If the individual does not respond with a repentant heart, then you must confront him or her with "the victim." If that fails, you must bring the person before the church. Matthew 18 is clear about this process, even though it is very tough to actually do.

> "Tough problems require courage and convictions— courage to confront the issues and convictions based on biblical principles. Too often, single adult pastors and leaders lack one or the other. Without courage, we fail our people. Without convictions based on God's Word, we fail our Lord."

Counseling Susan

I would begin by saying that no one is perfect in this world. "We all stumble in many ways" (James 3:2). Even though Dr. Taylor is a Christian leader, he still stumbles and sins. I would seek to help Susan understand some of the issues relating to sin in the world and our constant need to depend on the Lord in all circumstances of life.

Next, I would explain to Susan my plan to confront Dr. Taylor personally and seek her permission to do so.

I would tell her that I would not bring her name up in the confrontation.

Finally, I would seek to maintain communication with Susan in the subsequent weeks. Her church involvement is vital at this time in her life. The greatest potential damage for Susan is that this situation might hinder her growth in the Lord. By maintaining contact with her, the Lord may use me to turn her discouragement into a vital learning experience.

SEVENTEEN

Helping Singles Heal Their Damaged Emotions

Helping the Emotionally Damaged Single Adult

by Rod Chandler
*Associate pastor at Oakview
Church, Centralia, Washington*

As I try to guide people toward healing, I attempt to find answers to the following questions.

How Serious Is the Damage?

Did one major event or a series of events bring it on? I believe there are basically two types of people with emotional damage: the *badly bruised* and the *crushed*.

Bruised people will usually heal "naturally," as do broken bones or minor cuts. In the healing process they primarily need someone to listen to them, hug them, and reassure them of God's love and peace. They need to be assured that they are valued, and reminded that God desires to lift off their load of guilt and set them free.

On the other hand, people who have been crushed present tougher problems. Some we pastors can help and others we cannot. Based on my experience, many crushed people need to be referred to professional counselors. As their pastors, we need to be especially supportive with our love and affirmation, making sure they know they are not being abandoned. But the counselor is often better equipped to help them recover. After all, what is our goal? To genuinely help people, or to always say yes?

Following are some clues that a referral may be needed:
• Progress has ceased.
• Progress gained during counseling sessions is lost between visits.
• You say the same things each visit.
• You are fatigued by the visits (or thoughts of them).
• You think you are the healer.

What Is the Person's Concept of God?

Is his God a loving Father or a distorted dictator? Does she believe that God created her uniquely and on purpose? Does he believe that God cares for him and really longs to bring him peace and inner healing?

I don't believe we should over-spiritualize every problem. But I am convinced that if the individual's concept of God is wrong, he or she is sealing off God's ability to heal. Clear teaching about the basics of who God is needs to be an ongoing part of our programming and counseling.

What Are the Individual's Self-Talk Habits?

Once when I was experiencing considerable emotional pain, a counselor challenged me to log and examine my self-talk to help me get a clearer picture of who or what was controlling my feelings and views of myself. The procedure was basically this:

1. Recognize any negative self-talk

(e.g., "I always do that wrong").
2. Note the event that triggered it.
3. Identify the technique used (e.g., oversimplification).
4. Admit how it made me feel.
5. Challenge the conclusion about myself objectively and intellectually.
6. Refute the negative conclusion on the basis of Scripture.

This discipline is a very helpful tool. It helps clarify any distortion between people's objective thoughts and subjective feelings about themselves. It also challenges them to use the Bible to renew their minds (Romans 12:2).

Am I Inhibiting the Person's Need to Seek God?

It is very easy for a wounded person to slip into a "doctor-patient" mind-set. When it comes to spiritual matters though, I'm no doctor. I'm just a person who was terminal with sin but then accepted Jesus.

While dealing with one young woman with a long history of depression, I finally enabled her to see that she didn't need to hear me quote biblical principles to her each week. She needed to read them, quote them, and memorize them for herself. The promises of God were for her to embrace, not for me to hand-feed her weekly. Now, she needs me much less and is open to God much more. Don't let your people make you God's exclusive voice for their lives.

Finally, remember that Jesus is the Messiah, not you.

Creating a Healing Environment for Your Ministry

an interview with French A. Jones
Counselor in Dallas, Texas

A former single adult pastor at Northwest Bible Church in Dallas, French Jones now counsels hurting people on a full-time basis. Nevertheless, he believes emotional healing is not the ultimate goal, but a means to a higher calling—that of making disciples. Here he encourages singles ministries to catch this vision.

What are damaged emotions and how do they affect single adults?

Damaged emotions are hurts from the past that affect someone's present and future. These hurts can stem from all kinds of things, but most seem to be relationship-oriented. Examples of relationship hurts include divorce, a broken engagement, or lack of fulfillment in dating. From my observation, divorce seems to be the most prevalent.

What can a single adult pastor do to help heal damaged emotions?

First, a single adult pastor should *recognize the need* to deal with individuals who are hurting emotionally. The need is so great that we sometimes think, "I could never do it all," and thus end up not doing anything. This kind of thinking is a cop-out. The Lord never intended for us to take on that weight ourselves. However, He did provide an environment for healing to take place: the church. We, as single adult pastors and leaders, must seek to foster the kind of atmosphere in our churches whereby singles who come to our groups will feel unconditional love and acceptance. This is foundational to helping people heal.

> "Emotional healing is not the goal. It's simply a means to the end that the individual will become emotionally healed in order to become a maker of disciples for the Kingdom of God."

How can a single adult pastor develop a healing atmosphere?

Leadership is the key. A healing environment within a singles ministry *must begin at the top and filter down throughout the leadership of the ministry.* At Northwest Bible Church, the senior pastor has made a commitment to assist me in creating this type of atmosphere. He talks about his commitment to singles in his sermons. The elder board and the leaders involved in our singles and singles again ministry also work to create a healing environment.

In addition to the top staff members, the single adult pastor *must train leaders* how to reach out to hurting singles.

What other resources can the single adult pastor utilize to help heal damaged emotions?

Too often the single adult leader feels a need to "reinvent the wheel" when it comes to ministering to hurting individuals. One of the main things a pastor can do is to be aware of counselors, psychologists, and medical personnel to whom he can refer those in need.

Knowing what I can and cannot do is a step in the right direction. Even though I might want to help someone, I may not have the training, education, experience, or time to help. In that case, the best thing I can do is to refer the individual to someone who is capable.

For example, Jane came to me for counseling, but after working with her for a number of sessions, I concluded that I needed to refer her to another counselor better trained in a particular area. With her permission, I first called the counselor and discussed Jane's need. Then I set up an appointment with the counselor for Jane to confirm by phone. The transition went smoothly, and she received the help I was not able to give.

Find out what is available in your area. Once you refer someone to another professional, keep in touch with the counselee to make sure the person is benefiting from that service.

How can the single adult pastor communicate to others his vision of healing damaged emotions?

It's difficult to communicate something you don't have. I want my folks to have the real disease, not just be inoculated. I want them to be motivated out of a love for our Lord and the desire for Him to use them to further His Kingdom. Emotional healing is not the goal. It's simply a means to the end that the individual will become emotionally healed in order to become a maker of disciples for the Kingdom of God. The vision must be lived out, not just by the single adult pastor but also by leaders who are sharing the vision. A vision without action is only a dream.

The vision I have for our group is to be a healing body of Christians who don't just "have the vision" but who are also "doing the vision." The blessing comes when I hear how much they enjoyed helping someone through a difficult time. When this happens, Christians experience the joy of ministry, my time is multiplied, the hurting individual receives help, and the Lord receives the glory!

Hang in there when things seem to be all wrong; the most fulfilling thing in the world is to be used by the Lord for His purposes. As we seek to help others grow in that process, they experience the joy as well. Keep your vision fresh, develop leaders who share the same vision, and trust the Lord throughout the entire process. After all, He is far more concerned for His ministry than we are.

PART EIGHT:

Divorce and Remarriage

ABOUT PART EIGHT

Few, if any, subjects create
more controversy within the church than
divorce and remarriage.

But regardless of where your church
stands on these issues,
in order to have an effective ministry
with single adults, the issues must be
addressed and resolved.

The reality is that today nearly one-half
of all marriages involve at least one
formerly married person.

In this section, several leaders—from various
theological perspectives—look at the trends,
as well as the divorce/remarriage issue,
and some of the possible implications
for a ministry with single adults.

Divorce in Our Culture

Interviews with Judith Wallerstein

Divorce: The Uncomfortable Bedfellow of American Society

Jim Smoke interviews Judith Wallerstein
Executive director of the Center for the Family in Transition, Corte Madera, California

What are the three biggest things you've learned about divorce during the past twenty years of study and research?

First, divorce has a long-term effect on children. Many of the consequences may not be noticeable at first. The ramifications of divorce can be like a sleeping virus, lying dormant for years. But then they will tend to crescendo when the young person reaches late adolescence and young adulthood.

It's at this stage in life when people begin establishing relationships with the opposite sex, fall in love, make commitments, form a family. The process of making all these adult decisions takes center stage. And that's often when the anxieties and concerns about the failure of their parents' marriage will surface and have a significant effect on their life.

Second, divorce is a crisis like no other crisis in the life of an adult. At first we thought we might be looking at a crisis similar to bereavement. But divorce has a much stronger effect, generally speaking, in terms of anger, jealousy, depression, rage, and the sense of having been rejected and humiliated to the core. One doesn't see this to the same extent in other life crises. It's clearly different and more extensive.

Third, the child's experience in a divorced family is entirely different from that of the adult. Children feel and see the divorce as a continuum in their experience that tends to shadow their whole growing-up period. It begins with the failed marriage, the dislocation of the family unit, and continues with the many stresses of the post-divorce period, even into adulthood. They tend to feel that they lost their childhood because of the parents' divorce.

On the other hand, adults see it in "chapters." Their first marriage was chapter one: "I made a mistake, but I hope to build something better to replace the marriage that failed." Rather than a continuum, they are more likely to see specific beginnings and endings. One needs to recognize that the child and adult experience divorce in uniquely different ways.

I don't know whether those are the three most important things I've learned, but they are the first three that come to mind.

From your vantage point, what do ministers and church leaders need to communicate to those who are divorced?

They need to say in every way they can, "You're not alone. We are here to stand by you, to support you." They need to convey the same kind of concern and the same kind of compassion that they do for families in any other kind of crisis. And they need to find especially effective ways to speak to the adolescents who often have nobody to talk with.

But my sense is that this doesn't happen very much. There's a negative reaction that seems to occur, consciously or unconsciously. The family feels they will be humiliated, or rejected, so they leave the church. And the minister feels uncomfortable, embarrassed; he stumbles along, not sure about what to do or say.

The bottom line is that—without anybody intending to do so—when the family needs support the most, they don't have it. In fact, divorce is the only crisis I can think of where the support falls away when the need is at its greatest.

For example, in death, everybody comes to offer support and condolences. From what we've learned recently about the grief process, that support may not stay around long enough. But at least people come. Neighbors come, friends come, a lot of people come.

But divorce sets up a phobic reaction. People are afraid that it's catching, that it's going to somehow expose the problems in their own marriage.

Death has rituals. You know what to say. It may be hard to say something in the midst of the tragedy and loss, but you generally have some idea of what to say.

But what do you say to the divorced?

> "The bottom line is that—without anybody intending to do so—when the family needs support the most, they don't have it. In fact, divorce is the only crisis I can think of where the support falls away when the need is at its greatest."

WILL THE HIGH DIVORCE RATE CONTINUE?
an interview with Judith Wallerstein

Do you believe that the next decade in America will see an increase or decrease in the divorce rate?

I think there is both *good news* and *bad news*. The good news is that it seems that one of the immediate effects of my book—as well as the ongoing ripple effect—is that there may be more thought given before people rush out to get a divorce. Many therapists are now telling me that people are coming in and standing on the threshold longer, hesitating to go through with a divorce. People are asking, "What is it going to mean to my children?" They appear to be giving the issues and ramifications of divorce more serious thought.

There's no more of the creative divorce of the seventies. That's passe. In the seventies the attitude was, "Everyone can do it. It's okay. Come on in, the water's fine!" It's too early to say if this more cautious approach will continue, but at least for now that seems to be happening.

The bad news, on the other hand, is that we have an entire generation of kids growing up in divorced homes. The divorce rate, at least in the past, has tended to be higher for such children once they become married adults. So we could potentially see a long-term climbing divorce rate in this country.

Do you express sympathy for the family? Or do you say, "Good. I'm glad you finally got rid of that person who was making your life miserable"?

Consequently, because most people don't know what to say, they say nothing. They walk the other way, cross the street. It would be nice to see the church taking the lead in providing a model of support to those experiencing divorce.

Why do we as a society still seem to be so uncomfortable with divorce?

This seems to be true even though it is highly visible on television and in the movies—every soap is peppered with divorce. But our national psyche still seems to struggle with it.

I believe it's because we are at a new place in human history, and most of us don't realize it. There's never before been a human society where marriages have broken up at the rate we are seeing it happen today. One out of every two marriages ends in divorce, and this is making us very uncomfortable. People are anxious about it. You seldom go to a wedding without somehow thinking, "I hope this one's going to last." So the fact that it is a common occurrence has not made it any less a source of shame or guilt. It has not become a comfortable bedfellow because, in our hearts, we're worried about the consequences.

That's why my book hit a nerve. It didn't say divorce is bad, per se. It simply said that divorce is serious and that it is accompanied by long-term consequences. I think we've known that. And I think we've been looking the other way because we haven't known what to do with this phenomenon.

We know in our bones that it isn't okay. And we also know in our bones that we're not going back. There's no

---

IS THE FAMILY DISAPPEARING IN AMERICA?
Judith Wallerstein answers . . .

I don't believe so. One of the bright spots in my research results is that—although divorce has difficult, long-term effects on kids—these children do not seem to be taking relationships lightly. If I had told you that these children were cynical, you would have said, "Of course." But these aren't the findings. It seems that they haven't given up on the family. This is one of the most wonderful findings. I think it's partly because the children have been so worried and concerned about their parents during their growing-up years. The majority of the kids I studied seem to be taking relationships seriously. They seem to be showing a great deal of concern for their siblings and for their parents. Their sense of relationship has not disappeared. They want marriage and commitment in their life, in their future. They believe that cheating on a mate is wrong. In some ways, they are much more conservative in their attitudes than their parents. And I think that is optimistic.

So it's not like the family is disappearing. But whether these kids will be able to put it together and make it work once they are adults will depend, in part, on what kind of help we can give them as a society, as the church. It's going to be an uphill battle for them. I truly hope that the church will provide them a healthy model of stability and support.

tremendous evidence that marriages were so great in the generation of our parents. So we really don't know what to do or where to go. I think this is a source of profound concern in American society. People are growing increasingly troubled about our staggering number of broken homes.

They know that the television image of divorce is mostly fantasy. It's not real. It seldom deals with the consequences. It's also interesting to note that the favorite TV programs are not about divorce but about families that stick together—"The Cosby Show," "Roseanne"—where the problems are solved in thirty minutes.

Let's say there is a couple who have been married for thirty or more years and then they get divorced. Their kids are grown and they have grandchildren. In other words, grandma and grandpa are getting divorced. How does this affect the adult children and grandchildren?

Historically, grandparents don't get divorced. They bake brownies and give out Christmas presents. But when it happens, it has a profound effect on the family.

Most of my research and writing has focused on the younger children of divorce, not adult children. But I get a lot of letters from people who ask, "Why didn't you write about me? My parents divorced when I was twenty-seven (or thirty-five), and it changed my life." That group has been very poorly studied. We need more research in this area. But what we can say is that the divorce certainly affects them deeply.

First, they feel drawn to move back to help their parents. Oftentimes, they have a parent who has really fallen apart. So they have the issue of "I've got my own children who need me. I've got my mother who is falling apart. What should I do?" There is a real physical and emotional pull. Should I leave my kids and my husband and go back a thousand miles and spend three weeks or months? It's a mess.

The second biggest thing people write me about is that it shakes their view of the stability and security of the home. It rocks them. They can't go home again. This is especially difficult when kids go away to college and then their parents get divorced. The kids feel—and often correctly—that as long as they were home they could hold the marriage together. . . . There are some significant issues that need to be dealt with here.

> **"There's never before been a human society where marriages have broken up at the rate we are seeing it happen today. One out of every two marriages ends in divorce, and this is making us very uncomfortable."**

What do you say to a fifty-five-year-old woman who comes in and says, "After thirty-five years, he's asking for a divorce." To a child you can say, "Your whole life is ahead of you." But what do you say to an older woman; especially when she's invested the major portion of her life in this marital relationship?

If she's had her entire life wrapped up in the marriage, then she's going to be in deep trouble. You have to try to help her think about other interests in life: maybe going back to school, looking at a new career, something she has always thought about doing. But it's also important that she get used to the idea that she may be single for the rest of her life. I don't think you need to tell her that; she probably already knows.

Sometimes I'm not sure she does. There's often this fantasy that someone, someplace. . . .

Yes. But I don't think it's the therapist's or pastor's job to disabuse people of hope, solutions, fantasies. In fact, let's help them keep it alive. True, it's unhealthy to build your whole life around an illusion. And if finding a man is the only thing she can think about, then she's in trouble. But to hold on to a hope is wonderful. Why not? It enhances life.

John Powell recently wrote a book called *Happiness Is an Inside Job*. The message is that happiness comes from within you, not from another person. Do you agree?

Only to a point. The fact is that we live in a world together. If you are totally dependent on outside circumstances for your happiness, that's one thing; but the truth is we need significant others in our lives. We were designed by our Creator to live this way. It is true for all of us, but it may be especially true for those facing the ills of growing old.

The Right to Remarry

The Case for a Redemptive Second Marriage

by **Harold Ivan Smith**
Founder of Tear Catchers Ministry, Kansas City, Missouri

Morton Hunt, author of *The Divorce Experience* and one of the leading U. S. researchers on divorce and remarriage, estimates that of those divorced, 85 percent of the men and 76 percent of the women remarry, most of them within twelve to fourteen months. Remarriage is not some abstract theory, but rather a reality that all single adult ministers and leaders must deal with.

The Singles Ministry Mission

In my opinion, one of the primary missions of a single adult minister is to help those who have failed to get back on their feet, to better equip them for strong, redemptive second marriages. It's clear from the statistics that the vast majority of those divorced will remarry. That leaves us in the church with the option to either ignore them, hoping the remarriage issue will go away, or to provide a healthy, supportive fellowship that can encourage and allow second marriages to be a magnificent expression of God's healing from brokenness.

When we don't provide this support, we in fact become party to the spiraling rate of second and third divorces. Unfortunately, the first option has been exercised too often. Our silence, avoidance, or timidity encourages many dating couples to avoid helpful, needed remarital counseling. They then make uninformed judgments that lead them to premature, unhealthy second marriages. The vicious cycle continues. If anyone needs premarital counseling, it is the previously married. We must help their scabs become scars.

Remarriage Debate in History

The remarriage debate is not a new one, as a quick look at church history will show. Some of today's well-known theologians would have us believe that the divorce/remarriage issue was clear-cut two weeks after the Resurrection. But the truth is, at no point in church history has there been lasting agreement.

As early as AD 140, Hermas and Jerome argued that apostasy, adultery, and idolatry were all adequate grounds for remarriage. But Origen and Chrysostom insisted it was permissible only in the case of adultery. (And even here we see a double standard. Men were not encouraged to take back their wife if she was the guilty party, while women were always expected to reunite with their fallen husband. This was partly due to their belief that sperm lived inside the woman for weeks or even months. So, if a man took his wife back after she had strayed, they could never know for sure who fathered their next child.)

Originally, the strong stand against second marriages applied only to clergy. It was still considered permissible for commoners and nonclergy. Then, Justin Martyr, an early church father, condemned *all* second marriages as sinful and adulterous liaisons. During this time the feelings against remarriage were so strong that the council of Neocaesarea in 315 forbade clergy to even attend a remarriage wedding. Furthermore, penance was required before remarrieds could take communion. (And in that day, it was believed that if you didn't take communion, you could not receive salvation. Thus began the remarrieds' "second class" status, which often continues yet today.)

There were even those who strongly opposed second marriages for the widow or widower. Tertullian (AD 160-230) disagreed with those who believed that remarriage was a defense against sexual temptation. He insisted that the marriage vow lasted forever, even beyond death, and that remarriage was never permissible under any circumstances. Other church leaders of his day accused him of heresy.

It's interesting to note that Tertullian's teachings thrived among many church leaders partly because widows and widowers who did not remarry normally willed all their property to the church. By the twelfth century the church had acquired nearly 50 percent of all the property in Europe—in part due to Tertullian's influence. But eventually the church began having trouble caring for so many widows, and therefore remarriage for them became increasingly more acceptable, even encouraged.

Finally, with Gratian's *Decretum* in 1142, we find a brief period of consensus against remarriage among our church fathers. But even then, for the right price, the clergy would find a loophole and grant a special dispensation allowing any person to remarry. Even Martin Luther, the father of the Reformation, made exceptions and granted second marriages providing they be kept secret. And the debate continues.

This brief look at church history is important to help us understand the deep roots of opposition to second marriages and to realize the debate will not be resolved by seminary graduates who pride themselves on nuances of the Greek.

> **"In my opinion, one of the primary missions of a single adult minister is to help those who have failed to get back on their feet, to better equip them for strong, redemptive second marriages."**

Considerations for Remarriage

When I remove myself from the age-old debate and seek to genuinely understand the overall teachings of Christ, I am convinced that remarriage—in most cases—is permissible. The primary conditions, I believe, are two:

- that the couple be willing to undergo serious, in-depth Christian counseling, and
- that they are convinced the decision to marry represents God's will for their lives.

In this counseling, I suggest these

five criteria be considered:

1. Have I forgiven myself?
2. Have I forgiven my former spouse?
3. Has enough time elapsed to exhaust reasonable possibilities for reconciliation?
4. Have I resolved all unfinished business from my first marriage? (For example, is there back alimony owed; are there jagged edges that can be mended? Some things may not be resolvable. What's important is that you have gone the extra mile to resolve everything possible.)
5. Do both I and my partner believe it is God's will and for His glory that we marry (or remarry)?

Certainly, if the counselee's attitudes and responses do not seem healthy—best noticed over several weeks or months of counseling—then I would point out those danger signals and require additional counseling and/or postponement of the remarriage.

We as ministers and leaders must not allow the world of the single-again to become an asylum for the "marital incompetent," in Morton Hunt's view, but a "school for the remarriageable." Good second marriages make contributions to our society and the church. Just observe that of Ronald Reagan and many others who have contributed greatly in our world.

As my colleague, Jim Smoke, has said, "Remarriage for some people is an *option*, for others it is an *opportunity*. If God is at work in your life, it will be a great opportunity."

In Search of a Conservative View of Remarriage

by Doug Randlett
College-career-singles pastor at Thomas Road Baptist Church, Lynchburg, Virginia

I began my ministry years ago as a minister of music. Over several years I evolved into an associate pastoral role, eventually acknowledging the call of God on my life to minister with youth and young adults. In these capacities I did that which was convenient—I put my head in the sand and ignored the issue of remarriage. Due to a conservative theological background, I began to reflect the attitude of a certain popular speaker who said no remarriage regardless. Then came my initiation into the world of single adults. Guess what? I had to develop a "from the heart" position on remarriage.

Choices for Remarriage

Two possible choices have been predominant during my years in the ministry. One is based upon the biblical fact that Jesus was hard on divorce. Jesus' standards aside, many of us chose a position of no remarriage for anyone, anytime, for any reason, to combat a rising divorce rate.

The other position was purported by

those who would lower the biblical standard. It's a position based upon the words *caring* and *loving*, which have been used to accommodate every marital hangnail that comes along. The position allows for easy divorce and remarriage. It is my belief that both positions are intolerable.

Jesus' Position
on Divorce and Remarriage

It is clear that Jesus was quite hard on divorce (Matthew 19:4-6). It was not His plan. However, a careful reading of Matthew 19:1-12 will reveal that Jesus permitted divorce in the case of adultery. This refers, I believe, to a life habit of adultery rather than a singular act.

According to 1 Corinthians 7:27-28, *the Bible permits remarriage where divorce is on biblical grounds*. John MacArthur, Jr., states that this passage speaks of those who have been divorced (no reason as to why the divorce), and that these may remarry without being in sin, provided the divorce is according to biblical grounds.

However, the most often asked question is, "What about me?" "What

---

OUR NEED FOR LESS DOGMA, MORE COMPASSION
by Larry Crabb
Founder of The Institute of Biblical Counseling, Denver, Colorado

I went to a large evangelical conference in Chicago recently. One of the seminars I attended was led by a man who had recently written a book on divorce and remarriage. Based on his many hours of exegetical study, he came down hard on divorce and remarriage. According to him there are almost never any biblical grounds for divorce—and even more so—never grounds for remarriage.

I don't agree with such a hard stance. This particular scholar had spent weeks studying the scriptural passages on the subject. But you can't learn the Bible only in a library. There the gospel becomes cold and technical. The Bible has to be lived out in the real world. Yet I don't want to go to the other extreme and change or adapt Scripture to fit whatever makes someone happy.

I believe the church must remain in tension on this issue. It's the tension between law and grace; it forces us to be sensitive to people and their real needs and hurts. We can make bold pronouncements where Scripture is absolutely clear. But in the realities of a fallen world, we have to maintain a very sensitive, compassionate attitude.

Unfortunately, within some groups, people who are divorced and remarried are denied opportunities to be recognized as valued persons. That's a terrible thing. Some people want to live by a lot of rules. I'm not opposed to having convictions in this or any other area. I have several myself. However, I want to see people valued and loved.

The final absolute is the love of God and the love of others. The Lord wants to move into people's lives and make them a tremendous blessing to others, no matter what their previous failures. There are certain things we need to be dogmatic about. But some people think they need a list of eighty-four fundamentals to be on target. My list is closer to ten. We need to be firmly dogmatic about fewer things.

about my situation? It isn't covered specifically in Scripture." Many in our singles ministries want to know if it is right to remarry—period. The answer is not always an easy one. A good understanding and application of Matthew 19, 1 Corinthians 7, and 1 John 1:9 will help.

Counseling Is
a Must, Not an Option

To answer the title question, we must counsel those looking to remarry. We may not always counsel to remarry, but we must counsel. There are specifically three cases where I would give counsel toward a remarriage:

> "Due to a conservative theological background, I began to reflect the attitude of a certain popular speaker who said no remarriage regardless. Then came my initiation into the world of single adults. Guess what? I had to develop a 'from the heart' position on remarriage."

* When divorce resulted from an unrepentant, adulterous situation (Matthew 19:9).
* When the divorce occurred prior to salvation (2 Corinthians 5:17).
* When an unsaved partner decided to desert the marriage (1 Corinthians 7:15).

All cases must be treated individually, based upon the unique nuances of that situation. I'm saying that I counsel not to remarry as well as to remarry. Remarriage is most often a viable option for our divorced singles, but not always. Be certain to have a sensitivity toward the Word of God and not just to the counselee.

Most second marriages will have a greater opportunity to glorify and honor God if we will take the risk to be open and honest in remarriage counseling. Depending on the couple involved, there are several issues to address in this counseling. Here are some areas I cover.

1. *A discussion as to why the previous marriage dissolved.* This gives some insight into further areas of need, and it gives me an opportunity to give guidance if there remain any loose ends.

2. *It is often necessary to deal with guilt.* For example:
* guilt over past sin,
* guilt over an unforgiving spirit toward a former partner,
* guilt over not accepting God's forgiveness, or
* guilt over the possible remarriage compounded by confusion over whether God can or will bless it.

3. *If a never-married partner is involved in this second marriage, I am careful to include that person in all counseling sessions.* Better that this person has a clear understanding of the failed marriage than that he or she blindly accepts it and faces a possible trauma later on.

4. *One session is given to the subject of assurance of salvation.* I have found that there needs to be an overall strong spiritual foundation for a second marriage (the lack of this foundation being a primary reason for most divorces).

5. *Along with the passages listed*

above, I present the biblical model of a marriage from Ephesians 5. This again provides added confidence reinforced by the solid Word of God.

6. *Time is spent on the subject of self-confidence.* Failed marriages often produce low self-assurance. There must be hope given for success in remarriage. Reassurance given here is a major step in providing for a productive second marriage.

Through use of the Taylor-Johnson Temperament Analysis, I noticed a need for bolstering the self-image of the divorced party. Building confidence is a major issue with me in remarriage counseling.

7. *Communicative skills are discussed.* In most divorce cases (if not all), communication skills were nonexistent or became ineffective.

8. *Finally, I counsel as to how this new marriage can be a positive contribution to the Christian community.*

Even though there may be a suffering of consequences (Galatians 6:7) due to past violations of the Word, 1 John 1:9 still offers hope for all sinners, not just those who blew it in a first marriage. God is the God of the second chance, third chance, ad infinitum.

One final warning. Our quest for giving hope must be based upon the Word of God and not upon our ability to rationalize. We must be able to call clean that which is clean and willing to call unclean that which is unclean. Out of this kind of thinking we can give appropriate, edifying counsel and offer hope—His hope—to our searching, hurting, divorced single adults.

How Long Should a Pastor Encourage Someone to Pursue Reconciliation?

an interview with David Seamands
Professor of pastoral ministries at Asbury Theological Seminary, Wilmore, Kentucky

How long should a pastor encourage single adults to pursue reconciliation after separation or divorce (assuming that neither partner has remarried)?

I think a lot depends on what the grounds for the separation or divorce really are. But let's lay some groundwork first. My general philosophy regarding this subject has been greatly influenced by Martin Luther and some of the theologians that followed him. Luther's general philosophy was this: Marriage is an indissoluble union except by death or its equivalent. Now, that's a free Seamands' translation.

Luther said that when Jesus gave the exception clause in Matthew 5:32—"except for cause of *porneia*"—it was not being given as a principle but as a "for example."

What is *porneia*?

It is the Greek word used in Matthew, which is usually translated to mean "adultery," the biblical exception for divorce. (It is also the word from which we get "pornography.") However, *porneia* is a much broader term than adultery. It's any form of sexual immorality or improper behavior that can cause the death of a marriage.

And what is the heart of a marriage? It is mutual, exclusive affection and commitment. Anything that breaks or destroys this relationship is the equivalent of death. It could be adultery, serious alcoholism, incest, physical abuse, emotional abuse, or as Luther said, "The willful, final desertion by the unbelieving partner." (See 1 Cor. 7:12-15.) It seems to me that *porneia* would cover any of these kinds of things, because each are the equivalent to the death of a marriage.

> **"Reconciliation can only be considered when there is a very sincere attempt by both parties for counseling and change."**

So the pastor should consider the cause of the "death" before counseling someone to reconcile?

Yes. For example, if something like alcoholism, physical abuse, or adultery is the basis for the separation or divorce, then although we seek reconciliation, we don't seek it at all cost. We must be realistic and not gloss over the facts. Reconciliation can only be considered when there is a very sincere attempt by both parties for counseling and change.

To get back together just for the sake of saying, "Well, we're getting back together," is a mistake unless some of the initial problems are openly dealt with and corrected. I've seen some real tragedies. I'm dealing with a case right now where the unbelieving partner (the husband) departed, and after a few years he became a Christian. The woman—in her zeal to reconcile—just said, "He's a Christian now, so we can get married again."

But it's an awful mess. A lot of the original personality factors that led to his alcoholism and promiscuousness were never really dealt with. The marriage is a real hell for this gal right now. She says, "I just presumed, since he'd become a Christian, that everything was going to be okay. If I had known, I would have been more cautious, set some conditions, and insisted that we get help before automatically assuming that we should get married again."

What about marriage today where somebody just decides he or she doesn't want to be married anymore?

From a Christian standpoint that's not an acceptable grounds for divorce, whether it's incompatibility or "I just don't have the feelings anymore." This is a case where both sides need to commit themselves to long, hard work and counseling. The door must be kept open for a long time and both parties should work extremely hard at attempting a reconciliation. This is also where the pastor should encourage reconciliation with intensity. Because many—if not most—of these marriages are redeemable and reconstructible. I do a lot of counseling for just this sort of thing.

You said the door should be kept open for a long time. I realize it would vary from situation to situation, but would a long time be a year? Five years?

It's so hard to give a specific time limit because everything is dictated by causes and circumstances. But there's a limit. I don't think one party can go on indefinitely maintaining an open door without some genuine, positive response from the other party. I think there's a lot of unreality and unnecessary guilt here.

The attitude I usually take with people is, "Okay, pray about this. Take it easy. Don't get involved with others, but put a time limit on the reconciliation effort. Go to a counselor and work hard. But if one or both of you are not willing to do that, then it's probably over." In the first place, within twelve or fourteen months—statistically speaking—from 50 to 75 percent of the men will be remarried. When a former mate remarries, the matter is closed. Reconciling the marriage is no longer a realistic option.

Then there are the Christian friends who guarantee that "if you just keep praying, God will bring you back together." It's unrealistic because a prayer like that involves another person's will. You cannot guarantee success to those kinds of prayers. God—although He certainly has the power to do so—does not make it a practice to dictate that we do something against our will. If He did so, He'd go zap and save everybody in the world right now. But He has *chosen* not to force His will upon us. He created us to make our

own personal choices.

Let me put the time limit this way. People must allow themselves sufficient time to be able to make a free choice. This is so they don't bury the hurt, garbage, and wounds of the first marriage under a second marriage. Whenever the time is, it has to be when they're able to say, "I'm over it. I can accept things as they are. I'm free to make a choice." To me that takes a minimum of a year or two. Probably two.

Let me just summarize what I think you are saying up to this point. If a person has divorced or separated due to the more severe problems of adultery, alcoholism, or physical abuse, then the pastor should not push hard for reconciliation in that situation. If God does a miraculous work in the other party's life and the person is able to show consistent, genuine change for the better, then that's a different situation. And reconciliation can begin.

That is correct. Furthermore, I would say, the Christian should take the initiative in beginning the reconciliation process. Send a letter, make a phone call, have a serious conversation either personally or through a mediator. Make the offer. Let the initiative be taken on the part of the believer. But if that is turned down, then the pastor should not be pushing and pushing.

To continue our summary, let's say a couple is separated more out of convenience; they just

decided they didn't love each other anymore. The pastor at that point should encourage both parties to pursue reconciliation for a longer period of time.

Yes. The pastor must also be willing to work with them or get them to a qualified counselor. It's commitment to long, hard work at this stage.

> "True, divorce was never intended. It was not part of the plan. Our failures go back to the Garden of Eden. But Jesus is realistic and forgiving. He knows we are frail and imperfect. We must face reality and get rid of some of this hazy guilt that surrounds us evangelicals, so that we can become redemptive."

I think I hear you saying that we in the church—along with the pastor—need to hold up the banner for reconciliation as long as possible without putting unnecessary guilt or bondage on the party who is attempting to reconcile.

You're right. I personally have an extremely high view of marriage and a high commitment to see it be as God intended. But there comes a time when we must be realistic and say, "All right, you've done all you can. The time has come to change your prayers. No longer pray for a reconciliation but that you will have the strength to do what is obvious, which may be to leave, or divorce."

You must have the strength to make a free decision and say, "Okay God, if you've got somebody else for my life, send that person along." That's often a hard thing to do. People tend to hang on to unrealistic hopes. Then they turn against God because He's not answering their prayers.

Has the church been guilty of teaching or encouraging unrealistic thinking?

We really have. As both a pastor and counselor I have picked up many of the broken pieces, particularly with women. The guy's gone, and she says, "Well, I know he's coming back." But the next thing she knows he's remarried. Then she comes and says, "Yes, but God told so-and-so that he was coming back, and I knew my prayers were going to be answered." So now what do you do?

There comes a time when you turn the corner, close the door, change the content of your prayers, and ask for the strength to face life alone, look for someone else, or ask God's guidance in a whole new direction. We need to help keep the guilt or unrealistic hopes from clobbering people.

Do you believe, based on your interpretation of Scripture, that once a person has attempted to reconcile and the door has been shut, that he or she is then free to remarry?

Oh yes. In Judaism, if you were divorced, you were totally free. Remarriage was never questioned. Forbidding remarriage is not a Judaic-Christian idea. I don't know where we get it, really. If the marriage is over, it's the equivalent of death, and a person is free. That's my interpretation of scriptural teachings on this.

Lastly, what advice do you have for those pastors or leaders who might be struggling with what role reconciliation should play in their ministry?

First, I see too few pastors who have really searched the Scriptures and read up on the subject. We end up with an emotional, hazy, inherited view that often is totally unfounded and unrealistic. I think serious exegetical study, prayer, and consulting with others are desperately needed. Then we need a better understanding of Jesus. He has a realism about Him.

True, divorce was never intended. It was not part of the plan. Our failures go back to the Garden of Eden. But Jesus is realistic and forgiving. He knows we are frail and imperfect. We must face reality and get rid of some of this hazy guilt that surrounds us evangelicals, so that we can become redemptive. Otherwise we do not redeem the situation but cause people to limp along, carrying unnecessary guilt for years.

Pastors really have to work at this. They've got to study it, pray about it, and work through it for their own personal ministry. It's a horrible task. Just today I said to my pastoral care class, "There are two things you must make up your mind about: (a) don't dare leave this seminary without an adequate theology of suffering, and (b) develop an adequate theology of marriage, divorce, and remarriage."

How are you going to face these issues?

FOR THE PASTOR: Three Conditions to Meet Before Counseling Someone About Remarriage

by Chuck Shores
Senior pastor at Ojai Valley Wesleyan Church, Ojai Valley, California

The couple is obviously in love. As they approach you after the singles meeting, you notice they are holding hands. Their words are ever so hesitant; their demeanor a little shy. He speaks first, with something of a grin, "God has done a wonderful thing in our lives. When I was divorced, I thought I'd never love again. But I've come to love her. Better yet, she says she loves me!"

"We were wondering," she breaks in, her eyes sparkling, "if you would be able to perform the ceremony?"

Decision time. Judgment day. You are on trial: your beliefs, your integrity, your ministry. The couple is on trial: their relationships of the past, their new relationship, their beliefs, their integrity, their future. Time to rule; time to decide. What do you do?

Having counseled numerous couples and performed over sixty weddings of single adults over the past few years, I have become more and more convinced that counsel concerning the issue of remarriage can properly be given only when three conditions have been met.

A Clear View of the Biblical, Moral, and Social Issues of Remarriage

Have you thought it through? Have you read the wide range of opinions given today? Are you familiar with the perspectives of people such as Larry Richards, Dwight Hervey Small, David Hocking, Chuck Swindoll, Jay Adams, or Roger H. Crook? Have you worked through Matthew 5 and Matthew 19 (and parallel passages), or 1 Corinthians 7, along with other relevant Scriptures for yourself?

Where, then, do you stand? Two prominent pastors in our area both took open stands on the issue. One said, "The Scripture is not clear, and good biblical teachers are on both sides. My principle is, 'when in doubt, don't.' Therefore, to be safe, I will not remarry divorced people."

The other said, "The Scripture is not clear, and good biblical teachers are on both sides. In such matters, I always come down on the side of grace. Therefore to be safe, I do remarry divorced people."

What is your position? Is it in line with the other aspects of your ministry? Are you in harmony with your pastor or director? Can you and your pastor, leaders, or coworkers speak with a unified voice?

James wrote, "Let not many of you

COMMUNICATING GOD'S FORGIVENESS TO THE DIVORCED
by Carole Sanderson Streeter
Author of Finding Your Place After Divorce

Last year, during a service at a church I was visiting, something happened which I had never seen. The pastor went to the pulpit and read the story of the prodigal son and the father who ran out to embrace his wayward son. Then the pastor said, "There is someone with us this morning who has not been here for quite a while. Many of us have been concerned and have prayed for him. Today we want him to know that we are glad he is back."

The pastor named the man and asked him to come to the front of the church. As the man came, the pastor went down near the communion table to meet him and to enclose him in the embrace of reconciliation, in the name of the congregation. Members were urged to greet him after the service and offer private encouragement.

The man's failing and absence were public knowledge. How fitting, then, that his return should also be public, as a seal of the forgiveness that had obviously already been sought and received. This pictured so well the horizontal element of forgiveness.

While I am not suggesting this form for divorced people, something needs to be done, in public as well as in private, to make sure that the forgiveness is not only sought and received, but also believed, by the divorced person and by the congregation. I know of one pastor who at times serves communion privately to a person in need of the healing touch of forgiveness. He also may pronounce an absolution from the guilt that divorced people often can't let go of.[33]

become teachers, my brethren, knowing that as such we shall incur a stricter judgment" (James 3:1, NASB). As leaders and pastors of single adults, we have a significant obligation to think things through honestly and clearly.

The Couple Believes It Is Biblically Proper for Them to Remarry

There are both marital and spiritual consequences for the couple. Confidence in God's will for their marriage will pay great dividends during the days of emotional stress that come to all relationships. Uncertainty about where they stand with God will play havoc with them. If the matter is dealt with honestly and openly, the assurance of having done God's will provides a stabilizing factor in the marriage. If, however, the issue is not clearly settled, the temptation will surely come (and it's a strong one in pressure situations) to think or say, "It was a mistake. It wasn't God's will for us to marry. We'd better undo the wrong we've done and divorce."

The couple's belief has spiritual effects as well. Infatuation often leads people to violate their conscience or to "rationalize" truth to fit their desires. The Apostle Paul warns that "whatever is not from faith is sin" (Romans 14:23, NASB). When individuals marry against their own understanding of God's will, they do great harm to their relationship with God, to themselves, and to their spouses. Counselors of single adults seeking remarriage must be as certain as possible that the couple is acting in accordance with honest, pure belief.

The Couple Is Ready for Remarriage

Real life issues must be faced and dealt with. Has genuine forgiveness been given and experienced? Have reasonable attempts been made toward reconciliation where it might be proper? Has enough time been given for the healing process to do substantial work in the divorced person's inner life and relationships? Are present obligations being faithfully performed? Does this couple understand marital love and how to successfully solve relationship problems? Have they discussed and agreed on the matters of finances, decision making, residence, discipline of children, and relationships with the ex and the ex's family?

These and other important matters need full exploration and reasonable resolution through preremarriage counseling well before entering into a new marriage. The responsible counselor will insist on the couple being truly ready.

In summary, I see three major concerns in counseling people considering remarriage: the counselor's beliefs about remarriage, the couple's beliefs, and the couple's readiness. When all three get the green light, then (and only then) are you free to respond, "Do your wedding? Why, yes. It will be a privilege!"

Counseling the Divorced Toward God's Best

by Jim Talley
Singles pastor at First Baptist Church, Modesto, California

Oftentimes, while on speaking engagements, I'm asked the age-old question, "How long do I wait before I can remarry?" After many years of counseling with separated and divorced couples, I have come up with the following answer: The question each person must ask is, "Do I want God's best for my life?" If the answer is yes, the question of time must be subordinated to the will of God. (This is assuming that the mate has not remarried (Deuteronomy 24:4).

A Desire for Hope

Many separated or divorced people live from one "kind" word to another from their ex-spouse, hoping it means they will get back together. I don't encourage them to make reconciliation their goal. (Reconciliation requires the cooperation of another individual who is beyond their control.)

But I do encourage them to make reconciliation a desire for which to hope and pray. There is nothing wrong with hoping, for with it comes faith, which is the substance of things hoped for, the evidence of things not seen (Hebrews 11:1).

Facing Reality

This time of separation or divorce is the time for them to work on their own life without waiting for any positive response from their ex-spouse. I encourage separated or divorced people to continue doing little, thoughtful things for their ex-spouse that show they still care, but to not expect anything in return.

Their focus needs to be on becoming the right person rather than finding the right person to remarry. The priority right now must be on their vertical relationship with God through Christ. As they develop a deeper walk with God, they're more likely to be able to communicate His love to their ex-spouse (possibly helping to restore the original flame that brought them together in the first place). As they begin to be stabilized spiritually, they are better equipped to be stabilized emotionally, financially, and socially.

Filing for Divorce

Once a separation has occurred, I give the following advice:
1. Don't file for divorce. If the spouse chooses to do so, then let it happen. Don't contest it. Avoid court as much as possible.
2. If there is a need for them to protect their assets or themselves physically, then file for a legal separation rather than a divorce.
3. Upon legal separation or divorce, I recommend that the person sign a written agreement with me stating that he or she will become a reconciler for six months (renewable for a second six-month period, but not

usually to exceed one year).

Webster's definition of reconciliation is: "To cause to be friendly, to bring back harmony."

Duration of Reconciliation

As mentioned earlier, I believe that each separated or divorced person should make a one-year commitment to be a reconciler, after which they are better able to sense God's direction and to know if there might be hope for restoration. Furthermore, I strongly encourage the divorced person not to leave the line of reconciliation until he or she can stand before God and say, "I have been faithful to my one-year commitment to be a reconciler. I have not dated or become emotionally or physically involved with another. I've done everything within my power to be friendly and harmonious with my ex-spouse. By my heart and my actions, I have been a reconciler."

Counsel and Support

During this year of reconciliation, I advise them to avoid those "helpful" people who try to introduce them to a "very special friend," or those who say, "Get on with your life. After all, you deserve it." The temptation to begin dating soon is often very strong. My counsel is that they develop a strong same-sex support system and/or a relationship with a counselor who will stand by them in their commitment to be a reconciler.

My Final Challenge

The saddest thing I hear is, "If I had known my ex-mate might change and be open to reconciliation, I would have waited. But now it's too late."

We as leaders must do everything we can to encourage our people to be reconcilers.

> **"I strongly encourage the divorced person not to leave the line of reconciliation until he or she can stand before God and say, 'I have been faithful to my one-year commitment to be a reconciler. I have not dated or become emotionally or physically involved with another. . . . By my heart and my actions, I have been a reconciler.' "**

PART NINE:

The Single-Parent Family

ABOUT PART NINE

The single-parent family
is one of the fastest growing family units
in America today.

In fact, there are nearly as many children
living in one-parent homes as there are
living in two-parent homes.

The church can no longer hold to the view
that "family" is what it was in the fifties and sixties.

This section features several leaders
who help us understand some of the specific needs
of both the child and the parent,
as well as how the church can be more effective
in providing a healthy, lasting ministry with
the single-parent family.

TWENTY

The Needs of the Single-Parent Family

Meeting the Needs of Parent and Child

by Bobbie Reed
Director of Agnew State Hospital,
San Jose, California

The statistics are sobering: Single parents have increased over 30 percent during the eighties; 50 percent of all married parents can expect to be single parents for some period in their lives; 17 percent of all children live in a single-parent family; and 50 percent of all children born today will live in a single-parent family for some period of their lives.

So what can churches do to make the best of a tough situation for the single-parent families in their congregations and communities? Basically, each church needs to assess the unique needs of the single parents in its congregation and plan to meet those needs. The responsibility for such programs should not rest solely with church leaders, however. Single parents can and must assume some of the responsibility for starting, maintaining, and expanding the necessary programs.

Here are some specific ways in which the Body of Christ can meet needs and uphold single parents and their children.

Focus on Children's Needs

Emotional Support

Initially, children often respond to living in a one-parent home by feeling rejected by the absent parent, by being angry at the change in the home situation, by experiencing guilt for causing the breakup of the marriage (a typical response in most children, not often based on facts), or by developing low self-esteem.

As we recognize these responses, we can minister to children in several ways. Guilt is healed through learning about forgiveness and being forgiven; rejection by acceptance; anger by forgiving; and a poor self-image by affirmation.

Role Models

Single parents often are quite concerned about trying to be both mom and dad to their children. But the most pressing concern I hear (about raising children of the opposite sex) is how to provide appropriate adult role models for the children. Male role models for boys are of particular concern.

The church can assist in this area in a variety of ways: by recruiting male Sunday school teachers; by encouraging families to "adopt" a single-parent family and include them in regular family outings such as picnics, trips to the zoo, or just getting together for dinner on occasion; and by enlisting men (married or single) in the church to serve as "big brothers" or surrogate father figures for boys from one-parent families.

Too often I hear stories from single

moms who say they've tried unsuccessfully to find a man in the church to be a big brother for their son(s). Often, they are advised to contact a secular organization, which (1) usually has a long waiting list; and (2) is not set up to provide Christian men who can give spiritual leadership to our children. Consequently, the church needs to respond to this need.

Interestingly enough, most single fathers with custody do not have any difficulty finding female role models for their daughters.

Acceptance

The stereotype of children from a one-parent family—unruly, impossible, potential juvenile delinquents—is not necessarily true. Studies show that in the long run the statistics are about the same for all children. However, it *is* true that children in crises—like adults—may behave in unusual ways. *Accepting the person is the first step toward helping to extinguish unwanted and unproductive behaviors.*

Help the Single Parents

Parents who have recently become single again are usually trying to cope with getting through their own deep waters—and being good parents at the same time. The strain is terrific. We can help by providing them with the following.

Respite. Taking the kids for an evening, or better yet a weekend, can be the best gift you could ever give a single parent. To be able to sleep in, read a book, listen to the quiet, or run errands alone means so much, and re-

news his or her strength for the challenge (and bedlam) of a single-parent family.

Resources. Organize a clothing exchange for single parents so they can swap children's outgrown clothing with one another to help save on that expense. Arrange a bulletin board or newsletter where parents can advertise needs, or their surpluses (extra furniture, a room for rent, services for a fee).

Also, *plan work days* where several members of the singles group gather at the home of a single-parent family and spend the day doing yard work, painting, repairs, or whatever is needed. By rotating the work days, all members can be given assistance with big jobs.

> "Taking the kids for an evening, or better yet a weekend, can be the best gift you could ever give a single parent. To be able to sleep in, read a book, listen to the quiet, or run errands alone means so much, and renews his or her strength for the challenge (and bedlam) of a single-parent family."

Child care. As soon as possible, a church needs to provide child care for all single adult functions—even weekend retreats. Faced with the choice of spending five dollars for child care or for groceries, food usually wins. The people who may need the fellowship the most are sometimes the ones who can least afford it. One group even arranged for daytime child care for parents who were going job hunting.

Support. Including several activities in the monthly calendar for parents and children together is a good way to meet the social, interactive, and recreational needs of the single parents. But, organizing a weekly discussion group where single parents can come to share together has consistently proven to be one of the most successful ways to minister to real needs.

As people share, a sense of community develops. People learn from one another and are reassured that they aren't the only ones who might be struggling just then. Often, the group can encourage another person simply by sharing how the same situation occurred in their lives. These groups also allow others to share in the joy of the parent's successes along the way.

Education. One way to be of service is to provide valuable information to single parents, from which they can acquire new parenting skills.

Sensitivity. Church leaders need to be sensitive to the existence of single-parent families. Mother's Day and Father's Day sermons should not focus on married parents only. Mother-daughter and father-son activities need to be planned and publicized in such a way that surrogate parents are provided for children in families where there is no mother or father in the home.

> **"Church leaders need to be sensitive to the existence of single-parent families. Mother's Day and Father's Day sermons should not focus on married parents only. Mother-daughter and father-son activities need . . . [to provide] surrogate parents."**

Providing a Ministry for the Single-Parent Family

by Doug Morphis
Counselor at First United Methodist Church, Wichita, Kansas

There was a period in my life when I was a single parent. I have also been involved in singles ministry for several years. Based on both my personal and professional experience, I offer some suggestions I believe will be helpful to the church in ministry with the single-parent family.

Affirm Single Parents

The church needs to affirm single parents by acknowledging that children can receive nurturing, love, and Christian values in single-parent homes as well as in two-parent homes. One way to communicate your acceptance of single parents is to encourage them to seek leadership roles in the church that will allow them to serve on decision-making bodies such as education committees, administrative bodies, and in planning for family ministries. This ensures that single parents not only sing in the choir and teach Sunday school, but they also have significant input and leadership roles in the church at large.

Encourage Single Parents to Share Their Spiritual Stories

Single parents often understand the power of God and the power of a supportive community in ways their married friends do not. Their stories are moving and inspirational; they can help others discover the power and grace of God in their own lives.

Support Single Parents in the Traumas and Transitions of Their Lives

There are times when single parents need extra attention—a lot of TLC, prayer, spiritual exhortation, and even financial help. To meet these special needs, churches should offer divorce- and grief-recovery groups, support groups for children of divorce and death, and even workshops for new parents, including single parents who have adopted or are unmarried parents.

Be Sensitive to the Difficult Issues in Single-Parent Families

Some particular issues need to be addressed by the whole church if it is going to minister to the needs of single-parent families.

1. *The other family.* Since many single-parent families are the product of divorce, there is usually another family in which the children spend time. Thus, the church needs to be sensitive to the fact that children from single-parent families cannot always participate in all the church activities.

For instance, children may want to join the church through a confirmation class that requires attendance, but they spend every other weekend in the other home and are unable to attend all the confirmation classes. In my church there is a divorce situation where the father is Protestant and the mother is Catholic. The father has weekend custody, so the kids are able to attend on Sunday morning. But the mother will not let the kids attend membership training or other church activities during the week.

The church must have a structure that allows the children's teachers to become familiar with each family situation and make decisions pertaining to attendance expectations based on each particular family situation.

Sometimes different parents may pick up the children after activities. It is important that the church set a policy about who can pick up the children and what should be done if the other parent comes by to pick them up.

2. *Holiday activities* such as Mother's Day, Father's Day, Easter, and Christmas may have to be adjusted for the special needs of the single-parent family, particularly when giving gifts is involved.

3. *Child care* should be provided for all events that the church sponsors for adults (board meetings, choir practice, seminars, retreats, and dinners), if you

> "Since many single-parent families are the product of divorce, there is usually another family in which the children spend time. Thus, the church needs to be sensitive to the fact that children from single-parent families cannot always participate in all the church activities."

want single parents to participate.

4. *Make scholarships available* for all events that cost money. This consideration will give single parents with limited finances the opportunity to participate.

Reexamine Sexual-Role Expectations

During my seven years of single parenting (before I remarried), most people in the church felt sorry for me. I was asked such things as: "How do you relate to your teenage girls?" "Can I sew that button on your coat for you?" "Would you like for me to fix a dish for you for the upcoming covered-dish dinner?"

These questions reflect a mind-set that says men can't do certain tasks as well as women. But in reality, I know single women who are very adept at discipline and house or car maintenance. At the same time, many single fathers are excellent cooks and homemakers. Maybe single parents can teach the church that God makes us human beings with the capacity to learn new tasks and that both sexes can be effective parents when given the opportunity and encouragement.

TWENTY-ONE

Children of Divorce

Ways the Church Can Help Children of Divorce

an interview with
Judith Wallerstein
Executive director of the Center for the Family in Transition, Corte Madera, California

What prompted you as a psychologist to get interested in the subject of children and divorce?

I think I've always been interested in looking at situations that nobody else has looked at yet. That challenges and excites me. When I first began laying the groundwork for this research, little study had been completed in this area.

It was during the early seventies, when I had just moved to California from a very stable community in the Midwest. (I had lived at the Menninger Clinic for seventeen years.) In California, I suddenly saw a landscape full of different kinds of families where divorce, separation, and remarriage were becoming increasingly common. This was the beginning of the divorce explosion that was to affect our entire society.

When you first began to write your book *Second Chances*, what were the one or two primary thoughts you most wanted to communicate in the book?

First, that we live with myths about this crisis called divorce. And that two of those primary myths are that

• divorce is short term in its impact and that every adult really can weather a relationship that's been broken, and

• that children are naturally resilient and will recover from the divorce experience.

I wanted to take on those myths because I thought they were getting in the way of our ability to develop programs and ways of helping the growing number of troubled families.

What should pastors and other church leaders be doing to effectively assist children of divorce?

First and foremost, they need to be available at the time the family breaks up. And they need to be able, without awkwardness and embarrassment, to say to a child, "Things are very hard right now in your family, and I know that. I hope it's going to get better. Let's talk about some of the things." By saying this, you give the child some hope, and you help him or her acknowledge that it is a very difficult experience, but that it's something that's okay to talk about.

You don't need to be a trained therapist to provide this nurturing, healing presence in a child's life. In fact, a pastor (or lay leader) can often be more acceptable and less threatening.

I don't think the church should have separate classes or groups for children of divorced parents. It is much healthier to have all types of kids learning, playing, doing some drama or art together. The primary purpose is to integrate these kids into the mainstream.

It seems that there is already a form of isolation that kids in single-parent families feel. How can that best be overcome?

Well, I think individual contact with a sympathetic adult is worth its weight in gold. What the pastor, leader, or youth worker has to know is that the divorced parents, with the best of intentions, are less available to their children. It's not that they are terrible parents. It's just that they can't do it all. They're oftentimes more stressed and strained after the divorce. Someone in some way—be it through the extended family or the institution of the church, school, or community organization—has to step in to help be a parent for the child during that critical period. Otherwise, the child is alone with all these terrible anxieties, wondering what's going to happen tomorrow.

The other thing I would say is to check back. Don't assume that a one-time effort will fix the situation. The thing about the divorced family is that it is more vulnerable. There are more crises and the single-parent family has fewer resources. So check back. "How's school going?" "What's happening?" Develop a follow-up program that keeps in touch with these children on an ongoing basis.

And when the youngster reaches adolescence, I think it would be ex-

---

WHICH CHILDREN ARE MOST AFFECTED BY DIVORCE?
by Judith Wallerstein

Who are the children—from preschool to college age—who are most affected by the divorce experience?

1. *Those up to age nine.* The children who have the hardest time at the outset are the young children: those up to ages eight or nine. This is because their physical care often gets disrupted, too. They are sent to three or four baby-sitters, and they don't know what's happening. They can be very frightened.

2. *Early adolescence (ages eleven through fourteen).* Later, the group that I find most vulnerable are the kids just beginning to move into adolescence as the divorce hits home. The family became weaker just at the time when they were experiencing a rise in aggressive and sexual impulses, at a time when the streets were calling. The issue of moving into adolescence just as the family is weaker is serious, and I think that would be very important for church ministries to address. This especially affects those kids ages eleven through fourteen. I'm very concerned about this group.

3. *All ages.* Every age group is affected by divorce in a variety of ways. No one's home free. What we found in our research was that divorce may sometimes benefit one of the adults in the family, but that it worked against the rest of the family members. They missed the stability of family life—and they were lonely, terribly lonely. The loneliness we see now in America is very pathetic.

But what was also clear is that, although a lot of people have a very hard time of it, they usually make it. It is not all doom and gloom. The majority of the kids that I studied found some way to make it through the tough stuff.

tremely helpful to be very old-fash-
ioned about it. Have a group of adoles-
cent kids talk about relationships and
discuss what "good" means. I did that
once talking about what sin means.

Discussions like this can be a big help.
Because the issue is, "Is my father a
good man? Do I want to be like my
dad or mom?"

I'm convinced that all adolescents

A KEY INGREDIENT TO A HEALTHY SINGLE-PARENT MINISTRY: RECOGNIZING THE NEEDS AND FEELINGS OF THE CHILDREN
by Dan Lundblad
Counselor at Blue Water Center for Christian Counseling, Port Huron, Michigan

It is estimated that 60 percent of children born today will live in a single-parent home at some time. Developing a holistic approach to the needs of the single-parent family is no easy task. It is, however, one of the most exciting challenges facing our churches today. A single parent recently shared this thought with me: "The people at the church always make the kids feel welcome . . . which helps me feel welcome, too."

Children will want to return to the place where they feel accepted. Realizing the impact children can have in their parents' decision to return to a singles group, may I offer these suggestions for developing your ministry with single parents.

Establish an environment where the children's feelings are accepted and where their need for healing, love, and belonging are acknowledged.

1. **A consistent monthly "family time"** is one excellent way to do this. Ours has been a common meal the first Sunday of each month where we recognize children's birthdays and achievements. At these monthly meetings children form friendships with one another and develop their own internal support system in the larger church body.

2. **A newsletter for children of single-parent families** could be developed with the help of older single-parent children. Teenagers need to be acknowledged for their contributions if they are to remain a positive role model for younger children.

3. **Mainstream single-parent children into the existing Christian education program.** I strongly believe that the second staff position in a single adult ministry should be a qualified children's worker who has a burden for the single-parent family. The successful inclusion of all children into the Christian education program will benefit children from both single-parent and two-parent families.

4. **Find ways to bridge single-parent families with two-parent families.** The inclusion of single-parent children into the activities of functioning two-parent family systems provides a model for successful interaction between men and women. Furthermore, these times of interaction and fellowship provide the single parent with the added support needed when parenting solo.

Today our traditional church programs are being challenged to incorporate the needs of the single-parent family. We are not called to rescue people from their problems; we are called to "bear one another's burdens, and so fulfil the law of Christ" (Galatians 6:2, RSV).

need more discussion like this than they are getting. This is an especially serious issue that needs to be discussed by kids from divorced homes.

What is something we could do to help children of divorce survive and grow in healthy ways?

Kids need mentors. Very few kids have one today. And children from divorced homes especially need them. I'm not talking about big brothers or big sisters. I'm talking about mentors, older adults who exercise a moral, intellectual and emotional influence, a teacher role.

Could this be like an important aunt, uncle, or grandparent?

It could be. It could also be an adult in the church or community. We found in our study that kids from divorced homes had very few mentors. They didn't have them in the church or the school. Although there were some who seemed to benefit enormously from mentoring grandparents, this was a small minority.

Mentoring can make a big difference. The kids in our study who had mentors stood out. One was a football star. His coach was his mentor. His coach loved him, the girls loved him, people came from all over to watch him play. He did very well with his supportive environment and a good coach for a mentor. Another person was a young woman who was a brilliant student in Chemistry. She had key mentors all along the line. But few kids have this kind of mentoring relationship.

What is the value of a mentoring relationship?

The mentoring relationship communicates that you are loved and have something of worth. It's also intellectual, a teacher-student relationship. There's the wish that you will follow in the teacher's footsteps. I'm a chemist—you'll be a chemist. I'm a football player—you'll be a football player. Or, maybe we both do stamp collecting. It's almost like a father-child or mother-child relationship around a particular line of interest. It's not just that you are loved but that you are also in some way my heir. You are carrying on an important tradition where we are both a part of the chain. This gives a child a tremendous sense of purpose, direction, and continuity. It's very exciting for a kid to feel that he has been selected for something special and unique.

The sky's the limit for all the various mentoring relationship possibilities. Pair up children and adults with similar interests. It can be anything from musical instruments to drawing or painting, stamp collecting, computers, or photography.

I'm not saying that the minister should take on the role of mentoring every divorced kid in the community. But it would be wonderful if the church

> **"What the pastor, leader, or youth worker has to know is that the divorced parents, with the best of intentions, are less available to their children. It's not that they are terrible parents. It's just that they can't do it all. They're oftentimes more stressed and strained after the divorce."**

constituency could be mobilized to have couples and singles take on a mentoring role with one or two children. It would do wonders to help provide stability and support for kids from divorced homes—and to help reverse the destructive divorce cycle.

Mentoring is one of the greatest things the church could provide children of divorce.

What do you see happening with blended families as we move into the future?

This is an area where we are having to learn as we go. One problem I'm seeing with blended families is that in many instances it seems to be a good marriage for the adults, but it hasn't been good for some or all of the children. The marriage may have included one of the children from an earlier marriage but not others. Or all the children might feel left out.

There are many times when the spouses in a blended family do not get along. But there are also families where the children feel that "the marriage is great for my mom, but it doesn't include me." And the kid might be right. If the child loses the parent that he felt closest to and ends up with a stepparent that he doesn't like or feel close to, then he could feel like he is ending up with nobody. Many of the kids in our study felt that way. They didn't have their own dad because he had left them. They felt their stepdad or stepmom was primarily a disciplinarian and not a loving person.

One of the big dangers in stepfamilies is that people are awkward or uncomfortable in their new role. In many cases I've observed, the stepfather was becoming much too strict, expecting this instant intimacy, instant obedience, instant conformity.

From the outside, it can look like a good marriage, a good blend. But we have to realize that we are dealing with a new kind of family. Learning to help blended families survive and be healthy is going to be a challenge. In truth, to be a blended family usually takes a lifetime.

> **"It would be wonderful if the church constituency could be mobilized to have couples and singles take on a mentoring role with one or two children. It would do wonders to help provide stability and support for kids from divorced homes—and to help reverse the destructive divorce cycle."**

Developing Support Systems for the Single-Parent Family

Don't Let Single Parents Slip Through the Cracks

by Willard Black
Founder and director of the Institute for Christian Resources, San Jose, California

Based on my experiences as a pastor, a Christian leader, and a single parent (for over ten years), here are some guidelines which will help congregations keep single parents from slipping through the cracks.

Offer help immediately. The new demands are overwhelming. Household management, income production, parenting, helping address the children's emotional needs—plus keeping up with their church and school activities—is a massive overload. Help is needed now.

Don't wait for the single parent to seek your help. Following divorce, death of a spouse, or a pregnancy outside of marriage, few men or women have the emotional energy to ask for help. Some new single parents are too hurt or humiliated to request support, even from close friends or family members. Be the initiator and make your offers of support as soon as possible.

Provide support based on specific needs. Before you meet with a single parent, imagine that you have just become one yourself. No longer do you have a spouse with whom you share household and parenting tasks, and your household income has been slashed from 30 to 40 percent. Now that you have a more realistic picture in your mind, you can better discern the most important needs of the single parent.

When Virginia, who has six children, was divorced after nineteen years of marriage, it could have been the end of the world for her financially.

She said, "Money was a problem right away." She had not been employed since she was first married, and there were no family savings. She did, however, belong to a church where several families got together and put a large sum of money in a long-term fund for her.

Each month, for several years, the church sent her a check. This assured her of having food on the table. Her need was understood, and her friends were on target.

Since needs vary considerably among single parents, individual assessments are needed to stay on target.

Specify the kind and amount of help you can give. Predictable help, either little or much, is often the best kind of help. And because it is unlikely that a few helpers can meet all the needs in a single parent's life, it is necessary to be specific about what you will do.

Will you give emotional support, or financial support? Can you visit in person, or on the telephone? If caring for the children, can you receive them after school, or will you keep them one weekend a month? Answers to such questions will clarify the expectations of the person being helped and will not overburden the helper.

Specific and predictable help not only meets obvious needs, it helps single parents define areas of their own responsibility. This gives them a greater sense of control over their own lives.

Commit help for an extended period of time. Needs of single parents often continue much longer than anyone would like. Most responses which fulfill a need take six months, or longer.

Bill needed an extended commitment of time to help him recover emotionally from his loss. He felt totally rejected when his wife left him. Four years later, I asked him what helped him most. He said, "Jim and Mary invited me over every Wednesday night for dinner and a Bible study. I was welcome to stay after that and watch television as long as I wanted to. They just asked me to lock the door as I left."

For nearly two years, Wednesday night was Bill's night at Jim and Mary's. This extended commitment of time, love, and hospitality helped him regain his self-worth.

Terminate help at the appropriate time. One message I repeat frequently to single parents in conferences is: "It's okay to be a consumer." Most of us would prefer not to be in a dependent position. It's more comfortable to be a contributor than a consumer. For this reason it is important to know when to reduce or end your support so that it is not awkward for either the giver or the receiver. Monitor the needs as they change, and keep communications open.

In congregations where appropriate care is extended to single parents, a particular leader—or a team of leaders—accepts the responsibility to see that care is given. An organizational structure and process is put in place to see that people are not overlooked.

It is true that some needs are met spontaneously, but this occurs only for people who are well established in their congregations. Marginal church members and those completely outside the church have their needs addressed only when formal attention is directed their way.

By following the above suggestions, single parents will find much of the support and encouragement they so desperately need. The church can, and must, perform an adequate ministry to single parents.

> **"Don't wait for the single parent to seek your help. Following divorce, death of a spouse, or a pregnancy outside of marriage, few men or women have the emotional energy to ask for help."**

Ministry with Single Parents Is a Congregational Affair

by Sandi Harding
Lay leader at Saint Stephen's Episcopal Church, Sewickley, Pennsylvania

The single parent carries tremendous emotional concerns and questions. "Are my kids and I still a family?" he or she asks. "If so, can we make this family work?"

Generally speaking, the church, while acknowledging these concerns, has been ineffective in providing the strong support system needed. In my opinion, single-parent families require fellowship with "whole" families in the church. The single-parent families' needs will not be met until the entire congregation is challenged to be involved.

The church often attempts to meet this need by building large singles "programs." The assumption that "single families will be cared for by the singles community" is an uninformed one. More critical to single families is an integration into the church-at-large, giving them a wider sense of belonging, a wider system of support and stability, and a wider circle for their own unique gifts of ministry.

I believe the church must do five things to begin truly meeting the needs of today's single parents.

Educate the Congregation

Singles leaders can do this by sharing and discussing the following key concerns and needs of the single parent.

Feelings of isolation. The number one problem of single parents is a feeling of not belonging. As families disintegrate, a loss of close relationships with other families will usually occur. The prior support systems are fractured and questions of self-esteem and self-worth arise: "Am I needed? Does anyone care?" Additionally, the still potent stigma of the "broken family" serves to increase the feelings of isolation.

Children are also isolated; especially, if a move has occurred. They leave familiar places and friends behind. New and strange responsibilities, coupled with feelings of loss, anger, and depression, further separate them from their peers.

Against these emotions, the single parents strive to prove their family is nevertheless okay. Often they will even turn down offers of help—at least initially—due to pride or fear. No parent wants to admit that "I can't handle things on my own."

Thus the overwhelming feeling among single parents is that they are all alone: There is no significant other to share in the joys, responsibilities, and discipline.

Role identity. The single parent is faced with a new challenge—playing the role of both parents. This creates confusion, frustration, and anger. The mother who previously served as the caretaker and source of affection must now be the breadwinner and disciplinarian, too.

Fathers generally have an easier time, as full-time child care often allows their daily routines to be less interrupted. However, they too discover new roles—shopper, launderer, and cook.

Children also demonstrate confusion over their identity. If allowed, they will attempt to take the place of the missing parent. Sadly, the remaining parent frequently encourages this reversal due to his or her own emotional needs.

Financial pressures. After a separation or divorce, financial pressures confront both women and men. However, studies show that men have more earning power and regain their financial loss more quickly. Women have a harder adjustment for several reasons. They may not have been working and now must seek employment or the embarrassment of government assistance. Approximately 90 percent of them make less than $15,000 a year; from this they must deduct the high cost of day care. Statistically, the level of income for women decreases 76 percent after a divorce, while the level for men actually increases 24 percent. Far too often, child support is never paid. This all adds up to being a tremendous stress on single mothers.

As the congregation begins to fully understand these needs and concerns, they are better able to provide practical, valuable help for the single parent. Such help does not necessarily require expensive programs, but simply the practicing of Christ's commandment: "Love one another as I have loved you" (John 15:12, RSV).

Provide Pastoral Support and Up-Front Teaching

People take their cues from the person in charge. If the pastor verbally recognizes the needs of single parents, the congregation is encouraged to show a more active concern as well. Sensitive presentation of the general and specific needs of single-parent families promotes this concern. Sermons can make use of single-parent illustrations, both biblical and modern.

Specific needs for clothing, appliances, housing, and other basics can be announced or printed for the church service sheet, newsletter, or bulletin board.

It is helpful to remember single parents on holidays, especially Mother's Day and Father's Day.

> "The number one problem of single parents is a feeling of not belonging. As families disintegrate, a loss of close relationships with other families will usually occur."

Special prayers might be offered for them. Also, they should be seen and heard; sharing the love of Christ with the congregation and telling how certain needs are being answered. In this the pastor takes the lead: If he or she accepts single parents, then others will follow suit.

Make Church Functions and Retreats Affordable

Single parents desperately need involvement with the church family.

Continually remind them that they are welcome at all church family activities. However, this may necessitate providing them with scholarship money so limited funds don't keep them from attending badly needed Christian fellowship activities.

Encourage People to "Adopt" a Single-Parent Family

Children of single parents need to be exposed to complete families in order to understand the relationship between husband, wife, and children. Since most single parents are mothers, it's important to provide strong male role models. To address this need, complete families can "adopt" single-parent families, including them in family outings or vacations, and frequently hav-

IDEAS FOR STARTING THE SINGLE-PARENT FAMILY MINISTRY

Support groups for single-parent families seem to work best when they grow out of educational programs. That's the opinion of Barbara Schiller, assistant to the director of single life ministries, Central Presbyterian Church, St. Louis. As a single parent and staff member, Barbara has developed two successful ministries in her church—"Broken Rainbow" for kids and "Just Me and the Kids" for the parents.

The foundation for these programs is a ten-to-fifteen-week educational program that provides practical tools to help single-parent families adjust to their new life. As relationships develop among classmates, the healing process accelerates and the class naturally develops into a small group that will stick together far beyond the termination of formal instruction.

Here are some topics such an educational program might include:

• Redefining the family
• Identifying and understanding the superparent syndrome
• Keys to helping children cope with separation and loss
• Independence and responsibility
• Dating as a single parent
• Developing healthy sexual identity role models for children
• Considering and understanding remarriage.

For more ideas and information, Barbara recommends that you consult the following books:

Just Me and the Kids, by Patricia Brandt (David C. Cook, 1985)
Surviving the Break-up, by Judith Wallerstein and Joan Kelly (Basic, 1982)
Helping Children Cope with Separation and Loss, by Claudia Jewett (Harvard Common Press-Boston, 1982)
How to Really Love Your Child, by Ross Campbell (Victor Books/Scripture Press, 1979)
The Parents Book About Divorce, by Richard Gardner (Bantam, 1982)
Stages, an excellent secular curriculum about families in transition. This was created, and is currently being used, by the Irvine, California, school district. This curriculum could easily be adapted as your own children's program. Contact the Guidance Projects Office, 31B West Yale Loop, Irvine, CA 92714, phone (714) 552-4882.

ing brunch together after church.

These traditional family times are generally lonely times for single-parent families. They will appreciate the love and concern that comes with such fellowship. To provide male models, some outings might be "for guys only."

Meet Needs Through a "Practical Advisor's Network"

Practical knowledge is hard to obtain for the parent struggling with learning a second role in a family. A system of practical advisors could be of great help in many areas. Financial advisors could help single parents set up a budget or apply for low-rate loans.

Counselor advisors could assist with individual and family counseling as well as with questions involving children. Job networking (how to write a resume or apply for a job) and home repairs (what to fix and how to do it) are other areas ripe for practical advice. Most churches have such expertise within their membership. Group classes or individual consultation could easily be arranged.

The challenge to minister with single-parent families will not get easier. Sadly, the vast majority of these families have little or no involvement in the life of the church. Now is the time to reevaluate our ministry to single-parent families and to provide them with the spiritual support and healing environment of Christ.

SINGLE MOTHERS AND HOMOSEXUAL SONS:
The Fears and the Facts

by **Bobbie Reed**
Director of Agnew State Hospital, San Jose, California

Across the country, many single mothers fear that their sons—lacking a father at home—may grow up gay. Some news items in the press have suggested that male children who grow up in single-parent homes are more likely to be gay that those who grow up in two-parent homes. I wanted to respond to these concerns, so I researched the subject. I talked to psychologists, gay men, and mothers of gay men; I read books and journals; and I talked to directors of Christian ministries that help homosexuals go straight. I found no significant correlation between homosexuality and being raised by a single mother.

The experts aren't in agreement about just what causes male homosexuality, but several factors may contribute to it. A lack of bonding with a father (or father figure) in the early years of life may cause a boy to grow up with a deep loneliness and desire for fatherly love and acceptance; he may try to meet that need by seeking sexual attention from men. However, most men who grow up without a father at home do not become gay.

Many fathers and sons fail to bond even though the father is present in the home. One gay man told me that his stepfather had physically abused him daily for six months before he was two years old. When his mother discovered what was happening, she left her husband and stayed away from men for years. The son grew up believing that men were cruel and women were kind, so he rejected the masculine part of his own character.

Another gay man traces his sexual preference to his clinging mother who made him the center of her life. As a child, he spent all of his free time with Mom. He failed to form close friendships with other boys and girls. As a teen, he wasn't comfortable with girls, but was drawn to quiet, introverted boys. At the same time, he admired the forcefulness and power of the more aggressive boys. This internal conflict led him to a homosexual lifestyle.

Homosexual experimentation that becomes a habit can also cause a homosexual lifestyle. When a behavior results in pleasure, the behavior will likely be repeated. So, a boy who experiences pleasure from sex play with an-

> **"Some boys raised in a single-parent home will become gay, and their mothers will tend to blame themselves for their sons' sexuality. As singles leaders, we must be sensitive, understanding, and prepared to comfort and counsel these mothers through their guilt and grief."**

other boy usually wants to play again and again. The boy often experiences guilt and shame, but if the physical pleasure outweighs the guilt and shame, the boy may become hooked on a gay lifestyle.

I have named factors that contribute to homosexuality, but it is very important to recognize that *most* boys who
• were raised by single mothers,
• were abused by fathers or father figures,
• had clinging moms, or
• infrequently experimented sexually with other boys, ARE NOT GAY.

As leaders of single adult ministries, what can we do to help single mothers deal with these fears? We can help them
• understand and acknowledge their fears,
• talk about their fears,
• become comfortable with their own sexuality,
• find positive male role models for their sons, such as teachers, big brothers, sports coaches, relatives, and friends,
• develop a strong network of friends for themselves and their sons,
• allow their sons' own blend of masculine and feminine characteristics to take shape,
• cultivate a good relationship between the sons and their father (if possible), and
• provide a strong spiritual foundation in the home.

Some boys raised in a single-parent home will become gay, and their mothers will tend to blame themselves for their sons' sexuality. As singles leaders, we must be sensitive, understanding, and prepared to comfort and counsel these mothers through their guilt and grief.

But in most cases, sons raised by single mothers will not become gay. In fact, those sons have a better father than any earthly father. Psalm 68:5 says, "A father to the fatherless, a defender of widows, is God in his holy dwelling."

PART TEN:

Contemporary Issues in Single Adult Ministry

ABOUT PART TEN

How do you deal with
a single adult in your group
who is living an immoral life?

Are Christian single men wimps?

What can you do to provide support systems
for single women who are tempted
to become involved with married men?

Should your single adults be tested for AIDS?

These are some of the contemporary issues
that are addressed in an open, honest
manner in this section.

TWENTY THREE

Love and Commitment

"Romantic Love":
The Barrier that Keeps Singles from Making Commitments

an interview with Robert N. Bellah
Professor of sociology, University of California, Berkeley

Why is it so difficult for people to make commitments today?

I think it's related to the strong emphasis in our society on individual autonomy and self-fulfillment as being the absolutely most important thing. Consequently, the moment one feels the group or individual is not contributing to one's own interests or needs, it's very easy to pull out.

The language of today is journey— "I'm on my journey. If you're not going with me, good-bye." It's very hard to get people who are in that mode to think of themselves as part of a "we" . . . to realize that there is no such thing as a journey all alone.

How did we get to this noncommittal place in our society?

There are several reasons. For one, it has to do with our emphasis on individual mobility, financial success, and a high valuation on personal achievement. This is all linked to such things as the importance of education. To get a good education today often requires that you leave your home and community. Furthermore, education often undermines your childhood faith.

It also has to do with the worship of self, which is obviously idolatry and quintessentially sinful. This cultural selfishness, in a deep sense, destroys the self as well as our relationships with others.

Remember the injunction "Love thy neighbor as thyself." There is nothing wrong with loving yourself in the economy of God first, and neighbor second. In that context, a sense of the worth of self is not absolute or taking precedent over others but, instead, is part of the total economy of love that is organized around God and gives great importance to the neighbor. This is how the self is really fulfilled.

However, when you forget about God, forget about the neighbor, and try to make the self absolute, you don't even have the self at that point. You just have emptiness.

When we lose a sense of connectedness to others in our society, we're tempted to think, "Well, the whole point is to get the next promotion to get more money to get more goods to create a little private world of happiness with me."

For single adults, what is the greatest barrier to making commitments?

One significant issue is the whole notion of romantic love, which is so prevalent in our society. By this, I mean the notion that there is one person out there who is the perfect person for you, and if you can just find him, you will live happily ever after. The truth is that if you believe that enough, then nobody will ever quite fit or measure up, and you will go on looking for Mr. or Mrs. right forever, never making a lasting commitment.

The truth is that the whole romantic love thing is 90 percent hokum because it's trying to make another person in a love relationship into a savior. There is only one Savior and He is Jesus Christ. No human being can bear that weight.

Because our notion of romantic love is unattainable—because it is blown way out of proportion—we as a society have developed a deep cynicism about love relationships. Consequently, many people become exploitive in their relationships, seeking only momentary pleasure. In some ways, that is the opposite extreme of seeking a savior in a romantic relationship. Both are unhealthy.

What do single adults most need from the church?

First, they need to be affirmed and accepted. Just because they do not fit into the traditional family stereotype, the church must not send the message that they are oddballs or out of step. In fact, I'm convinced that the more the church accepts singles, and the more single adults can find people in the church they can count on, the more likely it will be for the single adult to move into healthy committed relationships. The irony is that the more singles are accepted for what they are, the sooner they will reach a point where they want greater commitment in their relationships.

Second, single adults—especially single parents—need the church; probably more than marrieds. In fact, all singles—because of loneliness—really need networks of other people. The church can be the best place for this network, for this badly needed supportive community.

What do we need more of in our relationships?

Forgiveness. There is tremendous encouragement and fulfillment in a relationship between two people who understand that they are not perfect. I don't think any marriage or other relationship can survive without forgiveness. We're never going to be perfect for the other person, no matter how hard we try. Being part of a church community —based on love and shared beliefs—helps us be more realistic with one another's shortcomings.

> "The truth is that the whole romantic love thing is 90 percent hokum because it's trying to make another person in a love relationship into a savior. There is only one Savior and He is Jesus Christ. No human being can bear that weight."

TWENTY FOUR

Dealing with Immorality in Your Singles Group

Dealing with Immorality Through Confrontation and Accountability

by Jim Talley
Singles pastor at First Baptist Church, Modesto, California

I n dealing with immorality, I operate on the assumption that many single adults—even those in evangelical churches—are sexually active (or have been in the last year). That's especially true for those in a dating relationship and seems to be well supported by most research I've seen as well as from my own observations as a pastor.

Second, I believe that God has called us to holiness. The church must take its biblical mandate to stand against immorality and to provide a support system for those desiring to resist the strong, ever-present cultural pressures today.

Taking the Pulse

Once a single adult has attended our singles ministry more than three times, either I or one of my leadership team meet privately with him or her to ask three questions:

1. Are you a Christian?
2. Do you have the assurance of salvation? Or, if you died tonight, do you know you would go to heaven? (If the answer is no on either question one or two, we invite him or her to pray to receive Christ.)
3. If you now are, or have recently been in a dating relationship, would you share with me the maximum number you have reached in that relationship?

   1 = look
   2 = touch
   3 = holding hands lightly
   4 = constant holding hands
   5 = light kiss
   6 = strong kiss
   7 = french kiss
   8 = fondling the breasts
   9 = touching sexual organs
   10 = sexual intercourse

I have asked these questions of nearly fifteen hundred singles a year for several years. Only one or two people per year refuse to answer. I look at it much like a doctor-patient relationship. If I know where the person is struggling, I am better able to minister effectively.

Relationship Instruction

Our next step is to encourage all of our people to enroll in our Relationship Instruction course, which relies heavily on accountability to the course instructor (usually a Sunday school teacher or lay leader). I believe strongly in accountability. Freedom comes from sharing with another mature Christian (James 5:16).

Participants commit to meet with their instructor twice monthly for four months. (This is not a premarriage course.) They also make a commitment to keep their relationship(s) below number seven on the chart. If they go to number eight or beyond, they commit to phone their instructor within twenty-four hours for counsel and support. In my opinion, the most effective thing we can do is get our singles into this monitoring program, so that we can have ongoing input into their relationships, helping them move away from immorality.

The Relationship Instruction course, which covers all aspects of healthy dating relationships, includes a section entitled "Dealing with Immorality." In this section there is a "Gaining Moral Freedom" chart where each participant agrees to record the occurrence of physical involvement that reaches level eight or higher.

Success, for us, is defined as lengthening time between failures—not sinless perfection. If, by the third recorded occurrence, there is no noticeable lengthening between failures—or if the assignments simply go uncompleted—we terminate the course for the individual and apply church discipline, which I will explain below.

The Relationship Instruction course is not *required* of our singles. At any one time only from 10 to 15 percent of our group are enrolled in the course. We also apply church discipline when needed with those not enrolled, if we observe a continual unrepentant or unwilling attitude to deal with the moral issues in their life. (With sixty lay leaders in our singles ministry, we are able to have good one-on-one relationships with most of our single adults.)

Applying Church Discipline

Before explaining our church discipline procedure, I should note that we've only had to dismiss about two singles per year. A change of heart usually takes place before dismissal is necessary. Seldom do we have people who are not genuinely seeking to grow in their relationship with God. That doesn't mean they will not fail; it means the attitude of their heart is right and that progress is evident.

When we apply church discipline, we follow the biblical guidelines of Matthew 18. Either I or one of my trained leaders goes to them first. The next time, two staff members go. If, after going to them two or three times (over a one-month period), we do not see any noticeable change of attitude, I make a recommendation for dismissal to the church staff. If accepted, it goes to the board of deacons, who actually have the responsibility for dismissing the individual involved. (By dismissal, I mean they can no longer be a member of the church, nor can they attend any singles function without repenting and going through restoration counseling.)

> **"Success, for us, is defined as lengthening the time between failures—not sinless perfection."**

We do not "spy" on our people to check up on their moral conduct. If they're not living right, it usually becomes very apparent by their response to counsel, in their willingness or unwillingness to submit to spiritual authority, and in their personal conduct and attitude. I firmly believe that when we teach the Word and proclaim holiness, the convicting power of the Holy Spirit always makes the truth known and the sin evident.

Our system may sound rigid to some, but the vast majority of our singles appreciate and thank us for it. As one single recently told me, "I've sought spiritual counsel and guidance many times before, but never once did someone have the boldness to confront me with my greatest struggles and failures and then provide support to help me do right. I'm so glad you did. Openly talking about it and having someone to be accountable to have helped me overcome and grow in my relationship with Christ."

That's the bottom line for us—to help our single adults become established in a holy lifestyle.

Balancing Moral Responsibility and Moral Freedom

by Terry Hershey
Director of Christian Focus, Inc., Seattle, Washington

It is clear from Scripture that the good news speaks of people who are both morally responsible and morally free. When moral freedom goes beyond moral responsibility, we have sin and immorality. How do we confront immorality while maintaining responsibility and freedom?

Our temptation is to remove the freedom, construct a system where the person is "not allowed" to sin, and define immorality by what we do or do not do. The result is legalism. We are comfortable with legalism because it takes the responsibility of making moral choices away from us and puts it on the church, the pastor, or the "list" our group created. In response to such a system, essentially Jesus said, "I don't care how 'pure' you are by what you don't do, you are still impure in your heart" (Matthew 15:16-20, author's paraphrase).

My assignment is to make this issue as practical as possible. Quite frankly, that is not easy, unless you choose legalism. But if legalism will not work, where can we turn?

Present a Biblical Theology of Sexuality

Let's use the true story of John and Jane (fictitious names). They were in love. John was a leader in one of our singles groups. They decided to move in together. Those are the basic facts.

Now, how should I confront their immorality in this situation? Prior to dealing with their immorality, there needs to be a foundation for establishing the ground rules. What are the perimeters for sexual expression? To whom are John and Jane morally responsible?

In our singles ministry we begin by regularly teaching a healthy biblical theology of sex. (This is taught as an annual Sunday morning series plus a Saturday seminar.) I put the subject before the people, emphasizing that the purpose of a God-created sexuality is to promote life. I would call the Bible "pro-life," not simply in a procreative sense, but in all areas—spiritually and emotionally. That which is pro-life is nurturing and will produce wholeness, health, and a sense of completeness. The opposite produces death. The biblical message is that my body can become an instrument of life or death.

The question of a true biblical theology becomes, "Will this or that particular behavior lead me toward life or toward death?" I no longer define morality (or immorality) by a checklist.

When dealing with this issue, I ask three questions of those who come to me (or of those whom I approach, as in the case of John and Jane):

- Is the behavior you are engaging in nurturing for both of you? (Or does the other person become an object to meet your "needs"?)
- Is the behavior healthy for both?
- Is the behavior wise? In other words, a kiss may be "legally" okay, but for some, it is non-nurturing and therefore immoral.

Ask for Repentance

This is the first step toward healing. In repentance, we take responsibility for who we are. During counseling, I see to it that the couple (or individual) is given the opportunity to be honest about their behavior(s) and their desire to change. Repentance that is verbalized allows me—and others—to offer support and encouragement. After John and Jane were honest in response to the questions, it was my job to create an environment for repentance, not penance. In legalism, one is motivated to look for "loopholes" in the system rather than to repent.

Extend Forgiveness

It must be verbally affirmed. "John and Jane, you are forgiven because of Jesus, and you are free to choose pro-life behaviors."

This cannot be a conditional forgiveness saying, "I will forgive you only if you promise to never do it again." Forgiveness says, "I release you from your past, accept you as you are, and even allow you the freedom to fail again." That's the mystery of the gospel. If we don't give our singles freedom to fail, we can't really forgive them.

I find it interesting that Jesus didn't forgive Peter based upon any conditions. The mystery of grace is that it releases us, knowing full well we may fail again. Forgiveness frees us. Legalism forces us to focus on our failure and the reality that we can never quite measure up. We then neurotically walk around concentrating on "not sinning."

Provide Creative Alternatives

Following a "confrontation" about immorality and a call for repentance, I set up three counseling appointments with the couple (or individual) to provide creative alternatives for their sexual urges. For example, making a

> **"Forgiveness says, 'I release you from your past, accept you as you are, and even allow you the freedom to fail again.' That's the mystery of the gospel. If we don't give our singles freedom to fail, we can't really forgive them."**

decision beforehand not to end up at the apartment alone, intentionally focusing on doing more creative things with other people, choosing ways to develop the friendship in pro-life ways.

John and Jane don't need their pastor to reinforce their tendencies toward failure. Instead, they need their pastor to pray with them and encourage them in their desire for pro-life. What if they fail again? I walk them through the four steps again. I don't see us running out of chances in 1 John 1:9. When Jesus forgave Peter, He also provided alternatives for Peter's focus. He told Peter to "feed the sheep" and to "not worry about John."

Finally, do I seek people out or wait for them to come to me? If they are in a leadership position, I go to them. As a leadership team we are called to model a Christian lifestyle. If there is no repentance, they are asked to step down from leadership. (I set up ongoing counseling appointments to affirm that we are rejecting the behavior, not the person.)

But with the regular membership, I seldom confront them. My duty before God is not to be a moral policeman of my singles. Rather, my duty is to declare Him and His gospel with clarity and honesty; then offer my people a chance to respond. (We do have a strong small-group ministry established that helps many of our single adults find help and support in making pro-life choices.)

Overall, my goal and purpose for this ministry is to create an environment for people to be both responsible and free.

Single Men

SINGLE CHRISTIAN MEN: Why the "Wimp Perception" by Women and How to Overcome It

by Dan Chun
Minister with singles at Menlo Park Presbyterian Church, Menlo Park, California

Some people, including many single women, think single Christian men tend to be wimps. Why does this perception exist, and what can we do to change it?

I do not believe all single Christian men are perceived as weak and nonassertive. However, I and other single adult pastors have heard single women say many times, "Where are all the good Christian men? Why don't the men in this group ask me out more often? Why do they seem so wimpy? I don't want to date nonChristian men but they are the only ones asking . . . and they seem so exciting!"

I don't claim to have all the answers, but here are some observations I've made over the past few years as I've had the opportunity to work full time with single adults. I've also include suggestions that I believe might be helpful for your group.

Christian Men Take Fewer Risks

I think one reason women might perceive a single man as wimpy is that in his sincere efforts and desire to be Christlike, a Christian man takes fewer risks. He wants to be spiritually mature and to not sin, so he plays it safe. He doesn't want to make mistakes, be tempted, and fall back into the world's ways.

Contrast that with the nonChristian guy who is outspoken and has a real lust for life. He doesn't worry about going out and having a few beers or seeing an R-rated movie. There is more freedom in his lifestyle because he has fewer moral guidelines to which he is committed. Consequently, many Christian ladies are attracted to the nonChristian because he appears more exciting, maybe enjoys a wider variety of magazines, books, theater, and movies than the ordinary Christian guy.

The Christian man, often out of his desire to be a better Christian, curtails some of his outside reading to focus more on the Bible and other religious books, attends fewer social or cultural events because he's involved in church, Christian seminars, and maybe a weekly study group. Thus the Christian renaissance man fades away.

The Christian single man also struggles with the risk of becoming sexually involved. In seeking to live a godly life, he may be fearful of leading a woman astray, of getting too involved physically. He may see "group dates" as safer (while women find them less romantic). Consequently, he may hesitate to even make the first phone call for a one-on-one date.

It's Hard to Date
Your Christian Brother or Sister

Another reason I think nonChristian men may often be more appealing to our single women is because we emphasize and teach that we are to treat one another as brothers and sisters. But when you think about it, it's hard to kiss your brother or sister! That may have a dampening effect on dating within the group.

Social Transitions
and Confusing Role Models

Generally speaking, men are going through a transition. Because of the feminist movement, many men don't know where they fit. It's the age where women ask men out for dates, and many men—especially the older ones—are not used to that. It's also a transition for the divorced man who expected to be a breadwinner and provider but finds himself without a family to provide for.

There is also the confusion of what it means to be a Christian man. The model of Jesus in the gospels is one of a man who weeps, who cares for people, and in many ways is sentimental, loving, and sensitive. But those characteristics in our society are viewed by men as feminine. So the Christian man struggles with how to match up the "Rambo" values of our society with the image of Christ.

Suggestions
for Helping the Situation

Encourage single women to value Christian men. First, we need to encourage our single women to fight the temptation to lower their standards. When women feel Christian single men are weak and less than exciting, they are tempted to allow their high standards to erode by seeking non-Christian men to marry or by being involved in a premarital sexual relationship. This erosion occurs because they are tired of waiting for years to find the right man. They start wondering if their standards are too high, if they are being too picky. Their biological clock is ticking and many long to be a mom. But they look around and notice that few of the Christian guys are asking them out for a date—and those who do seem to lack "excitement" or refined social skills. The pressure is on the woman to make some choices.

But there's a long-term gain in waiting for a Christian man. In very practical terms, if we claim that Jesus is our best Friend and the Lord of our lives, and the One who has saved us from our sins and the messes we've gotten ourselves into, then don't we want to share our most important Friend and Lord with our spouse? If we can't share this most important Person and lifestyle, then we are setting ourselves up for a poor marriage—possibly, even divorce. The divorce rate is high enough already, so why increase the odds?

That's usually the way I approach it with my singles. It doesn't work just to say, "The Bible says." Advice needs to be very practical. I remind them that if they are building a house, make sure to get the foundation right.

Encourage single men to be in a small group. We need to make a concerted effort to get our men involved in covenant or small groups that pray, share, and study the Bible. They need the opportunity to meet on a regular basis—men with men—just to share their concerns, lower their masks, and talk about their insecurities about women, work, and their faith.

Many times singles join small groups to meet members of the opposite sex. But I'm convinced that men usually feel more free to talk about their real feelings when there are no women around. When they meet on a regular basis, the trust level goes up, the self-esteem rises, and they are more likely to work from strength rather than weakness. Because of that strength, the men can take more risks, and in being together they realize they are not alone. You can go from that refuge, have a date, then come back and say it didn't work or it did, and know you are okay either way.

Find creative ways to bring adventure into their life. Something I picked up from University Presbyterian Church in Seattle, Washington, is the concept of "God's Desperadoes" or "Robin Hood and His Merry Men." This is where you get a group of guys together for the purpose of doing secret ministries for the entire church family.

> "Another reason I think nonChristian men may often be more appealing to our single women is because we emphasize and teach that we are to treat one another as brothers and sisters. But when you think about it, it's hard to kiss your brother or sister! That may have a dampening effect on dating within the group."

Yes, Christian covert operations! They look for someone in need and then clandestinely go help solve that need.

For example, they might take a woman's car and have it washed, oiled, cleaned, gassed, and brought back without her knowing it. They just leave a note that says, "God's Desperadoes." This is an excellent way for single men to build camaraderie and to help them recapture some of their adventuresome spirit and excitement by finding a need and filling it.

Keep men in a visible leadership position. We are all painfully aware that more women come to church than men. But a downspiraling effect can occur if more women are visible in leadership roles than are men. This lack of visible male leadership makes men less likely to attend. Men won't continue coming to a singles group just because there are a lot of women there. Men respond best to other men in leadership. That's why we always make sure we have at least one male emcee.

Phil Kotke, a marketing expert, shared at a Fuller Seminary management conference that one main problem in the church is that we are not going after the men. Most church marketing appeals to women more than men. We simply have to make a concerted effort to go after the men. This means our singles social calendars need to reflect manly events. We need baseball games, white-water rafting, climbing the summit, retreats for men only, men's barbecues, and Bible studies. Potlucks alone won't cut it.

Encourage your singles to embrace

the adventure of front-line Christianity. As I said earlier, it can seem that nonChristians have more pizzazz. But one thing I try to teach is that this is only surface pizzazz. I strongly believe that if you are Christ-centered, you have the most pizzazz. When you become a Christian, it's like being Indiana Jones. You are on a mission for God, and it means being involved in the drama of helping and saving people from the forces of evil. It takes all of your mind and energy to plan it.

As Christians, we should go out on a limb—for God. Our faith in Jesus Christ empowers us to do things that we otherwise would not dare to even think of doing. In my church, the singles fellowship is perhaps the most active of all the groups. On Thanksgiving morning, they're the ones at the shelters serving food to the homeless. At Christmas time, they're the volunteers packing and delivering gifts to the needy families the church has adopted. During a weekend singles retreat, the Sunday school is in real need because many of the regular teachers are on the retreat.

I'm proud that our singles will drive two days to Mexico to help an orphanage. They'll take underprivileged kids on a weekend campout. They'll use their week's vacation to go to South America on an evangelistic outreach.

If you have single Christian men who are playing it safe, maybe you do have wimps. Challenge them to become God's Desperadoes, and I think you'll eliminate the wimp factor.

Men and Marriage

an interview with George Gilder
Author of **Men and Marriage** *and* **Wealth and Poverty**

In this interview, best-selling author George Gilder addresses the issue of single men, discussing these questions and others:

• *Should the church play "matchmaker" and be involved in arranging marriages?*
• *Are single men adrift without a marriage partner?*
• *Do single women determine the sexual conduct in a relationship?*

What is the most important thing that the church needs to understand about single adults?

That most singles want to get married. Marriage is a very honorable goal that shouldn't be disparaged or dismissed. Single adults in the church should not be embarrassed to pursue marriage.

Some people involved in single adult ministry teach that singleness—biblically speaking—is a high calling. Saint Paul and Jesus Christ are referred to often as single adult role models. How would you respond to someone who says that singleness is as high a calling as marriage?

The vast majority of single adults do get married. Their actions speak louder than any words that might celebrate singleness. Obviously, people can make a wonderful vocation out of all kinds of situations, including singleness. It is one way people can be used by God.

But at the same time, I don't think singleness should be considered equal to marriage. Generally, I think it is a less fulfilled condition. The state of singleness should not be especially sought after or celebrated—unless it is part of some very special vocation like the Catholic priesthood.

> "One thing that does not help is to preach about how wonderful singleness is. I think that's a subtle lie. For example, this teaching implies that women in their twenties should not be concerned with finding a husband. But they should be."

Are you saying that single adult pastors/leaders should encourage their single adults to get married?

Yes. Single adults need help in getting married. Our society doesn't offer it. Young adults are often thrust into big, relatively impersonal cities and communities with very little guidance. They desperately need help from the church in finding people of similar moral commitments and aspirations. I believe it is a fully legitimate role of the church to help arrange meetings—and to some extent, marriages.

How much should the church play "matchmaker"?

As much as is effective . . . and it isn't always. It requires a subtle, delicate touch. But this difficulty shouldn't cause the church to dismiss the role of pairing up singles.

One thing that does not help is to preach about how wonderful singleness is. I think that's a subtle lie. For example, this teaching implies that women in their twenties should not be concerned with finding a husband. But they should be.

Young single women have the unique power and opportunity to get married, which passes rapidly as they move into their thirties and beyond. They also have a relatively limited window of opportunity to bear children. That's a fact of life that some leaders seem to deliberately obscure. To imply that they've got all the time in the world doesn't help young women.

Neither does it help to imply that single men should not be diligently preparing for the responsibilities of supporting a family. The church that teaches singleness as a virtue can potentially cause an injustice to single adults by making them think marriage is an unholy pursuit.

One struggle many churches have is in attracting single men. Why do you think this is?

One of the primary reasons is that single men tend to drift. They don't have the kind of clear goals and attachments to community and to the larger issues of human life that married men do. But this means they need the church that much more. I believe most of them unconsciously feel this need, but they have to be forced to recognize it. Single men know there is a gap in their lives, but they are not quite clear as to just what this gap is. That gap must be filled with the gospel. That is our challenge.

Do you have any suggestions on how the church might be more effective in reaching single men?

I don't profess to have all the answers, but here are some suggestions:

1. *Strong leadership*. We need strong leaders who can attract single men—leaders who will stand up for what they believe in without embarrassment or self-righteousness. Men are attracted to this type of leadership.

Furthermore, the minister must always understand that beneath the bravado of secular single men, there is real vulnerability and need. The challenge for the minister is to break through that bravado in a nonoffensive, inviting manner.

2. *Openly discuss moral concerns.* Although many have not as yet recognized them as spiritual concerns, most single adults have real moral concerns. Today there is a tremendous gaping emptiness in secular society. There is no moral anchor or pillar. If the church can become the place where people go to discuss matters of importance in the world—without being intimidated by dogmatic preachers—it will be more effective in reaching single men.

3. *Accept single men as they are.* I know when I was single, I was resistant to categorical preaching. At the time, I was quite open to the church and even receptive to much of its teachings. But if somebody just came out and said categorically that I should

never sleep with a woman before marriage, I would have turned them off.

Remember where most single men are coming from—the mind-set that the secular world encourages. Don't expect them to understand Scripture at every turn or to profess the inerrancy of the Bible. These are things that they will usually come to recognize later rather than sooner. Allow them room to question, to disagree, to doubt, and to discover the truth as they grow. Don't force-feed.

4. *Attract single women.* One of the greatest motivators for single men to come to church is to have single women who want to get married instead of just "play the field." I'm convinced that most single men really are looking for good, moral women. Recent statistics about what men seek in a mate back this up.

One major theme in your book *Men and Marriage* is your conviction that man needs a wife. Why?

Children are man's link to future generations and in many ways the embodiment of his own future. Without connection to woman, man is estranged from the very chain

"The so-called sexual revolution has attempted to convince us that women should be as sexually active outside of marriage as men; anything else implies a double standard. I am not implying that men should be more sexually active; there is clearly no moral or biblical justification to suggest this. However, I am saying that when women, in particular, become permissive, society pays a great price."

of nature and the essence of biological continuity. Only through loving a woman can man gain connections to specific children who allow him to partake in the importance of life beyond his own immediate needs and desires. Only through marriage can men participate in the moral order of the family.

Furthermore, it is often through family that a man begins to recognize the value of the church and his own relationship with God. That's why I believe marriage is so critical to man as well as to the ministry of the church.

Do you think men need marriage more than women?

Yes. I don't mean to paint all men with a broad brush. There are many exceptions to what I'm about to say. Often men without marriage are a greater danger to themselves and to society than are women without marriage. This is statistically supported both in American and in most cultures around the world. Unmarried women may be frustrated and unhappy, but they are much less likely to be neurotic, violent, sick, addicted, or alcoholic than are unmarried men.

Does the church need to talk to single men differently than to single women?

In some areas, certainly. The so-called sexual revolution has attempted to convince us that women should be as sexually active outside of marriage as men; anything else implies a double standard. I am not implying that men should be more sexually active; there is clearly no moral or biblical justification to suggest this. However, I am saying that *when women, in particular, become permissive, society pays a great price.*

What women (and the church) should remember is that men will always "love them and leave them" if women allow it. It's always been true, and it always will be. Even if you ignore Scripture and look at life purely from a sociological point of view, women cannot allow themselves free sex.

The woman is the only one who can stop this male cycle of "loving and leaving." From my observation, when the church speaks to single men, it won't get very far by telling them not to be sexually active. Sure, it can say that to the few who are already committed to Christ. But the others will usually be reached more effectively by women— not through preaching. Some idealists may not like what I'm saying, but look around. A man's entire orientation— his body, his sense of himself in the world—consists of pursuing women and winning them. It can be a destructive drive when he is left to himself. But it becomes very useful to the women who know how to channel this drive. It is through these male desires that the woman can help bring about moral changes as well as marital commitment.

But women can only channel men's drives when they say no to sex outside of marriage. The church must teach this with a passion.

In what ways do men and women differ sexually?

Man's whole sex drive is toward

short-term pleasure. Sexually he has no other inherent goal. On the other hand, a woman's sex drive is long term. Arousal takes longer and lasts longer. Pregnancy lasts nine months. The breast-feeding and nurturing of the child goes even longer. All of this is part of the woman's sex drive. It has long-term commitment written all over it. The man's sex drive does not.

It is the role of women to persuade men to give up their short-term sexual interests and commit themselves to the long-term issues such as supporting children. If this role is not performed by women, it won't be performed. If the woman fails to say no, fails to channel man's natural short-term sex drive within the context of marriage, then there is a major breakdown in society.

The single woman needs the teaching and encouragement of the church to say no. The church must give her the confidence to say no and help her realize she's probably not going to find many men who are already wonderfully domesticated. It's a hard role for the woman. But it must be viewed as an opportunity rather than an obligation. In this she needs the support of the church.

Are you saying that single women have primary responsibility for sexual conduct outside of marriage?

Yes. I don't mean to imply that men have no responsibility here. The Bible certainly does not let them off the hook. And, clearly, there are many responsible, moral single men around the world. But generally speaking, in any culture, it is the woman who primarily determines sexual conduct. If she doesn't say no and doesn't steer the man toward long-term commitment, he will not move toward monogamy. In this respect, it is the responsibility of the woman to change the man.

This is where many church leaders think I'm wrong. But I genuinely believe that today's church must do a better job of teaching women to say no. The male species, generally speaking, will not be celibate spontaneously. If the woman is sleeping around, the man will not impose monogamy on himself.

The church can and must teach women the benefits —not only spiritually but sociologically and culturally—of saying no to sex outside the bonds of marriage. This is one of the ways the church can indirectly reach more single men.

> "When monogamy breaks down, powerful, older men dominate more than one young woman, whether marrying or exploiting them. Then young single women aren't available to young single men who are left out. When this happens—as anthropologists can show you—there is almost always an increase in homosexuality."

Concerning single adults, what do you see as the primary problems that have developed in our society due to the fact that women have become more promiscuous?

There are several things:

1. *Breakdown of monogamy.* Throughout history, men have desired

to have more than one wife. Our culture has not allowed men to have harems, but as women become more sexually permissive, men are able to meet their desire simply by having a series of young wives.

A typical stereotype is the older man leaving his wife for the younger secretary. Men marry younger women and younger women marry older men. With free sex, men have no reason to commit "till death do us part." On the other side, young women see no need to marry "for richer or poorer, for better or worse" when they can easily find someone who is already richer and better—often a married (or formerly married) man. Young women are able to marry success and power, and older men are able to fulfill their dream of polygamy.

The consequences are that older women are abandoned and many young single men have a hard time finding marriageable women in their age range. When you have a greater than normal number of young single men and older divorced women, you have a tremendous strain on society.

2. *Poverty and crime increases.* Young single men commit the vast majority of all crimes, and they earn just a little more than half of what a married man who is the same age with the same education, qualifications, and experience earns. They appear to be less committed to a productive role in the world.

Poverty grows because there are more single mothers. Female-headed families comprise nearly all of America's poor. The children in these single-parent homes suffer, as does the nation's economic prosperity, making this one of the primary social crises of our time.

3. *Homosexuality increases.* This is another consequence of the large number of young single men and older divorced women. Homosexuality is not some inborn tendency or innate propensity toward other men. It is something that men choose as a result of the short-term male sex drive gone awry.

When monogamy breaks down, powerful, older men dominate more than one young woman, whether marrying or exploiting them. Then young single women aren't available to young single men who are left out. When this happens—as anthropologists can show you—there is almost always an increase in homosexuality.

Around the world there is a correlation in ethnographic tables between societies with polygamy—which essentially means powerful men can have more than one wife—and societies with conspicuous homosexuality.

I don't mean to imply that single men need to be discouraged about their possibilities for marriage. In my opinion, any man who really wants to get married and is ready to love a woman can find one. But a broad sociological problem has developed, and it affects many single men who may not even realize they're being affected.

What can the church do to help solve these problems?

The church must remain confident and firm in its teaching that marriage is both holy and crucial in society. By upholding marriage, the church is not only catering to a particular scriptural dictate, it is also performing an absolutely crucial function in our culture.

Marriage must be one of the major banners of the church. A lot of people imagine that marriage can exist outside of the church. It may exist but it cannot survive. Marriage is much more than a consumer contract. It is a sacrament, a sacred institution. What has made marriage survive down through the centuries is its holy character.

Do you anticipate that divorce and the breakdown of monogamy will continue to increase?

No. I think the pendulum is swinging back. I believe this is happening because the increase in divorce has slowed for the time being, and there is the continual spread of evangelical churches. The evangelical movement certainly has its ups and downs, but the general upward thrust of this movement seems quite clear, and I think it will continue to prevail.

Editor's note: In the book *Men and Marriage* (Pelican), Gilder did not support his argument from Scripture or theology because his book research preceded his conversion.

My Response to George Gilder: Don't Blame Single Men for Everything

by Harold Ivan Smith
Founder of Tear Catchers Ministry, Kansas City, Missouri

It is one thing for a book to ignore Scripture, as does George Gilder's *Men and Marriage*; after all, it was written before he became a Christian. However, this interview with him on the same subject could not possibly, in my judgment, represent a New Testament understanding of marriage, mission, or evangelism.

His interview responses are a particular blend of right-wing Republican rhetoric, Mormonism, and Judaism. It is well written and appeals to a particular mind-set, but is also full of little illogical "holes" in which a less-than-careful reader can disappear.

I have read the interview numerous times; I have carefully read his book. I am still wondering how James Dobson and *Christianity Today* could find this man's writings so appealing.

When asked what is the most important thing the church needs to understand about single adults, Gilder answered, "That most single adults want to get married." After eight years in single adult ministry, I believe the most important thing the church still needs to understand is that single adults must *first* be accepted as first-class citizens. Then, I believe, the church must find a way to tap their incredible resources for mission and ministry.

Yes, I agree with Gilder that "the vast majority of single adults *do* get married." However, they do not *stay* married. Why? Because many have not been exposed to the basic New Testament doctrine: wholeness is found in Christ Jesus —and not in marriage. Too many of them attend churches where they will never be fully accepted into the life stream of the congregation until they are married.

> "Gilder needs to take a big whiff of reality. There are 7,266,000 more single women than there are single men. And if God isn't Mormon, Christian leaders have to deal with that imbalance. This simply means that singleness had better have the potential for being wonderful and fulfilling, or there are going to be a lot of angry women."

If the church could help them come to terms with their singleness, more of them would be ready for the responsibilities of marriage.

Simply, Gilder argues that "everyone ought to be married. The men and the women and the boys and the girls." He would rewrite the *Westminster Catechism*, which has stood for two hundred years: "What is the chief purpose of man? *To get married, legitimize his sexual drive (because he cannot possibly discipline it in any other way), have 2.3 kids, a boat in the driveway, an IRA, and vote Republican."* I will admit that it is preachable in many evangelical churches today—but it is not biblical.

It would be one thing if Gilder's ideas were new. They are not. Theodore Roosevelt tried this same doctrine of *suprafamilialism* in the 1910s; only Roosevelt argued that anyone who didn't have at least ten children couldn't be much of a man or a Christian.

A simple reading of Scripture shows that singleness is equal to marriage. I wonder what Gilder thinks about eternal life: Will he be comfortable there, since everyone will be single?

But the most objectionable part of his logic is his declaration that "preaching how wonderful singleness is" is "a subtle lie." *Lie?* Isn't that a bit too much? Simply put, as a divorce researcher who has sat in hundreds of restaurants and watched married couples eating in complete silence, I think Gilder's binoculars were pointed at the wrong object.

If marriage is so "wonderful," according to Gilder's logic, why are more people not *staying* married? And why are there so many desperately lonely and unhappy married people?

"A fully legitimate role of the church [is] to help arrange meetings" for matrimonial purposes, Gilder argues. The fully legitimate purpose of the church is to "go and make disciples of all nations, baptizing them in the name of the Father and of the Son and of the Holy Spirit, and teaching them to obey everything I have commanded you" (Matthew 28:19-20, NIV).

Did Jesus "command" marriage? Hardly. Did anyone in the New Testament "command" marriage? One could argue that the Apostle Paul did in saying "it is better to marry than to burn," but anyone with an understanding of Paul's teaching would know that he taught it is better to be under control than to be burning in the first place.

No, the command is this: "Seek first his kingdom and his righteousness, and all these things will be given to you as well" (Matthew 6:33, NIV). But there is no guarantee of marriage—or for a lasting marriage—for anyone these days.

Gilder's research is based on a fundamental error. He argues in his book, and alludes to it in the interview, that almost every problem in the world is caused by single males; if they would just get married, stay married, and raise their sons to follow the steps of "dear old dad," what a wonderful world this would be.

Well, Gilder needs to take a big whiff of reality. There are 7,266,000 more single women than there are single men. And if God isn't Mormon, Christian leaders have to deal with that imbalance. This simply means that singleness had better have the potential for being wonderful and fulfilling, or there are going to be a lot of angry women.

On the other hand, I do agree with much of what Gilder had to say on how the church could be more effective in reaching single men. Maybe Gilder's ultimate contribution to the church will be to spark a helpful debate on these issues.

Married Men, Single Women

Single Women and Affairs—Who Is Vulnerable?

an interview with
Catherine S. Smith
Clinical psychologist,
Pasadena, California

I n the following interview, Dr.
Smith addresses these questions:
• What type of single woman is
most likely to become involved
with a married man?
• How can someone best counsel
the single woman involved?
• What can single adult pastors do
to provide an effective support
system for women in their groups?

**According to researcher and au-
thor Laurel Richardson in her
book *The New Other Woman*, 60
percent of married men will have
a sexual relationship with an
unmarried woman by the time
they are forty. Based on your
experience as a Christian clinical psychologist, do you think
Richardson's statistic would also
be true among those in the
church?**

I think it's somewhat high. At the
same time, I don't think it's totally out
of line with the church population, especially among those under thirty or
forty. One difference is that many in the
church may be more likely to have an
emotional affair—one that is not con-
summated in a sexual relationship. But
overall—based on the shoptalk of
Christian therapists and ministers I
know—marital infidelity is a significant
problem in the church.

**What type of single woman is
most likely to become involved
with a married man?**

Based on my experiences, there are
basically three types: (1) the competent professional, (2) the woman who
is fearful of being totally absorbed by a
man, and (3) the woman who is going
through a major transition. Here's a
look at each of these types.

*The competent, professional single
woman.* She's what I would consider a
high risk. She's busy and has little time
to form strong, healthy relationships
with other single adults. Because of
pressures in the church to get married,
many singles have a "supermarket
mentality." I've often observed single
women—especially competent professionals—who decide at first meeting if
a single man is "eligible." Based on a
superficial observation, they often
decide he's not compatible and go on
to the next person.

Good relationships can grow only in
a casual, getting-to-know-one-another
friendship. They can't by deciding on
the second date if he's marriageable or
not. No wonder so many single adults
(both men and women) are unable to
develop deep, intimate relationships
with members of the opposite sex.
They simply don't give them time to
grow.

Thus, the single woman's life, to a
large degree, revolves around her

work. And what often happens, over a period of time, is that she develops this relationship with a married man, which begins totally safe and unpressured. However, the relationship gradually becomes deeper, more intimate, and vulnerable. The woman then begins to feel that she's found something wonderful, something she's never found in a conventional relationship. And that's the real danger; she begins to believe she can't find this level of intimacy in a conventional relationship.

The single woman fearful of being absorbed by a man. (This woman often overlaps with the competent, professional woman.) Often the stereotype of a typical married couple in the church is of a strong, outgoing man and a quiet, submissive wife with little or no identity of her own.

Many of today's single women—maybe even subconsciously—believe that if they get married, they too will have to become quiet and submissive. They are fearful of losing their identity. (Many divorced women are also fearful of this because they've come out of a marriage where their husband believed the stereotype and insisted that they live it out.) It's this fear that being totally controlled by the man is necessary for a Christian marriage, a marriage where two people become one—and the husband is the one.

Thus, some women seek a quasi-marriage. They get emotionally involved with a married man who can't ultimately reciprocate. They think it helps them maintain control over their life.

The single woman in transition.

Anyone who is going through major life changes—a divorce, death of a close friend, change in job or location, or loss of a parent—is vulnerable. This is especially true of women. Sometimes a married man can seem more secure and reassuring during these times.

What advice do you give to a single woman who is involved with a married man?

First, I explore with her why she is there. And to be quite honest, I don't accept as an answer "the great male shortage" excuse. That excuse is a way to not take responsibility for our choices. It buys into the assumption that women always need to marry a man who is more powerful, more competent, and older—someone who can take care of them. When women consider younger and/or less-successful men, there really is no male shortage.

I find out why she's in the relationship. What needs are being met that she believes are not going to be met someplace else? Once those needs are identified, I vigorously

> "Often the stereotype of a typical married couple in the church is of a strong, outgoing man and a quiet, submissive wife with little or no identity of her own. Many of today's single women—maybe even subconsciously—believe that if they get married, they too will have to become quiet and submissive. They are fearful of losing their identity. . . . Thus, some women seek a quasi-marriage. They get emotionally involved with a married man who can't ultimately reciprocate. They think it helps them maintain control over their life."

work to help her find other ways to have those needs met.

As a therapist, I don't see myself in a position to tell single women what to do. Instead, I push them in a confrontational, loving kind of way by asking, "Do you want to make that choice, and are you prepared to live with the consequences of that choice?"

> "Allow and encourage single women, as a group, to talk openly about what it's like to be thirty and single, to have sexual feelings, to have feelings of lust, to really be turned on by a particular guy. *The more those thoughts are kept secret, the more likely they will be carried out.* Sharing secrets with others is one way to develop accountability."

What will some of the consequences be for single women who choose to be involved with a married man?

Several come to mind. First, for those in the Christian world, it separates them from friends because they have this secret they can't tell anyone. It's taboo. So it damages friendships; it isolates.

Second, it sets up this fantasy of what a good man is. Because the married man is only involved for short periods of time, he can be exceptionally warm and supportive. So they begin to develop unrealistic expectations of men in real life.

Third, they stand a good chance of being miserably lonely and depressed on holidays. He's home with his wife and kids. But the single woman feels he should be with her.

Fourth, it puts their future on hold. Oftentimes the married man promises that he will leave his wife. By doing so, he is implying that the single woman will have a future with him. But statistically, that very seldom happens. Normally, the man will leave his wife immediately after the affair begins . . . or not at all.

And finally, it fosters a self-fulfilling prophecy that the only way her needs can be met is with an already married man. That sets up some very damaging patterns.

Earlier you talked about the importance of finding out the single woman's needs. Can you give an example of how you would do this?

Let's say she says, "I need 'that' [whatever 'that' may be] in my life." I start by helping her break down what "that" is. What does "I need 'that' in my life" mean? Does it mean she doesn't want to go to parties alone, or that she's tired of going to weddings by herself? Does it mean she wants someone who cares when she comes home at night? Does it mean she's tired of always feeling like she has to be the strong one, or that she wants someone with whom she can express her sexual needs?

As long as it's, "I don't have a man; I need 'that,' " it's too nebulous. All you can do is feel powerless to help her, and all she can feel is bad about it. Determine what is the "that" in that. It will help empower both of you to better discover her needs and healthy ways to begin meeting those needs.

(But remember that none of her needs will be met perfectly—in any relationship. That's mythology.)

What is one creative alternative you would offer to a single woman struggling with some of these needs?

I'd suggest she work as hard in her friendships as in her romantic relationships. While I was single—I married at age thirty—I learned how healthy it was for me to invest in my friendships, whether I was dating or not. Friends gave me someone to talk with after a long day. I also had a roommate who was a good friend. She cared about me if I was sick, and she was wonderful to talk with.

Relationships are essential, but you don't have them unless you invest in them. Intimate friendships with men and women help us be single and help us be married. Invest in people, then you will have friends to hold you when you need to cry, and to celebrate with you when it really matters. Friendship takes a major commitment of time; unfortunately, not everyone's willing to do that.

What would you say to single adult pastors who want to develop a support system for the single women in their group?

First, I would ask them to acknowledge the fact that all of us have clay feet; all of us are vulnerable. Second, I would suggest creating an environment where their single women can get together and talk openly about their different temptations. We don't have places where we can do that often enough.

Allow and encourage single women, as a group, to talk openly about what it's like to be thirty and single, to have sexual feelings, to have feelings of lust, to really be turned on by a particular guy. *The more those thoughts are kept secret, the more likely they will be carried out.* Sharing secrets with others is one way to develop accountability.

I would tell pastors to help their singles deal openly with their sexuality. Help them differentiate between sexual feelings and love, help them deal honestly with their desires to be held and taken care of.

Helen Gurley Brown, editor of *Cosmopolitan* magazine and author of *Having It All*, encourages single women to be involved with married men. (See next page.) How would you respond to her advice?

Her advice strikes me as exactly the opposite of "having it all." Rather, I would say it's advice for men who want to have it all—the wife at home who cares for the kids and the bright, attractive woman on the side. I guess I see it as a position where the women are ultimately saying, "I'm going to make a fundamental compromise. For whatever reason, I can't (or won't) have a normal, healthy marriage relationship, so I'm going to settle for next best."

Compromises in life are a reality. We all have to make them. But my question to the single women is, "Is this the compromise you want to make?" I believe there are many better, more satisfactory compromises.

I counsel quite a number of single women who are—or have been—involved with married men. If they were all wonderfully happy, fulfilled women, I might be tempted to think being involved with a married man is an acceptable compromise—except that the Bible is quite clear on this subject. But they are not happy and fulfilled, at least not for long. The compromises and choices they have made carry a heavy price tag. From my perspective, it's not worth it.

If you were a single adult pastor or leader, what would you do to help reduce this single women/married men problem?

I would talk to the women in my group, tell them this seems to be an issue on the national scene, and ask for their perspective. I'd ask them to help me understand the vulnerabilities that make it such a temptation for some women and how much of a problem it is in their circle of friends. And I'd ask them for suggestions on how our singles ministry could be more helpful in providing positive support.

SECULAR INFLUENCES ON SINGLE WOMEN

(Editor's Note: This article helps illustrate some of the popular influences on single women in our society today, even Christian single women.)

Helen Gurley Brown is founding editor and guiding light of *Cosmopolitan* Magazine, one of today's most widely read women's magazines. In Brown's 1982 book *Having It All,*[34] she gave the following advice to single women.

"I don't see how a single girl can survive without an occasional married man to fill in the gaps and stave off hunger during the lean days. Many people (especially married women) feel married men are off limits totally, for moral reasons (you ought not confiscate somebody else's property) and practical ones (he can never see you Saturday night, goes home, even on Tuesday night, right after dinner—or before).

"True, true, true, but to me avoiding married men totally when you're single would be like passing up first aid in a Tijuana hospital when you're bleeding to death because you prefer an immaculate American hospital some unreachable distance across the border.

"This is my reasoning about married men: (a) When you're single, it's important to have heterosexual male companionship. You must connect with men. (b) All the connecting doesn't have to be with somebody you could marry. (c) You should not go without sex too long. (d) Married men need you and are some of the homiest, appreciatingest, lovingest, most accomplished of our men sexually, and are there during a drought. (e) You can 'use' them selectively, to sleep with if you're lonely. Some take you to marvelous places; especially those on expense accounts away from home.

"No, I never considered husband-borrowing immoral because I didn't pick the husbands, they picked me, and if it weren't me they'd pick somebody else.

"What about her? I never worried about her. She's got a problem but you aren't it. He is it. A cheating husband will cheat with somebody—you are not that special."

I might also try to put together a panel discussion for one of my group meetings. The panel could include a married man and woman, a single man and woman. They—with a good moderator—could discuss relationships, temptations, and solutions. They could also discuss the pressures in our society to have instant gratification. Again, if the subject can be honestly and openly discussed in a healthy, constructive way, it will help decrease the problem.

Can a single adult ministry really make a difference? Is the problem so big and overpowering that no singles ministry can expect to have any effect on single women/married men relationships?

Certainly, there are social and individual pressures that make it very hard for any one ministry to fix things up. But each ministry can have a positive impact on the situation.

For starters, simply raising the issue in this interview has already helped make an impact. If each ministry will also find ways to raise the issue and discuss the problem, it would help people realize they are not the only ones who struggle in this area. It allows people to start talking. The more you talk about things in a healthy, constructive way, the less you will be taken by surprise; the less things will sneak up on you; the more you will have a chance to honestly think through the consequences of your choices.

How the Changing Workplace Affects Single Women/ Married Men Relationships

by Harold Ivan Smith
Founder of Tear Catchers
Ministry, Kansas City, Missouri

Clearly, for America's 33 million single women, "a good man is hard to find." Moreover, considering that there are 7,266,000 more unmarried women than unmarried men, the competition is not evenly balanced.

Four factors appear to be fueling this phenomenon.
1. The mortality rate between sexes favors females.
2. In an era of high divorce, men tend to remarry more quickly.
3. Men have a preference for marrying women from four to ten years younger than them.
4. There are a growing number of females in the workplace, particularly in management. Of the 1.5 million managers and executives who have never married, 40 percent are female.

It's hard to believe that just one hundred years ago, one owner of a carriage and wagon works thought himself liberal for offering male employees one night off a week "for courting purposes" (two nights if he regularly attended church). American business has traditionally argued that the workplace was no place for romance. No longer. Workplace romance is flourishing, and companies are granting grudging acceptance—if not blessing—to the fact. Research has found that American singles spend eight hours of company time monthly on their social life.

Savvy Magazine, in a survey of 1,125 women, found that the workplace is the most popular place for women to meet potential husbands.[35]

Some researchers are calling this "the heiress problem." Where do women with strong academic and business experience and economic independence find their prince charmings in a "husband pool that is sparsely stocked and heavily fished"? Author and researcher Laurel Richardson observed that the single men who are left "tend to be those who are the least well-educated, least well-off, least well-suited occupationally, and most prone to mental and physical illnesses."[36]

Other researchers agree with Richardson's sobering thesis. One said that "given the demographic constraints, many single women who accept the goal of heterosexual couple-

---

STEPS TO HELPING SOMEONE HEAL FROM AN AFFAIR
by Barry McClay
Singles ministry leader, Harrisburg, Pennsylvania

1. *Confront the person(s) involved, if necessary.* People in pain often avoid reality. When required, we must confront them with the truth, in love. To be silent is often to be uncaring. Jesus Christ touched people where they were. He wasn't shy with the woman at the well, or intimidated by the adulterous woman's circumstances in John 8. As "wounded healers" we must reach out to the people involved.

Take the following action if you know a married man involved in an affair:

- Confront him honestly and offer your support. Your boldness may shock him into choosing his spouse and improving his marriage.
- Team him with healthy, nurturing role models who will teach strong marriage principles by word and example.
- Assure him of God's forgiveness.

If you know a single woman involved in an affair, follow these steps:

- Offer a loving and understanding support group. Connect her to another woman who is qualified to become her "spiritual advisor." Accountability—with love—increases security.
- Discuss openly and honestly with her the issues and motivations that led her into the relationship. Get to the heart of the matter, then help her find ways to meet those needs in healthy and nurturing ways.
- Assure her of God's forgiveness.

hood will have to turn to socially disapproved ways to achieve it."

Why Are These Relationships Developing?

First, for many women, getting married is not their primary goal. They want to "get ahead" or "get established" in their careers.

Initially, single women in the workplace view men in one of three ways: as mentors, colleagues, or friends. Richardson observes that "with socially-acceptable rationale, the single woman's erotic attraction may grow free of guilt or undue expectation."

A married man offers an added element of control. One woman observed, "I know I can close the door when he leaves because the relationship does not control my entire life."

Thus many single women believe they can juggle an emotional intimacy with professional aspirations. Such relationships offer men a continuing supply of fresh sexual partners as well as an opportunity for intimate female friendships.

How Should a Singles Ministry Respond to These Married Men/Single Women Affairs?

1. *Address the problem.* Many young, naive single women argue, "It can't happen to me." The testimony of many in Richardson's research is, "Oh

---

I might also add that it is a good idea to teach your single women how to tell if a man is married or not. Sometimes married men will get involved with single women while professing to be single themselves. Encourage the women to ask these three questions of new men in their lives:

• Ask for his home phone number.
• Ask for his home address and hint that you might drop by sometime.
• If there are still questions, call his place of business and tactfully inquire.

2. *Focus on self-esteem needs.* Single women involved with married men usually—to one degree or another—have devalued themselves as persons and potential future marriage partners. To help single women see themselves as God sees them is obviously a great way to help them begin building a healthy self-esteem. Our heavenly Father sees us as valuable, lovable, forgivable, and changeable.

An additional note: From my experience, it seems that many of these women have not yet recovered from a previous marriage. Divorce recovery must be more than a course we offer; it must be a healing process we invite people into.

3. *Learn how to touch, and teach others to do the same.* Many single women say they accepted the advances of married men because of their need for touch and affection. Perhaps we need to address this issue more in our ministries. A "high-tech" society requires "high-touch." Jesus could allow a known former prostitute to wash His feet because He could differentiate between love and lust. We need to teach how to be intimate without being sexual.

4. *Pray.* Let us not forget prayer—the dynamic force that penetrates the issues of our lives and brings about change in people. Maybe our first step should involve praying to God, who has demonstrated again and again His power to change and renew us into the persons whom He created.

ARE ALL THE GOOD SINGLE MEN GONE?
by Connell Cowan and Melvyn Kinder
Authors of **Smart Women, Foolish Choices**

Many times we hear single women comment that the "good men" are all taken. Or that married men somehow always seem more attractive than single men. There is a simple explanation for this. Married or "attached" men are not that different from single men—they just behave differently. When a man feels secure in a relationship, he is able to act in a much looser, freer fashion with other women; conversely, men and women who are single tend to behave in tighter and more self-conscious ways with each other. This is why the singles-bar scene often seems so shallow and unattractive. The "good ones" are not all married; it's just that the security and confidence that marriage provides allow them to act in a more natural and relaxed way than their single counterparts. Let those nervous, shy single men find a woman to connect with and they blossom into "good" married men, too.[37]

yes it can!" All single adults should be sensitized to the warning signals as well as warned of the consequences; that is, pregnancy and firing. Many corporations still favor a double standard: The man will stay and the woman will be terminated.

The woman should ask, "Am I being provocative in my dress, attitudes, or office humor—even in an attempt to fit in?" Barbara Gutek's landmark study of sex in the workplace reported that many women believe women workers dress to be attractive—even sexually attractive. Gutek argued that many do so because they believe they will be better treated by colleagues if they are attractive.[38]

The subject is also appropriate for group discussion because many males don't know how to respond. Colleague pressure urges them to make subtle come-ons to females. Yet, they need positive male models.

2. *Respond through counseling.* Some women give off subtle signals, which can be radically misinterpreted (this is a common defense by many men in sexual harassment cases). The "poor me, who would notice me?" pose may really be a subconscious pleading that can best be tackled through counseling.

3. *Respond through subgroups.* Some churches have responded with "accountability" groups for career-oriented, professional women. Gutek suggests that there are subtle differences between blue-collar sexual harassment and coworker sexual intimacy as experienced by upper professionals.

Some of these relationships develop in what I call "project intimacy," during which colleagues put in long and late hours and develop a dependency that would not be found among regular nine-to-five employees. Or they have positions that require overnight travel (this is one reason many employees like to hire single adults; they are more free for overnight assignment). When tempted, the single woman may be hundreds of miles from a support group.

4. *Work for full compensation.* Women on the average earn sixty-two cents for each dollar earned by a male. The single woman (particularly the single parent) needs that big sale or promotion. The temptation is always that "the ends justify the means." Moreover, the lower-paid woman may find it hard to say no to a superior's sexually intimate advances or hints. She needs the job too badly.

Perhaps those who espouse the yuppie mentality—"Do whatever it takes to get ahead"—should be told that some of the costs are too high.

5. *Work to attract more men to single adult groups.* The perpetual problem is that women outnumber males in single adult fellowships. Moreover, a certain percentage of men who do participate are not deemed suitable potential mates, nor do they offer the networking contacts many single women desire as they "shop around" for a group in which to invest themselves. That is not "snootyism"; it's reality.

Sometimes the single adult leader may need to refer a single adult to another group that might more adequately meet the individual's needs. Some will attend other groups occasionally to fill this need.

6. *Work to short-circuit the response.* Women want to be praised for job achievement based on their merit. The subtle inference "she slept her way to the top" taints and follows one's resume. Moreover, it is not men who tend to be unforgiving but other women—particularly strong feminists.

I believe Laurel Richardson is correct in her assessment that the problem is

not going to go away. Single adult groups are called "to serve the present age, calling to fulfill," in the words of the old hymn. That means dealing with the cruel reality that a good man is hard to find.

The strongest single adult ministry is rooted in a biblical understanding of discipleship and a healthy understanding of the reality of the work world.

Passion and Love: What's the Difference?

by John Splinter
Associate pastor and director of singles ministries at Central Presbyterian Church, Saint Louis, Missouri

In dealing with the area of sexuality, whether at a Sunday school level or in small groups, it is helpful to differentiate between sexual encounter, intimacy, and love. (Singles groups can usually find many professionals of varying backgrounds to come and address this issue.)

Thinking that the two are somehow related, people often seek love but settle for passion. Sometimes they are related, but in the case at hand—a single woman with a married man—*the probability is that the woman's needs for emotional intimacy and connectedness are being bartered against the man's sexual objectives.*

In differentiating between passion

and love, the singles leader can help his people by asking the following questions:

1. Is the leadership in the relationship being provided primarily by God or by hormones?
2. Are one or both parties being rescued—or rescuing someone else—from some painful situation?
3. Is the relationship being based on a positive, productive friendship, or is it an escape from singleness and loneliness?
4. What age difference is there, and what does that tell the single woman about herself?
5. How close is either party to a past relationship?
6. Is either person rebounding from a recent relationship?

When relationships are held up to the light of God's Word, *the more rationalization used to justify what's happening in the relationship, the more probable that it is not God's best for the people involved.*

Talking About AIDS

QUESTION 1: In This "Age of AIDS," What Advice Do You Have for Those Who Work with Single Adults?

Three Leaders Share Their Advice

MY RESPONSE:
by Harold Ivan Smith
Founder of Tear Catchers Ministry, Kansas City, Missouri

There are several things I would suggest for every single adult pastor.

1. *Start with a major dose of reality.* Don't assume that a high percentage of your single adults are celibate. Get your head out of the sand. It is very likely that there are singles in your group who have dangerous sexual biographies. There may be others in your group who are having a hard time keeping their head on straight when it comes to sexual decision making. Don't ignore the issue. AIDS continues to spread in the heterosexual community. And just because they attend your church does not make your single adults immune.

2. *Go to a bookstore and get at least one good book on AIDS.* Get the facts. Know what the disease is all about, so you can adequately and intelligently talk about it with your single adults.

3. *Warn about the consequences.* Over the next few years most single adults will know someone with AIDS. They will have probably even helped bury a friend, relative, or coworker who died from AIDS.

4. *Find a ministry.* Have your singles "adopt" an AIDS patient in your community. Love them. Or care for a family who has a son or daughter with AIDS.

MY RESPONSE:
by Ron Sunderland
Research fellow at The Institute of Religion, Texas Medical Center, Houston, Texas

First and foremost, the leaders need to be educated. I believe there is an enormous responsibility in the local church to ensure that single adults are fully aware of the nature of this crisis. But the leader cannot do an adequate job of this unless he or she is informed. It is vitally important for single adult leaders to understand the nature of this virus and its transmission, as well as how it is not transmitted.

Second, they need to understand that this is no longer just a gay issue. Heterosexual transmission is fast becoming a major concern. It is true that current cases of heterosexual transmission are more concentrated in areas such as Newark, New Jersey, and New York City. But the related effect on the heterosexual community is ever-widening—and will continue to be so at an alarming rate.

Third, AIDS is even becoming an issue for churches in the smaller communities. True, most AIDS cases currently begin in the big cities because that is where young people from the smaller communities go to find work. But many families in smaller communities are now beginning to bring their sons and daughters home to die from this disease. As this begins to happen at an increasing pace all across the country, the AIDS crisis suddenly becomes more personal.

MY RESPONSE:
by Jim Talley
Singles pastor at First Baptist Church, Modesto, California

First of all, recognize the fact that many single adults are sexually active. From my years of counseling and working with singles, my guess is that—across the board—approximately 50 to 60 percent are involved with someone sexually during any given six-month period. That's the reality and we need to operate from that premise.

Second, find out which singles in your group are sexually active. The only way I know how to do this is to ask them one on one. I do this in my counseling, and I ask this of all my leaders. I also ask any of my singles who are involved in a relationship. A lot of people consider me to be a moral policeman. But according to Hebrews 13:17, those of us in leadership have a responsibility for the spiritual lives of those God has given to us. If I'm concerned about their spiritual life, I need to be concerned about their sexual life, too. It clearly affects their spiritual life. Many singles pastors are unwilling or reluctant to delve into these areas. Consequently, the spiritual lives of their single adults are suffering.

Third, remind singles again and again that there is no such thing as "safe sex" outside of God's boundaries. To encourage your singles to use condoms is ungodly and immoral. Our role is to call people to biblical, moral guidelines to purity.

QUESTION 2: Should Pastors Take an Active Role in Encouraging Their Single Adults to Be Tested for AIDS?

Three Leaders Share Their Advice

MY RESPONSE:
by Harold Ivan Smith

I am not in favor of a mandatory, nationwide testing policy. However, I think it's a very fair policy for pastors to require AIDS testing during premarital counseling. My main concern with this is that it may not be soon enough. The potential for heartbreak is greater if a couple doesn't discover the cold truth until they are just about to get married. For that reason, I think it may be wise for pastors to encourage their single adults to be tested if they have been sexually active outside of a marriage relationship during the past ten years.

There are many individuals who wonder if they might have AIDS, even though they're not in a high-risk category. For these people, realizing that they are not infected, through testing, can be an incredibly reassuring experience. I'm not referring to hypochondriacs here, but to people who have been involved sexually and cannot be certain about the history of their sexual partner(s).

This can also be a great opportunity for the pastor to address this issue: "Whatever you've done in the past, God has spared you from AIDS. Now, how are you going to conduct your life from this point on to make sure you continue to test negative? What are the values and spiritual commitments that will typify your life?"

MY RESPONSE:
by Ron Sunderland

I believe the time has now come (or very soon will) when the clergy must begin asking premarital counselees if either one has ever been at risk to contract the HIV infection. This is certainly true for those in the larger cities—especially those on the East and West coasts. In those areas, pastors need to be asking the question sincerely and routinely. I don't believe the clergy has the luxury any longer of avoiding this. The growing AIDS crisis forces us to take some responsibility in helping our dating or engaged couples to explore this area fully.

But even if few or none of your single adults are found to be at risk, the subject of AIDS and a person's sexual history raises the broader issue of how to be good stewards of our gift of sexuality. What does mutual responsibility mean with respect to sexual behavior? What are the values and guidelines that emerge from a study of the Christian Scriptures—or even from a study of Greek theology? Where is the balance between personal freedom and placing others at risk? "Safe sex" is not really the issue here. Instead, the issue is how we are to discipline our sexuality. The AIDS issue raises these questions and offers an excellent opportunity for leaders to make it a matter of discussion with their single adults.

MY RESPONSE:
by Jim Talley

As a church, we actively *require* AIDS testing for two groups of people:
- all couples in premarital counseling,
- all single adults over age twenty-five who have ever been sexually involved.

This is not a negotiable item, in my opinion. If they are dating someone, we ask that they share the test results with their partner. The reason it is not required of those under twenty-five is simply a matter of mathematical progression. The older one is, the greater the potential number of sexual partners and, consequently, the greater the risk.

We *request* AIDS testing for single adults under twenty-five. However, if we know from their history or personal admission that they have been sexually active, our "request" would become a little firmer.

I'm also for a national mandatory testing policy. It's very odd that in the United States, if a person tests positive for syphilis, a public health officer interviews that person and asks for all the names and addresses of sexual partners so, they too can be tested. Due to this effective method of control, we've had no deaths from syphilis in forty years. Now we have an even deadlier disease, but we are so concerned about people's privacy that we are foolishly preventing effective AIDS control.

Should We Talk About Condoms?

by Harold Ivan Smith
Founder of Tear Catchers
Ministry, Kansas City, Missouri

S
ome things will never be shown on TV," said a conservative friend of mine. I used to think he was right. I'd seen advertisements for constipation remedies, female douches, tampons, and Cross-Your-Heart bras on prime-time television. But condoms? Then last week I watched Phil Donahue throw packaged condoms out to his studio audience.

I have two strong memories of condoms from adolescence. One is daring a buddy to walk into the local drugstore and buy a box. The other is of a group of boys, all of us with our faces plastered to the storefront window, watching as he proceeded to do just that, and of Mrs. Hawkins, the druggist, catching us.

Suddenly, condoms are big news. The AIDS epidemic has made that a reality. Dr. C. Everett Koop, the former surgeon general of the United States and an evangelical Christian, wrote in his now-famous report on AIDS that "unless it is possible to know with absolute certainty that neither you nor your sexual partner is carrying the virus of AIDS, you must use protective behavior—i.e., a condom, from start to finish."

Syndicated columnists like Bob Greene and Roger Simon are writing columns with titles like, "AIDS changes singles' dating." And a cartoon in the *San Francisco Chronicle* shows a couple sitting on a couch, he at one end, she at the other, their hands touching. He is reading the *Joy of Safe Sex*. She says, "Okay . . . what's next?" He answers, *"That's it."*

And it's not men who are buying condoms. It's women. AIDS is now the number one fear of women in the United States. Contraceptive companies' ads are now targeting women.

A Mentor Contraceptives' ad has a startling young woman saying, "I never thought I'd buy a condom." Then the ad copy reads, "Let's face it, sex these days can be risky business, and you need all the protection you can get." The last line reads, "So why take your fears to bed?"

However, the real bomber ad is from *Lifestyles*. She's young and pretty, with curly blonde hair—speaks right into the camera. "I never thought having an intimate relationship would be a matter of life or death. Yet, because of AIDS, I'm afraid. AIDS isn't just a gay disease, and everybody who gets it dies. The surgeon general's office says proper use of condoms can reduce

> "For several years, J. R. Ewing has been seducing 1.4 women per hour on *Dallas*. Last year researchers found 20,000 sexual scenes on prime-time TV (not counting soap operas). And nobody uses any protection or suffers any consequences. Sexually transmitted diseases, including AIDS, can no longer be avoided by the church."

your risk, so you'd be crazy not to use them." But the final words hit hardest: "I'd do a lot for love [and a million singles nod in agreement] but I'm not ready to die for it."

So what's a singles pastor to do? He doesn't want his singles to be sexually active, but neither does he want to hear, "I wish you had warned me." For your own sake, and the sake of your singles, take at least these three steps:

Become Informed

For several years, J. R. Ewing has been seducing 1.4 women per hour on *Dallas*. Last year researchers found 20,000 sexual scenes on prime-time TV (not counting soap operas). And nobody uses any protection or suffers any consequences. Sexually transmitted diseases, including AIDS, can no longer be avoided by the church. Dr. Koop has dedicated a considerable portion of his time and energy to educating the church about the problem of AIDS.

Do yourself and your single adults a favor: read the report. You can order a single copy by writing for the *Surgeon General's Report on AIDS*, at AIDS, P.O. Box 14252, Washington, DC. The material is public domain and may be reproduced in part or in full. Another report, *Answers on AIDS*, is available from the American Council on Science and Health, 47 Maple St., Summit, NJ 07901, (201) 277-0024.

Don't Assume It Can't Happen in Your Church

I've talked to pastors who say, "Oh, that wouldn't be a problem for my singles." AIDS is no longer only a "gay"

WHO'S AT RISK?
by Harold Ivan Smith

Many of today's sexually active single adults—especially those who are not gay or drug-users—have convinced themselves that the threat of AIDS need not affect their sexual behavior. That is why Harold Ivan Smith, in his book, *Questions Singles Ask*, developed a series of "Before Bedtime Questions." As Harold says, "Many single adults still believe they are not at risk. But the truth is that every act of intercourse brings them closer to danger. It's like the more lottery tickets you buy, the better chance you have of winning."

For those single adults in your community who may think "normal heterosexual intercourse" is still risk-free, have them consider these questions before getting involved in a sexual relationship. It hopefully will cause some of them to think again.

Before Bedtime Questions
1. Is he/she bisexual? Would they admit it if they were?
2. Has he/she had a blood transfusion during the period from 1975 to 1985?
3. Has he/she ever experimented with intravenous drugs?
4. Is he/she hemophiliac?
5. Has he/she had sex with any of the above?
6. Does he/she know all the answers to questions one through five above for all of his/her previous sexual partners (since 1979)?

disease. In the words of Dr. Koop: "The risk of infection increases according to the number of sexual partners one has, male or female. The more partners you have (or have had) the greater the risk of becoming infected with the AIDS virus."

No one is immune from the realities of AIDS. Your nicest girls (and guys) can be infected with the AIDS antibodies by making only one mistake. Given the sexual activity of single adults that we know about from counseling, what is our responsibility?

Consider Discussing Condoms

A "Just Say No" campaign is a good place to begin, but don't stop there. Teach morality, but face reality.

You may not choose to distribute condoms in Sunday school, but consider using the national magazine ad on condoms as a basis for small-group discussion. Be prepared to openly discuss the consequences of sexual relationships as well as the counsel they need to hear concerning protection.

If you have single parents of teenagers in your group, help them educate their teens about the danger of premarital sex.

I believe AIDS is one of the biggest social challenges single adult ministries will face as we enter the next century. Your single adults receive wrong information from the media, from coworkers, from hearsay. They deserve to hear the naked truth from you.

> **"No one is immune. . . . Your nicest girls (and guys) can be infected with the AIDS antibodies by making only one mistake. Given the sexual activity of single adults that we know about from our counseling, what is our responsibility?"**

PART ELEVEN:

Budget
and Promotion

ABOUT PART ELEVEN

Here's a look at two of the "nuts and bolts"
areas of any successful singles ministry.

How can you increase your singles ministry budget?

What ways can you improve your
exposure in the community?

Several experienced leaders share their
insight and knowhow.

TWENTY - EIGHT

Singles Ministry Budget and Finances

The Financial Benefits of a Healthy Singles Ministry

by Bill Flanagan
Minister with singles at Saint Andrew's Presbyterian Church, Newport Beach, California

I don't know of any other ministry in the life of the church that can be more cost-effective—from a purely dollars-and-cents perspective—than singles ministry. When someone tells me they can't afford a singles ministry, I tell them they can't afford not to have one.

If you are a good singles pastor who understands the importance of integrating singles into the life of the church, the singles ministry will pay for itself and more. The upfront money to hire a staff person and launch a healthy singles ministry is an excellent investment that will yield a many-fold return in both ministry and finances.

First, the church needs to be aware of the adult population in the area. Single adults will comprise somewhere between 30 and 60 percent of any given community. If the percentage of single adults who participate in your church is less than the percentage of singles in the community, then your church is not reaching a significant segment of its "mission field."

I don't believe in a singles church any more than I believe in a church of just married people. But if the church's membership is seriously out of balance with the community, then there is a need to reevaluate ministry methods and objectives. The way to attract singles to the church is to make a place for them, to invite them, and to integrate them into the church body.

The church that builds a healthy singles ministry will do at least three things:
1. Actively bring and invite singles to be a vital part of the church.
2. Recognize the particular needs and concerns of single adults.
3. Develop ministries to address those specific needs.

It is important to note that an effective singles ministry is not just a "satellite ministry" where singles are stuck off in some corner or treated as though they are in a leper colony. A truly healthy ministry will integrate singles into every facet of the life of the church. When singles are integrated and made to feel a welcome part of the congregation, they will give back to the church in many ways. (The key word is *healthy*.)

A strong, healthy singles ministry can become one of the most cost-effective ministries in the church.

Financial Dividends of a Singles Ministry

Before I go further, I want to clarify something. Some may read this as a crass, unspiritual way to view a ministry. It is not my intent to communicate to anyone that increased income can or should be a motivation for developing a ministry with single adults. But it is my intent to help nullify the excuse that some church leaders use when they say they cannot afford a single adult ministry in their budget. After nineteen years in singles ministry, I'm convinced that a church can afford such a ministry. In fact, it can become a profitable investment.

When I interviewed for my position here at St. Andrews Presbyterian Church, I told the leadership that their financial investment in a new singles ministry—my salary, the expenses to establish the office and program budget—would all be recouped within three years. I was wrong. It took us only two years. There were that many new single adults funneled into the life of the church.

One myth I would like to debunk is that single adults don't have any money. Of course many don't, especially single mothers. But single adults can clearly be a significant financial resource in the church.

Here is a brief look at how our singles ministry has more than paid for itself.

Increased Membership and Giving

In the eight years I've been here, we have attracted many people through our various singles ministries.

Because we are meeting needs, these people say, "There's something real here, something authentic." Many of them ultimately choose to plug into the life of this church. (Today approximately 40 to 45 percent of all adults joining our church are single adults.) Many of them would have never be-

come involved here if it hadn't been for the singles ministry. It was their doorway into our church. Many of them are now married, have families, and continue to be a vital part of our congregation. A number of them are also now in key church leadership positions.

In addition, those who join our church make pledges and give regularly. Since we don't keep track of what each person gives, we don't know the exact amount of their offerings. But even if the single adults pledge and give less than our average member—and I don't think they do—they would still be bringing considerably more dollars into the church than we are spending in our total singles ministry.

If I were ever forced to justify my singles ministry purely from a dollars-and-cents standpoint, I could do it by citing the increased membership and giving to the church through pledges and tithes alone. In fact, I can show a financial profit. (We have between 120 and 160 single adults join our church each year. Our average giving per adult member is between $400 and $500 annually.)

In addition to this increased income,

> "When I interviewed for my position here at St. Andrews Presbyterian, I told the leadership that their financial investment in a new singles ministry—my salary, the expenses to establish the office and program budget—would all be recouped within three years. I was wrong. It took us only two years . . . [due to] the increased membership and giving to the church through pledges and tithes alone."

they have brought tremendous energy into the church. This is a value that cannot be counted in dollars.

> "In less than six months so far this year, we've made a $4,000 profit from our divorce-recovery classes. This profit says to our church leaders that there is something exciting and meaningful going on. Here's a program that is not even trying to make money, but because it is meeting people's needs, it is generating a financial surplus."

Class Offerings

My current program budget is about $20,000 a year. This does not include salaries, but it does include everything else: literature, postage, money for speakers, and other miscellaneous expenses.

We have three classes that meet on Sunday mornings. The classes take an offering each Sunday that goes directly into the general church budget. Last year, that offering totaled approximately $15,000. Thus, these classes alone pay for at least 75 percent of our program budget (and this is just from a loose-change offering).

Divorce-Recovery Workshop

Our divorce-recovery program is also a source of profit. We never intended to make a profit in this ministry, but because of its success and the numbers now attending, a profit is realized. We charge $20 for a six-week class. This money includes the book, refreshments, advertising in the newspaper, and a dinner for our leaders.

In less than six months so far this year, we've made a $4,000 profit from our divorce-recovery classes. This profit says to our church leaders that there is something exciting and meaningful going on. Here's a program that is not even trying to make money, but because it is meeting people's needs, it is generating a financial surplus.

Special Gifts and Donations

Another source of income is gifts above and beyond the normal giving. For example, I received a $4,000 check from a single man, an attorney, who had gone through our divorce-recovery program. He said, "I just want to tell you how much your ministry has meant in my life." Over the years I've received many gifts like this—although most were not as large—from people who just want to say thank you and express their appreciation for our being there when they were needing help.

These gifts go directly to the church office and are counted as donations to the church rather than to the singles ministry. Consequently, at the end of the year I can remind our church leadership of tangible evidence of how this ministry is touching people's lives.

Retreats and Special Events

In addition to the above revenue sources, we have many special events and retreats throughout the year. Our total in-and-out dollars in this area is around $200,000 annually. If you just plan for a very slight profit on each event, you can generate considerable extra income. Although we don't rely on this income heavily, I know of several other singles pastors who say they can fund all or most of their singles ministry budget just from this source. Because of income opportunities like this, many singles ministries have become self-supporting.

Although increased church income is not the reason for establishing a ministry, I think it's helpful to point out to those who are budget and cost conscious that investing in a healthy singles ministry can pay dividends both financially and spiritually as you become a sanctuary for wholeness and healing.

From $0 to $100,000 in Six Years— Increasing the Singles Budget

by Timm Jackson
Minister with singles at Second Presbyterian Church, Memphis, Tennessee

When Timm Jackson became minister with single adults at Ward Church near Detroit in 1978, he had no operating budget beyond his salary. Within six years, his annual singles ministry budget was over $100,000 per year and growing. During this same time period, average weekly attendance in the singles ministry at the church grew from less than 100 to more than 800. Here Timm explains some of the reasons behind this budget increase.

While I was at Ward Church, money for the singles ministry came from the church budget and offerings designated for this ministry. (The church forbid fund raising.)

During the period from 1978 to 1984, both components of our budget increased dramatically. By 1983, the church's budget allocation from the general fund for the operating costs of the singles ministry had increased from zero dollars to $51,000. And by 1984, designated gifts to the singles ministry for that year totaled $50,000—nearly half of our $100,000 budget.

What convinced church leaders to spend more on the singles ministry? And what motivated members of our congregation to contribute more to this work? For one, they saw that we were meeting genuine needs and developing a quality ministry. But our church leaders also saw that the singles—once their needs were being met—were actually giving more to the church than the church gave to them in terms of dollars budgeted.

And their giving didn't slow down thereafter, despite a leveling off in the church's budget for singles. In 1988, when the singles ministry was still spending around $51,000, the singles gave more than $80,000 back into the general church fund through Sunday school offerings and gifts received at our regular Friday night activities. In other words, the singles generated nearly $30,000 more than was spent on them.

Why Has Our Ministry Become Financially Healthy?

Although I must admit it is sometimes a mystery to me, I believe there are four reasons why we have developed our financial base:

The single adults have emotional ownership of the ministry. Singles like to pay their own way. In my opinion, the church should never subsidize the singles ministry. All the church should do is provide start-up, opportunity, encouragement, and spiritual support. If singles sense ownership, they will give exceedingly of both their time and money.

> **"Our church leaders saw that the singles—once their needs were being met—were actually giving more to the church than the church gave to them in terms of dollars budgeted. . . . The singles generated nearly $30,000 more than was spent on them."**

Scratch where people itch and they will respond. Our people give because we focus on meeting their needs. We deal with things they struggle with or have questions about. When people personally experience the value and benefits of a ministry, they will be generous givers.

Give them an opportunity to be part of something that is bigger than they ever dreamed possible. Helping them catch a vision of what they can be and do with God's help is so important. It's more important than most of us realize. When single adults are successfully challenged to reach higher, to participate in some meaningful project or activity that helps change lives, that stretches them and they will be willing givers.

Produce a top quality ministry. We go after the leaders in our community. When we reach the sharpest people in town, the others will follow. But the leaders are generally talented and sophisticated, so we must be too. For example, when we have a special program, we design a stage set that would compete with a professional TV studio. We will not accept mediocrity. We push for professional quality in everything we do. Consequently, not only do the people come, but they also bring their friends and exhibit a willing desire to contribute financially. We seldom have to even talk about money.

TWENTY NINE

Advertising and Promotion for Your Singles Ministry

Effective Advertising on the Cheap

by Bill Pentak
Minister with singles at Sagemont Baptist Church, Houston, Texas

Have you ever noticed how our Lord always had a way of arresting the attention of others? Wherever He was involved in the work of ministry, He was either changing lives, causing riots, or challenging the status quo. Jesus was rarely, if ever, ignored.

That's why it's an absolute tragedy to find churches and single adult ministries that are casually neglected by the very people they are so desperately trying to reach. It seems, sadly, that the only attention the Church of Jesus Christ has managed to receive has come, lately, from the widely circulated stories—so reminiscent of daytime soap operas—of recently fallen television evangelists. It's a sad fact of our times that, when it is noticed, the church gets into the papers for all the wrong reasons.

Without question, you and I have more tools at our disposal to spread the gospel message than any of our predecessors ever dreamed of. At the same time, however, far too many single adult ministries are slowly starving away due to a lack of visibility either within their respective churches or in the communities in which they exist.

This crippling problem usually stems from either a lack of understanding by single adult leaders on how to properly advertise their ministries (advertising is one of the practical courses that seminary *doesn't* teach) or the opinion on the part of some, perhaps within their ministry, that advertising is somehow evil.

Effective Advertising

While our adversary undoubtedly uses Madison Avenue advertising techniques to sell sensual wares to the world, advertising in and of itself is not worldly. It is nothing more than a modern form of communication, a means to whatever end you choose to direct it. It is, in other words, an effective communication tool whose use depends solely upon the hand that wields it.

Sadly, while many spend their time debating its use in the church, our adversaries are using its effectiveness to sell a despairingly empty lifestyle to single adults by the tens of millions. It is high time, I think, for us to take this tool into our hands and use it to reach singles with a message that they are "complete in Christ" and that places exist where they can be accepted for who they are.

Effective advertising can do absolute wonders for your ministry. Not only will it generate more visitors for your ministry, it will also influence your community's opinion about the work you do. When I left my post as college minister at First Baptist of Houston to become minister with single adults at Sagemont Baptist, I walked into a ministry that had suffered declining attendance because it had no singles minister. My initial task was to reach our community with a message that Sagemont Baptist was beginning a brand-new ministry with single adults.

The fundamental question I asked was how I could capture the attention of Houston—all the way from south of downtown to the Clear Lake/NASA area. I decided to kick off our ministry with a "no holds barred" Sunday school rally featuring a contemporary Christian band, a catered breakfast served on real china, and a message from the new singles minister. At that time our attendance was averaging somewhere between eighty and ninety. Our "hallelujah" goal that Sunday was 200. (In its heyday, the singles ministry had never run over 150, so our goal was an ambitious one.) I planned a media blitz utilizing several different forms of advertising. Publicity for the event reached more than 1.5 million people in the Houston metropolitan area. As a result, on Sunday morning, June 15, 1989, our "grand opening" saw the arrival of more than 350 single adults!

Most astonishing was the discovery that our most effective techniques— the ones that reached the most single adults—cost well under $100! Herein lies one of the true challenges in promoting our ministries. Anyone can generate mass appeal with a wheelbarrow full of money. The challenge is to grab the attention of others with techniques that are at the same time effective *and* affordable. This involves not only doing things right, but also doing the right things. In my experience, this means using direct mail and carefully written news releases as two of the most effective and cost-efficient methods of promoting a ministry.

Direct Mail:
Low-Pressure Communication

In a recent Roper poll, 2,000 adults were given a list of twenty-one different daily activities and asked to rank them according to what they enjoyed most. Sixty-three percent of the respondents said the one thing they most looked forward to was getting their mail.

Contrary to what most people would have you believe, people enjoy getting "junk" mail! This illustrates one reason direct mail has been found so highly effective. Adults primarily enjoy this "daily activity" because it gives them an opportunity to consider new information without feeling the pressure of a sales job. Direct mail is, in other words, psychologically nonthreatening. A personal phone call or a visit from your ministry may be intimidating, but single adults can sit back, kick off their shoes, and read their mail in a relaxed atmosphere at their own convenience.

> **"Most astonishing was the discovery that our most effective techniques —the ones that reached the most single adults—cost well under $100! Herein lies one of the true challenges in promoting our ministries. Anyone can generate mass appeal with a wheelbarrow full of money. The challenge is to grab the attention of others with techniques that are at the same time effective *and* affordable."**

It's effective because it communicates a message at a time when the receiver's defensive barriers are down.

You will also find direct mail advantageous inasmuch as it allows you to speak to a large number of people at one time. I urge the pastors who attend my promotion seminars to put as much time and effort in the preparation of their church promotional materials as they do preparing for their Sunday sermons since it is likely that far more people will read the church's mail that week than will be in attendance Sunday morning to hear the weekly message.

Finally, direct mail is very effective since it is a more enduring form of advertising. Although radio and television have the potential to reach vast markets, they are by their very nature fleeting. (Thirty seconds later your advertisement is gone.) Direct mail has a much longer "shelf-life." Several weeks after our grand opening rally, for example, one single adult who was unable to attend earlier joined our ministry. During a "down" period in his life, he visited our ministry because he came across an "old" promotional piece we had mailed to his home weeks earlier.

> **Imagine a more difficult task than to be a recruiter for the armed forces. If they advertised the way many of our churches do, our volunteer army would be a disaster. They don't emphasize the "what" (six weeks of pure punishment in boot camp and a six-year enlistment). They tell you the benefits of enlisting. They admonish that "Uncle Sam wants YOU!" and that he wants to help you get your education, learn a career, and see the world.**

Writing a Direct-Mail Piece

Using direct mail is probably nothing new to you. Most single adult ministers keep a current mailing list of "members" and "prospects." Most direct mail, however, is poorly written. When writing copy for direct mail or any form of advertising, remember certain basic guidelines in advertising copywriting.

1. The most important is to *write the ad from your target audience's point of view*. Don't forget that the most important word in the English language is the word *you*.

2. This means, furthermore, that the bottom-line key to persuasive communication is to *tie your message around your audience's personal needs*. Most promotional material, unfortunately, is simply a regurgitation of who, what, when, and where. Spend more time emphasizing the why. *Tell them why they should come.*

3. *Explain the benefits they will receive from coming to your ministry.* One direct-mail piece we did, which was also reduced for a newspaper ad, admonished singles to "find encouragement for today and hope for tomorrow."

Imagine a more difficult task than to be a recruiter for the armed forces. If they advertised the way many of our churches do, our volunteer army would be a disaster. They don't emphasize the "what" (six weeks of pure punishment in boot camp and a six-year enlistment). They tell you the benefits of enlisting. They admonish that

"Uncle Sam wants YOU!" and that he wants to help you get your education, learn a career, and see the world.

4. *Be positive;* never use religious jargon (if you want to communicate in a language the nonchurched can understand).

5. *Proofread* your material.

News Releases

By far and away, the most important promotional tool for my ministry has been the use of the news release. With it I have received free advertising from newspapers, periodicals, and radio stations that otherwise would have cost thousands of dollars.

A news release is essentially a one-page news brief that covers the broad details of an event I am trying to promote. (See example.) I'm careful to keep it brief and to the point, covering the five *"w's"* (who, what, where, when, why) of good reporting. I title the news release and put the most important information in the first paragraph. (If you don't catch the reporter's interest right away, he or she probably won't read the rest.) I put "For Immediate Release" on the right side of the brief and include the date of its issue underneath. The release also includes the name, title, address, and phone number of a "contact" person in case a reporter has any follow-up questions. I send this out at least ten to fourteen days in advance of the event to every media organization in and around the city of Houston.

At the same time, I am continually building a mailing list of every publication, newspaper, locally based periodi-cal, and radio and television station in the Houston metropolitan area. I start-ed this list by scanning the area phone books. Now, whenever I walk into a grocery store, newsstand, or any other place of business, I pay close attention to any new start-up publications in our area. I buy copies of such publications and ask my secretary to find out the name, department, title, and address of the staff member who handles local news and publicity. I then add him or her to my mailing list, which now in-cludes more than 100 media people in our metropolitan area.

For our opening rally, for instance, I sent a news release to every one on our media mailing list, and for the top two newspapers in our city (the *Chronicle* and the *Post*), I included a black-and-white glossy photo of our guest artist. The *Chronicle* ran the pho-to with a caption on the event (which would have cost at least $800 for a sim-ilar-sized ad) and the *Post* made men-tion of it in the community calendar. The *Pasadena Citizen* ran a story on the rally, and we received coverage on KSBJ and KHCB, the top two Christian radio stations in this market. The total cost for all this coverage was little more than the price of a first class postage stamp!

Recently, I was put in charge of pub-lic relations for the biggest church-wide event we have—the annual "Wild Game Extravaganza." I sent out a press release packet. It included a press re-lease on special "Wild Game" logo sta-tionary, copies of all promotional mate-rial, and a ten-minute professional video, which was produced two years previously. (The copies we sent to the local television stations were duplicated on one-inch video tape.) Cecile White, religion editor for the *Houston Chronicle*, was so intrigued that she personally did a story on the Extravaganza, interviewing several guests and members of our church who were present. That next Saturday, the front page of the largest newspaper in Texas ran a "teaser" to entice readers to look in the religion section for a story about the "Wild Game Extravaganza" at our church. The en-

Singles Ministry
NEWS

Contact:
Bob Redding
Sagemont Baptist Church
11323 Hughes Road
Houston, TX 77089
(713) 481-8770

FOR IMMEDIATE RELEASE
MAY 22, 1989

Sagemont Baptist Church Launches City-Wide Singles Ministry with Gabriel in Concert June 4

On Sunday, June 4, Sagemont Baptist Church will launch its new city-wide singles ministry with a rally featuring Gabriel, a contemporary gospel band. The rally will take place at 11:15 a.m. at the Sagemont Singles Center, 11514 Hughes Road (at the corner of Hughes and Southbelt).

Guests will enjoy a catered lunch and a message from Bill Pentak, Sagemont's new minister with single adults. They will also be given a four-month special events calendar and single adult promotion packet.

For more information, call our 24-hour hotline at 922-1010, ext. 60.
To make reservations for child care, interested singles may call the single adult office at 481-8770.

–30–

tire front page of the religion section was covered with a color photograph and a feature article, which took almost two full pages. That kind of coverage would have cost us literally thousands of dollars. What it took instead, however, was careful planning and forethought about the kind of story that might interest a reporter.

Preparing News Releases

When producing a news release, remember to use eight-and-one-half-by eleven-inch plain white paper. (Reporters aren't interested in what it looks like, they're interested in its content.) I've also learned that it's good to put the personal home phone number of the "contact" person on the release. That tells reporters they can call the contact person at their own convenience. When sending a photograph, be sure to provide a high quality black-and-white glossy photo. Also, rubber stamp your organization's name and address on the back of the photo. If they choose to file it, they'll know who to contact later. Don't expect to get it back.

Use of News Releases

Finally, when using news releases, remember these vital guidelines.

1. *Don't overuse them.*

2. *Use news releases for those events that have the best capacity to draw a crowd.* If you send your newspaper editor a release for every event you have in your singles ministry, he or she will eventually file them in the wastebasket before they're ever opened.

3. *Don't take it personally if after all this work, the major paper in your town doesn't run anything.* Don't forget, the editors of a paper are looking for news, and depending on how desperate they are to fill up their edition, news is whatever the editor says it is. (This will vary from day to day, depending on the other news items needing coverage.)

4. *Recognize that you are competing with every other organization in your area that has a social calendar.* Since many of these organizations regularly meet on the second Saturday of the month, for example, plan your really big events during a month that has five weeks and plan it during the fifth week. You'll have a lot less competition for attention.

Advertising can be, without doubt, one of the most effective tools your ministry has for reaching out to single adults in your area. Contrary to what you may think, the kind of exposure you desire does not require a large advertising budget. What it does require, however, is a basic understanding of which methods to use, how to get your message to the proper people, and how to frame it in such a way that they will read it and use it.

> **"Advertising can be, without doubt, one of the most effective tools your ministry has for reaching out to single adults in your area."**

How Targeted Advertising Can Help Build Your Ministry

by Rich Kraljev
Minister with singles at New Hope Community Church, Portland, Oregon

In the late seventies, I attended a workshop at the Crystal Cathedral where I heard Jim Smoke share how his singles ministry had grown to over 1,000 singles a week. I was impressed! Just a handful of singles were attending my church at the time. Even so, I made it a goal that with God's help our church would reach similar heights. It seemed like an impossible dream at the time, but that dream eventually became a reality.

The success of New Hope Positive Singles has been explosive. Of the church's 3,200 active members, 30 percent are single adults. Much of this success has been due to our ability to communicate to the unchurched public the need-meeting ministries we offer.

Prior to becoming a pastor, I spent ten years working for a major airline. It was there where I first understood the power of advertising. I discovered that in order to reach people you must go where they are and let them know you have what they need! Even Jesus was acquainted with the power of advertis-ing. He knew that too much at the wrong time was harmful to His purposes (Mark 5:43, 8:30; Luke 5:14).

I'm convinced that if you're interested in fulfilling the Great Commission, the use of advertising media is a must. The following six steps will help you develop a strategy for advertising your single adult ministry.

Identify Your Market: Whose Attention Are You Trying to Capture?

This is *always* step one. Many singles groups get off on the wrong foot because they fail to establish a clear-cut idea of who they're trying to reach. They wallow in mediocrity because they aim at nothing and hit it.

My brother is an automobile executive who sells Buicks. He has discovered that the average Buick buyer is fifty-three years old, financially stable, and generally conservative in his views. He advertises in a manner that attracts this group of consumers.

As a single adult minister, how do you determine *your* target market? First, gather your leadership together for a brainstorming session. Develop a one-sentence statement of direction and purpose for your ministry. For example, our purpose at New Hope is "to reach the unchurched thousands of singles in our community for Jesus and to help heal their hurts and build their dreams." Everything we do is governed by this statement.

Next, find out the specific characteristics of the people you want to reach. I've learned that the majority of people described in our purpose statement don't go to church, are divorced (80 percent), are in the age range of twenty-five to forty, and are raising kids while holding down jobs. In their spare time they are trying to build relationships. Most of them are really hurting and are frantic for help.

Advertise in Places Where Your Market Looks for Help

Over the years, I've advertised via television, radio, and newspaper. All three are powerful, but I've found the printed word gives the best results. Why? Because of its staying power and circulation. Print doesn't disappear over the air waves, and is often passed from friend to friend. Many have come to our ministry because a caring relative or acquaintance clipped out an ad and gave it to them.

The newspaper you choose is also important. Inexpensive ads may not be as big a bargain as you think. I choose to run ads in our state's largest newspaper. It may cost more than some of the so-called bargain papers, but I find confidence in knowing that one out of two people in my community read it.

The section of the paper you advertise in is just as critical. The church page is wonderful, but unchurched people don't read it. Some of my most successful ads have been placed where the unchurched look for direction and guidance: next to "Dear Abby," by the TV listings, on the sports page, and by the daily horoscope.

Commit a Percentage of Your Budget to Advertising

At times I've set aside as much as 70 percent of my singles budget for advertising. Although that may sound irresponsible to some, I know that those advertising dollars are not wasted because the returns come back in the most precious of commodities—people. The harvest is in people finding Christ and lives being transformed.

An additional benefit of spending dollars for advertising is that, as it brings in more people, your financial base will increase. This in turn helps pay your newspaper advertising bill. Good advertising *always* pays for itself many times over.

> "The church page is wonderful, but unchurched people don't read it. Some of my most successful ads have been placed where the unchurched look for direction and guidance: next to 'Dear Abby,' by the TV listings, on the sports page, and by the daily horoscope."

Effective Advertising Has Cumulative Results: One Shot Advertising Doesn't Work

A singles minister friend of mine, whom I had encouraged to do more advertising, called one day to announce failure. "I ran one ad and it didn't work," he said. I wasn't surprised. Several years ago when I first began my singles ministry ad campaign, I went twelve weeks without one new person. I was ready to give up when on the thirteenth week our first visitor arrived at the door.

Print ads have a snowball effect—the more you advertise, the more momentum you develop. One single man who came to our group told me that for ten weeks he cut out our ads and taped them to his refrigerator. The eleventh week he took the leap and came to one of our activities. In order for advertising to work, you must commit yourself financially and creatively to a long-term program.

Highlight the Ministries that Meet the Real Needs of Single Adults

This is a list of some of the ministries we've developed over the years:
• Divorce Recovery
• Separation Survival
• Single Parent Support Group
• Children of Divorce Classes
• Free Professional Child Care
• Sports Ministries
• Counseling Center
• Social Activities
• Retreats and Camps
• Big Brother and Sister Outreach
• Helps and Service Exchange
• Grief Recovery
• Positive Preaching
• Book Ministry

These are what we advertise and what people respond to. If your ministry is small and you offer only one or two of those things, just advertise what you have. As people come and find Jesus, are healed and begin to grow, they begin to provide the base for new areas of ministry that will eventually draw others. The possibilities are limitless. The key is to let people know what you have.

Use Clean, Sharp Graphics and Language that Stir Excitement and Draw Attention

I'm a big fan of doing things first class for the cause of Christ. Two mistakes Christian organizations often make in their advertising are the use of somber, lifeless graphic design, and language that is cloaked in Christian buzzwords. The goal is to *communicate*! At New Hope, we communicate by presenting a sharp, clear, positive image in language the unchurched person can understand.

Some of you may be saying, "But I'm no graphic designer. What do I do?" I'm not a graphic specialist either. Most of my ideas I borrow. I read magazines, newspapers, and other printed material on a regular basis. I watch for well-done ads in newspapers and magazines and try to learn from them. What are the elements that made this ad catch my eye? If I find án idea I like, I clip it and file it for possible future use.

To make sure the language you are using in your advertisement is understandable to the lay person, make a rough copy and show it to a nonChristian friend. If he or she understands it, you will know it is something that the general public can relate to.

If you need assistance with layout, you will find that most major retail advertising newspapers are more than happy to help you. They can take your rough ideas and make them photoready at little or no cost to you.

Making Word-of-Mouth Advertising Work for You

by John Etcheto
Minister with singles at Reno Christian Fellowship, Reno, Nevada

Experts agree that one of the most effective advertising methods is personal referral—"word of mouth." But good word-of-mouth advertising does not just happen. It's created. It's not just a one-shot project. It is an ongoing process, a mind-set. Here are three things I've found helpful in maximizing word-of-mouth advertising in our singles ministry.

CONSISTENCY...
Remind, Remind, Remind

Key one is consistency. You must consistently remind the members of your singles group to tell others about your programs and to bring new people to activities. A very visual reminder is to leave an empty chair on your platform or in some other visible place during your singles functions. Encourage your singles to think of someone they know whom they could invite to "fill the empty chair."

CONVENIENCE...
Positive Pocket Pass-Alongs

The second key to word of mouth advertising is convenience. Make it easy for people to invite others to your activities. Your brochures and pass-along materials should be upbeat, positive, and bright. They should include clear directions or maps. People can't come if they can't find you.

One of the most effective aides my singles group has developed for word of mouth advertising is an expanded business card. The card contains the standard information on its face and a map to the church on its back. The card is twice as big as a regular business card but is folded to standard size. When opened up, the space inside acts as a minibrochure. It gives expanded information on our goals, objectives, and programs. Because of the size, these cards are convenient to pass out and easy to carry.

Another effective word of mouth advertising tool we use is an idea we borrowed from the singles ministry of Trinity Baptist Church of Santa Barbara, California. We include two copies of our monthly activities calendar in the mailings to our singles group. With the calendars is a note asking the person to pass one along to a friend.

COMMITMENT...
Telling Takes Time

The third key to word of mouth is commitment. The word of mouth process takes time. It does not generate large crowds at first. What it does generate is superior retention. People who come to your group through personal referral are far more likely to stay than those attracted by other forms of advertising.

List of Contributors

Ash, Mary Kay, is founder and owner of Mary Kay Cosmetics, Dallas, Texas.

Avlakeotes, Bret, a graduate of Dallas Theological Seminary, is single adult pastor at Fellowship Bible Church of Park Cities, Dallas, Texas.

Bellah, Dr. Robert N., is professor of sociology at the University of California, Berkeley. He is the author of *Habits of the Heart*.

Bennis, Warren, a psychologist, is professor of management at the University of Southern California School of Business Administration.

Black, Willard, a single parent and former pastor, is founder and director of the Institute for Christian Resources, Inc., San Jose, California. The Institute provides education resources for Christian living with an emphasis on family adjustments and social issues.

Bradshaw, Dr. Charles, is vice president of communications for Wycliffe Associates, Orange, California. He is also president of The Bradshaw Group, a consulting firm specializing in organizational development and planning from a Christian perspective.

Chandler, Rod, is associate pastor at Oakview Church, Centralia, Washington. Prior to his current posi-

tion, he was director with single adult ministries at Trinity Church, Lubbock, Texas. He received his master's in administration from Willamette University, Oregon.

Chun, Dan, is minister with singles at Menlo Park Presbyterian Church, Menlo Park, California. He received his doctorate of ministries and M.Div. from Fuller Theological Seminary. Prior to becoming a pastor, he was an award-winning film-maker and a journalist for a CBS news affiliate in Honolulu, Hawaii.

Cowan, Dr. Connell, is a clinical psychologist with a practice in Beverly Hills, California. He is a graduate of the University of Houston. Dr. Cowan has coauthored *Smart Women, Foolish Choices* (Clarkson & Potter) and *Women Men Love—Women Men Leave* (Clarkson & Potter) with Dr. Melvyn Kinder.

Crabb, Dr. Larry, is the author of several books, including *Inside Out* (NavPress) and *Understanding People* (Zondervan). He is the founder of The Institute of Biblical Counseling and is the chairman of the counseling program at Colorado Christian College, Denver, Colorado.

Crist, Johnny, a graduate of Fuller Theological Seminary, is senior pastor of Vineyard Christian Fellowship, Atlanta, Georgia. Prior to accepting his current position, he served as single adult pastor at MetroChurch, Edmond, Oklahoma. His doctoral dissertation was on singles ministry in the church.

Dycus, Jim, is senior associate minister of education at Calvary Assembly of God, Winter Park, Florida. He has authored *Not Guilty: From Convict to Christian* (Harper & Row) and coauthored *Children of Divorce* (David C. Cook).

Dyke, Jim, a graduate of Fuller Theological Seminary, is minister with singles at Grace Church of Edina, Edina, Minnesota. He served previously as minister with singles at College Avenue Baptist Church, San Diego, California. He has had articles published in *Christianity Today*, *Single Adult Ministries Journal*, and *Youthworker Journal*.

Eaton, Chris, is executive director of Single Purpose Ministries, an interdenominational ministry for single adults in the Tampa Bay/Orlando areas of Florida. He is president of Bridge Builders, Inc., a national consulting group that helps churches develop short-term missions teams and is a coauthor of *Vacations with a Purpose: A Planning Handbook for Your Short-Term Missions Team* (Singles Ministry Resources/NavPress).

Eliot, Dr. Robert, is a cardiologist in Nebraska who was quoted in *Time* magazine.

Etcheto, John, is singles pastor at Reno Christian Fellowship, Reno, Nevada. He is currently completing a graduate degree in counseling.

Fagerstrom, Doug, is minister with single adults at Calvary Church, Grand Rapids, Michigan. He serves as the executive director of the National Association of Single Adult Leaders (NSL). He is the editor of *Singles Ministry Handbook* (Victor Books).

Ferm, Deane W., former chaplain at Mount Holyoke College, is the author of *Alternative Lifestyles Confront the Church* (Seabury Press).

Flanagan, Bill, is minister with single adults at Saint Andrew's Presbyterian Church, Newport Beach, California. He is an adjunct professor at Fuller Theological Seminary and is the author of *Developing a Divorce Recovery Ministry: A How-to Manual* (Singles Ministry Resources/NavPress).

Foster, Dr. Timothy, is a licensed psychologist who received his degree from Rosemead Graduate School of Psychology, La Mirada, California. He is the author of *Called to Counsel* (Oliver-Nelson).

Franck, Dennis, who previously served as pastor with single adults in Montana and Nebraska, is singles pastor at Bethel Assembly of God Church, San Jose, California.

Gilder, George, a Harvard graduate, is the author of *Naked Nomads,*

Sexual Suicide (revised edition titled *Men and Marriage*) and *Wealth and Poverty*, a critique of Reaganomics. He writes regularly for *The Wall Street Journal, National Review,* and *Harper's* and has been featured on "Good Morning America" and Dr. James Dobson's "Focus on the Family" where Dr. Dobson called it "one of the best interviews [on their national radio program] in the last five years."

Gonzales, Georgia Coates, has been actively involved in singles ministry leadership in San Diego, California. She is a former staff member with Campus Crusade for Christ.

Graves, Cliff, a graduate of Fuller Theological Seminary, is associate pastor at Christ Community Church of the Reformed Church in America, Carmichael, California. His responsibilities include single adult ministry.

Graves, Mary G., a graduate of Fuller Theological Seminary, is associate pastor and minister of single adults at Solana Beach Presbyterian Church, Solana Beach, California.

Hageman, Randy, serves as associate pastor of First United Methodist Church, Lufkin, Texas. The single adult ministry is one of his responsibilities. He holds a master's of divinity degree from Perkins School of Theology, Southern Methodist University, with special course work in the area of single adult ministry.

Harding, Sandi, a registered nurse and single parent, is a lay leader at Saint Stephen's Episcopal Church, Sewickley, Pennsylvania.

Hedges, Charlie, a graduate of Western Seminary, is single adult pastor at South Coast Community Church, Newport Beach, California. He is a coauthor of *Call It Love or Call It Quits: The Single's Guide to Meaningful Relationships* (Worthy/Word).

Henderson, Gary, is a licensed marriage, family, and child therapist with L.I.F.E. Counselling Center, Monrovia, California.

Hershey, Terry, is director of Christian Focus, Inc., based in Seattle, Washington, a ministry that develops curriculum and training on relationship issues for the local church. He is a popular speaker and the author of several books, including *Beginning Again* (Thomas Nelson), *Young Adult Ministry* (Group Books), *Go Away, Come Closer* (Word), and *Intimacy: The Longing of Every Human Heart* (Harvest House).

Hurst, Rich, is a well-known speaker and singles ministry consultant and is singles ministry director at Crystal Cathedral, Garden Grove, California. He previously served on the singles ministry staff at University Presbyterian Church, Seattle, Washington. Rich is a coauthor of a book on leadership training for singles ministry.

Jackson, Timm, is singles pastor at Second Presbyterian Church,

Memphis, Tennessee. He previously served as executive director of the National Association of Single Adult Leaders (NSL) and founded Single Point Ministries at Ward Church, Livonia, Michigan.

Jones, French A., is a counselor in Dallas, Texas. Before establishing his counseling practice, he served as a single adult pastor at Northwest Bible Church, Dallas.

Jones, Jerry, a graduate of The University of Tulsa, is the editor and publisher of *Single Adult Ministries Journal* and director of Singles Ministry Resources, Colorado Springs, Colorado. He is the author of several books, including *Baby Boomers and the Future of World Missions* with Dr. Jim Engel (MDI) and *Beating the Break-up Habit* with Dick Purnell (Here's Life).

Kent, Dr. Lawrence W., is pastor of evangelism and singles at First Presbyterian Church, Flint, Michigan. He received his doctorate of ministry from Pittsburgh Theological Seminary.

Kinder, Dr. Melvyn, coauthored *Smart Women, Foolish Choices.* (Clarkson & Potter) and *Women Men Love—Women Men Leave* (Clarkson & Potter), with Dr. Connell Cowan. A graduate of UCLA, he is a clinical psychologist in Beverly Hills, California.

Kraljev, Rich, is minister with single adults at New Hope Community Church, Portland, Oregon. He previ-

ously worked in marketing for a major airline.

Larson, Ray, former pastor to singles at Capitol Christian Center, Sacramento, California, is now senior pastor at Bethel Assembly of God, Redding, California. He is the author of *Seasons of Singleness* (Gospel Light) and a coauthor of *When the Womb Is Empty* (Whitaker House). His B.A. in theology is from Southern California College.

Last, Scott, is minister with single adults at Emmanuel Faith Community Church, Escondido, California. He holds a Th.M. degree from Dallas Theological Seminary.

Lundblad, Dan, is a counselor at Blue Water Center for Christian Counseling, Port Huron, Michigan. He specializes in working with the divorced and single-parent families.

McAfee, Lisa, is a coauthor of *How to Start a Beginning Again Ministry* (Merritt Media).

McClay, Barry, is a business man, singles ministry leader, and lay counselor in Harrisburg, Pennsylvania. He formerly served as single adult pastor at Central Assembly of God, Raytown, Missouri.

Morgan, Andy, is director of Single Point Ministries at Ward Presbyterian Church, Livonia, Michigan. He has a B.A. in theology and history from Oral Roberts University, as well as graduate studies at McCormick Theological Seminary and Trinity Evangelical Divinity School. His articles have been published in *Solo*, *Charisma*, *Single Adult Ministries Journal,* and *Leadership Journal.* He currently hosts the only call-in talk show for singles in the nation: Solo Flight.

Morphis, Doug, a counselor in Wichita, Kansas, is the author of *Divorce Recovery Workshop* (Discipleship Resources). He previously served as minister with single adults and small groups at First United Methodist Church, Wichita.

Palser, Barry, is the pastor with singles at Happy Church, Denver, Colorado. His B.A. in Christian ministry is from Southwest College, Waxahachie, Texas. He is the author of *Singles—Dynamite in Today's Church* (self-published).

Pentak, Bill, is minister to single adults at Sagemont Baptist Church, Houston, Texas. He has a degree in communications studies from Baylor University and is a candidate for a master's of divinity from Southwestern Baptist Theological Seminary.

Petersen, Paul M., a graduate of Wheaton College and Gordon-Conwell Theological Seminary, is minister with single adults at Highland Park Presbyterian Church, Dallas, Texas.

Randlett, Doug, is college-career-singles pastor at Jerry Falwell's church, Thomas Road Baptist Church, Lynchburg, Virginia. He is also a professor in the religion department at Liberty Baptist University.

Randolph, Mary, is director of the singles ministry at Asbury United Methodist Church, Tulsa, Oklahoma. She is a certified lay speaker of the United Methodist Church and a member of the Jurisdictional Task Force for Single Adults.

Reed, Dr. Bobbie, is the author of several books, including *Single Mothers Raising Sons* (Thomas Nelson) and *Single on Sunday: A Manual for Successful Single Adult Ministries* (Concordia). She is currently director of Agnew State Hospital, San Jose, California.

Richards, Dr. Lawrence O., is the author of more than fifty books, including *The Believer's Guidebook* (Zondervan). He holds degrees from the University of Michigan, Dallas Theological Seminary, and Northwestern University.

Richwine, Jim, who has a counseling degree, serves on Dr. James Kennedy's staff as minister with singles at Coral Ridge Presbyterian Church, Fort Lauderdale, Florida.

Rydberg, Denny, is director of University Ministries at University Presbyterian Church, Seattle, Washington. He is the author of several resources, including the *Lifestyles* single adult curriculum (David C. Cook).

Schiller, Barbara, is assistant to the director of single life ministries at Central Presbyterian Church, Saint Louis, Missouri. As a single parent, she has developed successful ministries in her church—"Broken Rainbow" for kids, and "Just Me and the Kids" for their parents. She leads single-parent workshops and seminars.

Seamands, Dr. David, is professor of pastoral ministries at Asbury Theological Seminary, Wilmore, Kentucky. He is the author of several books, including *Healing for Damaged Emotions* and *Putting Away Childish Things* (Victor).

Shores, Chuck, is the senior pastor of Ojai Valley Wesleyan Church, Ojai Valley, California. He previously served as singles pastor at Skyline Wesleyan Church, Lemon Grove, California.

Sims, Jack, is president of B.O.O.M.E.R.S., a consulting firm formed to help the church reach young adults. He was previously on staff with Campus Crusade for Christ and was assistant pastor to Rev. John Wimber, founder of Vineyard Christian Fellowship, Placentia, California.

Smedes, Dr. Lewis B., until his recent retirement, was professor of theology and ethics at Fuller Theological Seminary, Pasadena, California. He is the author of several books, including *Choices: Making Right Decisions in a Complex World* and *How Can It Be All Right When Everything Is All Wrong?* (Harper & Row).

Smith, Dr. Catherine S., is a clinical psychologist with Associated Psychological Services, Pasadena, California. She holds both a theology and a psychology degree from Fuller Theological Seminary. In addition to her practice, she is director of counseling for Arcadia Presbyterian Church and serves as an adjunct faculty member at Fuller, teaching "Psychology of Women" and "Women and Therapy."

Smith, Dr. Harold Ivan, a popular speaker, is the founder of Tear Catchers, a Ministry of Compassion, Kansas City, Missouri. He is the author of several books, including *I Wish Someone Understood My Divorce* (Augsburg/Fortress), *You and Your Parents* (Augsburg/Fortress), and *Tear Catchers* (Abingdon). He holds a doctorate from Luther Rice Seminary, Jacksonville, Florida.

Smoke, Jim, a long-time leader in single adult ministries, is the author of several books, including *Growing Through Divorce* (Harvest House) and *Growing in Remarriage* (Revell). He is the founder and director of The Center for Divorce Recovery, Phoenix, Arizona. He travels extensively as a seminar and retreat speaker.

Splinter, John, is associate pastor and director of single adult ministries at Central Presbyterian Church, Saint Louis, Missouri. He is the author of *Second Chapter* (Baker), which is a programmed course for divorce recovery. He has a master's in pastoral counseling.

Streeter, Carole Sanderson, is the author of *Finding Your Place After Divorce* (Zondervan).

Suggs, Rob, has been a regular cartoonist with both *Leadership Journal* and *The Door* for several years. (He's the man behind Brother Biddle in *The Door,* a running feature from 1980 to 1988.) He is also a minister with single adults at Second Ponce de Leon Baptist Church, Atlanta, Georgia.

Sunderland, Dr. Ron, is a research fellow at The Institute of Religion, Texas Medical Center, Houston, Texas. He is the author of several books, including *AIDS: Personal Stories from a Pastoral Perspective, AIDS in the Church,* and *A Manual for Pastoral Care.*

Talley, Jim, is single adult pastor at First Baptist Church, Modesto, California. He is the author of *Too Close Too Soon* and *Reconcilable Differences* (Thomas Nelson).

Tillapaugh, Frank, is senior pastor at Bear Valley Baptist Church, Denver, Colorado. He is the author of several books, including *Unleashing the Church* (Regal).

Van Loan, Bill, is associate pastor at Arcadia Presbyterian Church, Arcadia, California. He has a M.Div. from Austin Presbyterian Theological Seminary, Austin, Texas.

Wallerstein, Dr. Judith, a psychologist, is executive director of the Center for the Family in Transition, Corte Madera, California (a nonprofit counseling center for families going through divorce). She is a graduate of Columbia University, Topeka Institute for Psychoanalysis, and Lund University in Sweden. Her book, *Second Chances: Men, Women and Children a Decade After Divorce,* reports on the results of the longest study of the impact of divorce on children and parents in the United States.

Westfall, Dr. John, a doctor of ministry graduate of Fuller Theological Seminary, is pastor of adult ministries at University Presbyterian Church, Seattle, Washington. He is the author of *Coloring Outside the Lines* (Harper & Row) and is a co-host for "Everyday People," a weekly radio program in the Seattle area.

Endnotes

1. Bromiley, Geoffrey W., *Theological Dictionary of the New Testament* (Grand Rapids, MI: William B. Eerdmans Publishing Company, 1985), pg. 1313. *Chera*: common greek usage is "widow" derived from a root meaning "forsaken"; *cheros* is used for "widower."

2. United States Census Bureau, Marriage and Family Department, Washington, DC (Document No. 301-763-7987).

3. Frankl, Viktor E., *Man's Search for Meaning* (New York: Pocketbook, 1963).

4. *The Holy Bible,* Nehemiah: Chapters 1-6.

5. Flanagan, William, "What I Wish I'd Known About Single Adult Ministry" (Carol Stream, IL: *Leadership Journal*, Fall, 1983.) (Adaptation). Reprinted by permission.

6. J. David Jones, "Single in America," *SOLO*, March/April, 1982, page 13.

7. McGavran, Donald A., and Arn, Winfield C., *Ten Steps for Church Growth* (San Francisco, CA: Harper and Row, 1977), page 35.

8. *Psychology Today*, October 1988, pages 39-42.

9. Richards, Lawrence O., *The Believer's Guidebook: The Christian Life from Aspirin to Zoos* (Grand Rapids, MI: Zondervan Publishing Co., 1983).

10. Ferm, Deane W., *Alternative Life-Styles Confront the Church* (New York: Seabury Press, 1983).

11. Hershey, Terry, and McAfee, Lisa, *How to Start a Beginning Again Ministry* (Merit Media, 1984). This book is out of print and the company is no longer in existence. It has been replaced by: Hershey, Terry, *How to Start a Beginning Again Ministry*, Leader's Manual (Woodinville, WA: Christian Focus, 1986).

12. Johnson, Roswell H., *TJTA: Taylor-Johnson Temperament Analysis* (Psychological Publishing, Inc., 5300 Hollywood Blvd., Los Angeles, CA 90027).

13. Bennis, Warren, "Effective Leadership: The Exception, Not the Rule," *U.S. News & World Report,* April 25, 1983, page 64 (adaptation).

14. Richards, Lawrence O., *The Believer's Guidebook: The Christian Life from Aspirin to Zoos* (Grand Rapids, MI: Zondervan Publishing Co., 1983).

15. Hershey, Terry, and McAfee, Lisa, *How to Start a Beginning Again Ministry,* Leader's Manual (Woodinville, WA: Christian Focus, 1986). (See footnote 11.)

16. Ash, Mary Kay, *Mary Kay on People Management* (New York: Warner, 1984) (adaptation).

17. *Psychology Today,* January 1982, pages 29-32.

18. SOLO, November/December 1979, page 10 (adaptation).

19. Simenauer, Jacqueline, and Carroll, David, *Singles: The New Americans* (New York: Simon & Schuster, 1982).

20. Williamson, David, *Building Power* (New York: Prentice Hall); Coleman,

Lyman, et al., *Serendipity Group Bible Study* (Grand Rapids, MI: Zondervan Publishing Co., 1986); Rydberg, Denny, *Building Community in Youth Groups* (Loveland, CO: Group Books, 1985).

21. "Single-cell anemia," see footnote 25.

22. Schaller, Lyle, *Assimilating New Members* (Nashville, TN: Abingdon Press, 1978).

23. See footnote 27.

24. "Ad hoc" committees: short-term commitment committees (see insert "Relational and Task—The Small Groups that Work" on page 188).

25. Dudley, Carl S., *Making the Small Church Effective* (Nashville, TN: Abingdon Press, 1978). Carl Dudley describes a "single cell" congregation in his book. He points out that the small church must be transformed from an overgrown small group into a congregation of groups, classes, choirs, circles and organizations.

26. Schaller, Lyle, *Assimilating New Members* (Nashville, TN: Abingdon Press, 1978), page 77. "Adult new members who do not become part of a group, accept a leadership role, or become involved in a task during their first year tend to become inactive."

27. Schaller, page 55. Notice the variety of groups that can exist in a typical local church: "These groups might include the youth fellowship that meets on Sunday evening, an adult Sunday school class, the women's organization, an evening Bible study group, a choir, the governing board, the Christian education committee, the pastoral relations committee that meets as a support group for the minister, or the group that comes over on the first Saturday of every month to clean the church."

28. Schaller, page 95.

29. Marty, Martin, Professor of Church History, University of Chicago, quote from a speech.

30. Crabb, Larry, and Allender, Dan B., *Encouragement* (Winona Lake, IN: BMH Books, 1986); Adams, Jay, *Competent to Counsel* (Oklahoma City, OK: Presbyterian & Reformed Publishers, 1970); Adams, Jay, *The Christian Counselors Manual* (Oklahoma City, OK: Presbyterian & Reformed Publishers, 1973); Crabb, Larry, *Inside Out* (Colorado Springs, CO: NavPress, 1988); Crabb, Larry, *Meeting Counseling Needs Through the Local Church* (available only to those participants in the basic seminar of The Institute of Biblical Counseling, 303-697-5425).

31. Foster, Timothy, *Called to Counsel* (Nashville, TN: Oliver Nelson, 1986). Reprinted by permission.

32. *NIV Bible* (Grand Rapids, MI: Zondervan Corporation, 1973).

33. Streeter, Carole Sanderson, "Communicating God's Forgiveness to the Divorced," adapted with permission from *Finding Your Place After Divorce* (Grand Rapids, MI: Zondervan Publishing, 1986).

34. Brown, Helen Gurley, *Having It All* (New York: Simon & Schuster, 1982).

35. "Sex and Success," *Savvy* (October 1985), pages 29-33.

36. Richardson, Laurel, *The New Other Woman* (New York: Free Press, 1986).

37. Cowan, Connell, and Kinder, Melvyn, *Smart Women, Foolish Choices* (New York: Clarkson & Potter, 1985), page 107.

38. Gutek, Barbara A., *Sex and the Workplace* (San Francisco, CA: Jossey-Bass, 1985).

Index of Subjects

Index of Persons

More Resources for Your Ministry with Single Adults

Contact Singles Ministry Resources
for a FREE catalog of all the best resources available
to help you build an effective ministry
with single adults in your church
and community.

Singles Ministry Resources
P.O. Box 62056
Colorado Springs, Colorado 80962-2056

Or call (800) 487-4-SAM
or (719) 488-2610